searching for soul

BOBBE TYLER

SEARCHING

for

SOUL

a survivor's guide

FOREWORD BY LUCIA CAPACCHIONE

swallow press ∽ *athens, ohio*

Swallow Press / Ohio University Press, Athens, Ohio 45701
www.ohioswallow.com

Printed in the United States of America
Swallow Press / Ohio University Press books are printed on acid-free paper ⊗ ™

16 15 14 13 12 11 10 09   5 4 3 2 1

A slightly different version of chapter 17 was first published in *Quadrant Journal:
The C. G. Jung Foundation of Analytical Psychology* 26, no. 2 (Summer 2006): 65–83.

Library of Congress Cataloging-in-Publication Data
Tyler, Bobbe, 1932–
Searching for soul : a survivor's guide / Bobbe Tyler ; foreword by Lucia Capacchione.
  p. cm.
Includes bibliographical references.
ISBN 978-0-8040-1118-1 (hc : alk. paper) — ISBN 978-0-8040-1119-8 (pb : alk. paper)
1. Conduct of life. 2. Wisdom. 3. Friendship. I. Title.
BJ1581.2.T95 2009
158—dc22

2009014796

To my children:

Jamison, Christian, and Cort,

who teach me still in all things.

Thank you.

Contents

Foreword

A century ago, Sigmund Freud, Carl Jung, and others breaking new ground in the field of psychoanalysis were forming somewhat similar theories about the unconscious part of the human psyche. On one thing they could all agree: if more people could diminish their suffering through an exploration of their unconscious, the world would be a happier and healthier place to live. So much progress was made in the ensuing hundred years that today most people value (if not urgently) a need for self-awareness in their own lives. We have also learned by now that there are dozens of ways to achieve self-awareness and that not all of those ways require the expertise of a therapist or a facilitator (of which I am one). If ever a book described the joys of living life as a result of "coming awake"—especially when the author had been cursed and desperate and blessed with her need to find the meaning of her self and her life –it is this book.

Searching for Soul is timely, arriving at a seemingly long historical moment of collective problems that cast their pall over all of us individually. Yet Bobbe Tyler's story is uplifting and encouraging. She believes that we must all participate in our lives fully conscious of our personal principles and values—first to find our own specific meaning and then to live with it in joy, because in living thus we change the entire world for the better. It is rare that one conscious person will change the world all at once, but I agree with Bobbe that at the very least each self-aware individual has the power to change the life of anyone who is in her or his orbit.

As an art therapist and an author, I have dedicated my life to sharing the healing power of writing with my books; Bobbe's work is a wonderful example of the results that can be achieved by writing about one's experiences. As I read her life story unfolding layer by layer, my heart was touched. The rigorous honesty and pleasing humility with which she looks into the mirror that is the written page inspires self-reflection. Though individual and personal, this is a universal tale of a woman finding herself by living the "examined life" so worthy of her work and by learning to accept the mystery of "what is."

Bobbe delves deeply into spirit and psyche as she follows a labyrinthine path through the many phases of her life. Speaking to women and men of every age, she writes of the search for her spiritual center during her troubles with marriage, of addictions (her father's and her own), of loss and learning in relationships, of a beloved sister's shattering problems with schizophrenia, and finally of the wisdom and aging that became the keys to her happiness. Yet the circumstances of her outer life serve only as a backdrop for a long, rich story about her inner life—how her psyche, fragile and "abandoned" to begin with, was transformed over time into the inner strength and beauty that mark her life today.

Her wise words inspired me to contemplate the cul-de-sacs in my own life, moved me to go deeply into myself and contemplate where I have been, where I am now, and where I am going. Some books appear at exactly the right moment in a person's life. I hope this is one of them for you, dear reader, and that Bobbe Tyler's story will lead you to write your own. May you treasure the wise counsel and healing words in this volume as much as I do.

Lucia Capacchione, Ph.D., A.T.R.

Art therapist and author of

The Creative Journal: The Art of Finding Yourself

and *Recovery of Your Inner Child*

Preface

For as long as I can remember I have searched for and read books just like this one. They were the straws I grasped to keep from drowning, the "voices" that prayed with me in the night, soothed my fears, and made all the difference in the world. Books like this were my manna in a time when there were fewer distractions in our culture; television, the Internet, cell phones, and iPods had not yet come along to divert one from the serious business of individual survival. Had that not been the case, I—who was shy and introverted and utterly lost as a child—would surely have foundered on the shoals of so much collective time consuming culture. As it was, I searched for, or was given, or "lucked into" *always* just the right book—the one whose story told of possibilities I could not have imagined, of loneliness conquered and the happiness I might one day feel. As I grew older, the authors of my survival became my family of choice. My tribe. My delight. My uncommon wealth.

I have always been a writer, yet before I could tell my own story, I first had to live my life. Not until my Gordian knots had all come unloosed and I was finally whole and healthy in mind, body, and soul would I be qualified to write what was my lifelong burning desire—one of those "just right" books that used to regularly save my life. The book is in your hands today because synchronicity influenced destiny to set my story telling in motion. As part of her research into the nature of wisdom, a friend pressed a set of "life review" questions into my hands—"The Harvesting Wisdom Interview"—and asked me to respond to them; her only instruction was, "Take as long as you like and go as deep as you can." I knew soon enough that I was writing an intimate discourse on self-discovery, a re-creation of an inner journey whose full meaning and substance would be revealed to me when I had finished my work. And so it was that in exchange for my considerable time and effort, I now enjoy a rare and valuable gift: my life—fully deciphered, whole, and comprehensible in all of its layers. Probing my past, plumbing my depths, I set about reliving the peaks and valleys of my story from seventeen different starting points and discovered that it was not just my story but *your* story, too. By diving as deep as I could go into the heart of my own particular darkness, I found again and again the essential meaning and purpose of every life. We are unique, so our stories will always be different on the transparent surface of life, yet the deeper I probed—beyond the "particular" to the level of soul—the more I was certain we are all one at our core.

I was stunned to find so much rich and complex material stored up in my psyche waiting to be expressed, but then I am surprised every day by what happens in the process of self-discovering awareness. It is thrilling to feel one's consciousness enliven and expand—one "sees" and understands and feels ancient, burdensome things falling away, leaving one lighter than air. I have never felt so free. With my friend's permission, the questions are included in the book as an appendix. They are not as simple as they seem; it will take you longer to answer them than you thought, but I assure you the results of your efforts will quietly change you inside and out. "Take as long as you like and go as deep as you can," and I can promise you this: the day will come when you know yourself more completely than you ever thought possible, and on that day you will hold your soul—like a precious jewel—in the palm of your hand.

Acknowledgments

My grateful and greatest thanks to Roberta Forem, without whose "Interview" questions this book would not be; to Dr. Lucia Capacchione, invaluable friend and publishing mentor; to Carla Riedel for her prepublication editing and story-teaching skills; to my faithful, endlessly patient readers, whose criticism and encouragement kept me writing, no matter what: Christine Wagner, Viktoria Holm Kramer, Peter Kemble, Catherine Haller, and Shirley Partridge. Special thanks go to Ohio University Press/Swallow Press director David Sanders for his enthusiastic response to the manuscript's content and to managing editor Nancy Basmajian, who untangled my prose and unmixed my metaphors with singular skill—and to the many unnamed others in the "village" it took to make this book.

Finally, I wish to thank the many authors whose names appear in the endnotes for their collective wisdom and merciful assistance with my life.

one

What do you mean?

> Perhaps she told herself, kneeling there, that "I would
> have to stop and think, to question my own position:
> 'What is man that Thou art mindful of him, O Lord?'
> What were we here for, what were we doing, what was
> the meaning of our lives?"

—Paul Elie

They were young in years, yet ripe enough to assume the heady, first-time excitement of pilfering. According to a plan conceived only minutes before the caper was on, my daughter, her best friend (older by a year), and my son (youngest of all and happy to be on the team) filched a lipstick apiece from our local drugstore. One at a time those brazen little bandits did their part of the dirty deed, then sauntered to and through the exit door and raced away—celebrating the success of their first *notable* heist all the way home.

The store owner, a decent, thoughtful man who knew my family nearly as well as he knew his own, had witnessed the mischief and opted not to humiliate the children in front of customers who might have known them (and me). Assuming rightly

I would wish to handle the incident myself, he approached me the next day when I came in for coffee and discreetly unreeled the whole sordid story. I thanked him for his kindness and opened my wallet to pay for the stolen goods, but he waved it away: "No, no, not necessary," he said, "I'm sure they won't do it again." I insisted he allow me to pay: *some* things are a given. Yet, as I lingered over my coffee thinking of ways I should approach my kids later that day, I felt the old fear and trembling of my early childhood and the possibility of doing them harm. On my way out, I told the owner I would be back later with my children in tow to submit their apologies, and asked if he would assist me by accepting their remorse with an appropriately measured response. "Of course," he said. "Don't be *too* hard on them, though," I added instinctively—but I needn't have worried; he would do it right.

When I confronted them with their no longer secret "secret," though, would I do it right? I used the time before they came home from school to soften the edges of my disappointment about what they had done. They were too young to deal with my first reaction, the one based on adult values that say stealing anything at all—even the seemingly insignificant—puts one's very soul in harm's way. The act defines you as a thief without honor, and that's not all. Until consciously brought to closure, it is possible that the lingering consequences of a hurtful act not yet repented will hang around in your psyche to remind you of itself for as long as you're willing to live with it. Many years ago, I discovered that someone close to me was a not-so-petty offender, and since stealing necessitates the twin sin of lying to establish one's innocence, I could never, down deep where it really matters, trust that person again. My wish—my need—is to forgive and forget when someone is less than honest with me, especially if some sign of atonement follows close behind the lie. But my *experience* is that when my unspoken but critically important assumption that you and I share similar principles is proved wrong, something (in me) breaks and the relationship changes.

But how could I preach hellfire and brimstone to my kids for stealing a lipstick when, given their ages (seven and eight maybe), they had done nothing more radical than to test the limits of their daring and courage in a spontaneous, thrilling, terrifying, and fairly harmless rite of passage? Too many years have passed now for me to recall my actual words to them before we all returned to the scene of their crime. I can only hope I made my case

Chapter one

effectively without being overly harsh. My father was much too severe with my sister and me about such things, so all of his "lessons" were lost in my more immediate need to defy him by yielding *not one teardrop* in exchange for the belt-marks he left on my bottom. Besides, I knew beforehand how mortified they would feel while facing the man they knew more as a friend than as someone who would squeal on them, so I felt a great tenderness for them in their predicament. Who among us hasn't stood fully exposed under a klieg light shining the truth on an indiscretion? My guess is that my kids gave up any further thoughts of crime, if indeed they'd had any, as they stood that day before their "executioner." Years later, they all regaled me with some of their teenage adventures—like racing cars on Mulholland Drive and "dipping into" drugs—which they had managed with good sense and great success to keep from me altogether. (God, did I ever thank you for that?)

What gives meaning to my life only now seems easy enough to discern. Truth, you may already have learned, is primary. If you don't tell the truth, your word is meaningless, and so, I guess, are you, in the sense that I'm not gonna hang out with you—because what's the point? I learned much about truth from my father. He once fooled me in jest, when, at age seven or so, I asked him the meaning of a word I needed to know for school. When I used his definition and was roundly teased for being light years off the mark, I felt so humiliated—and *betrayed*—that I never did forgive him for "lying" to me. When I was seventeen, I became engaged to my friend Johnny—a really nice guy I knew damned well I would never marry, but whose ring (with its itty-bitty diamond) I wanted to show off to my friends. Scared to death by what I had done, I wanted out, so, compounding my treachery, I concocted a story to persuade that really nice guy that our breakup was his fault. When I admitted to my father what I'd done, he insisted that I go "right *now*" and tell Johnny the truth—no, *not* on the phone, face-to-face. I shook with shame as I apologized to Johnny for telling him a serious, hurtful lie, but afterward I felt clean—and light as a feather—for the first time in weeks. Gathering up courage to "save my soul" wasn't easy to do at seventeen, but all credit goes to my father in this instance, for teaching me—in one lesson and for all time—a principle that quickly became deeply meaningful to me.

So I learned that both your word *and* mine have to be rock solid before I can feel good about either one of us. After truth come many more civilities—

What do you mean?

tolerance, generosity, compassion, and humility—that matter a great deal to most of us. They are the better qualities of our nature that make us respectable human beings, give meaning to our species, and keep civilization more or less afloat. Looking back, I would say that what gave meaning to my life evolved. It was cumulative. What seemed important in the books I read, the people I met, and my own life experiences moved in and out of favor with me, changing as I changed, until the values that grew strong in meaning to my life simply took up permanent residence as parts of my identity. Early on, depending on the set or sets of life skills I was practicing at the time, I would have said that what gave my life meaning was "my education," "my marriage," "mothering my children," or "advancing my career." All of them lent meaning because my intentions—to do well and make a difference—had been in each case worthy. But these were life roles, after all, and life roles, even the most important ones, come and go, wax and wane—they have lives of their own, so in one sense their meaning to a life is temporary. They all enlarged my worldview, increased my curiosity, and expanded my consciousness. But there came a time with each of them—usually after I had gained proficiency or was forced to abandon a role altogether (both my marriages, for example)—when my interest and energy and happiness had peaked and were waning and I would know it was time to move on. Always I would find—or it would find me—a new and different challenge ready to launch me on another adventure. Over the years, I got used to the rhythm of that process. I understood it, came to count on its predictability, and was quite content to think that what gave meaning to my life *was* this ongoing process and it would continue to renew my interest and my energy—and my happiness, of course—all the way to life's end. I was wrong. Jungian analyst James Hollis says:

> Depression at midlife is very common. It seems that there is a
> necessary and inevitable collision between the false self, reflexively
> cobbled together as a reaction to the vagaries of childhood, and
> the natural self [the person we are meant to become]. This colli-
> sion of opposites is suffered as a neurosis. Those who choose to
> remain unconscious of the task their suffering signifies will
> remain stuck.[1]

Chapter one

When I read those words, I was fifty-two years old, and something had shifted in me that was effectively stripping me clean of the "happiness" I had worked so hard to achieve and had come to believe was mine to keep. It had started with feelings of anxiety, turned dark, and settled in as a pervading sense of dread. It seeped through every crack in my psyche, absorbing light and defeating the power of my will. I could find no cause. My mind trolled for anything that could fix me, arcing a search in all directions and sweeping my past for clues: I was pretty much "cobbled together" as a child, no doubt about that—a mass of tangled wires in search of a motherboard comes to mind. But post-childhood, I had spent ten exceedingly grueling years "under repairs" in therapy—straightening wires, rebuilding some parts, uncrossing circuits, and such. So when sanity finally arrived (they said), I pronounced my self and my work "done"—she's a go. So might this *really be* a midlife crisis? I thought those happened in one's forties; I thought I had circumvented mine.

I took another look: I was married and divorced for a second time in my forties. The "happiness" part hadn't lasted—again, though I had been certain we could overcome the thousand different ways we were so different. Soon, I was offered a terrific job in the most important film company of that era, which at the time was located in my favorite city! I accepted, of course, and in a matter of weeks the haunting sadness of another failed marriage had lifted. I was thrilled, challenged, busy, and happy again—for a couple of years. Then everything in my life upended. At first, only a hint of something gone wrong, followed by increasingly ominous signs—the dread I mentioned, and finally the incontrovertible fact: I was in thrall to a sickness that was slowly killing my spirit and draining energy from every body part. Before long, I was spending too much time by myself—too frequently with a glass in my hand, my thoughts fixed on the once-solid lines of my biography sliding off its pages. All that had once given meaning to my life was floating away, disappearing into the drab gray of days passing by without notice, one indistinguishable from the next. Every part of me—save the solitary, barely breathing instinct taking note of the whole pitiful process—was lost in the throes of a great ennui. One does not forget such a time as that, nor will the mind's eye soon lose its image of the flat, ashen vastness that was my prison: a place without walls or horizon, extending into infinity.

What do you mean?

I found respite only in the workplace. My job was complex, requiring focus, precision, and a pleasing personality. Like a robot programmed to simulate a human likeness, I went through the motions—acting out the days, returning to what little was left of myself at day's end. I had pursued happiness all my life as a goal of learning well and trying my best: Why had happiness never lasted? What had gone wrong after all my work to get life right? What deep hole in me required so much more than I could feed it? And why, after all my years of therapy, could I not find the mercy to spare myself this unrelenting self-flagellation? These were the questions that dogged the hours I spent at home, to which my answer was always the same: I was suffering the fruits of all my failures with a full-blown depression. But even then, without Hollis to teach me otherwise, it would not have crossed my mind that I was stuck in a midlife crisis I had *not* circumvented, but denied. And that last divorce? It was only one piece in a sack full of denial that I would need to drag out of my unconscious and shine a light on, because the long con was over.

Ironically, the fear that my mind might succumb to its paralysis helped to keep it alive. I knew just enough about depression to realize that I had no time to lose in finding a remedy. Yet, was it even possible to compel my incredibly resistant mind to overcome its own inertia? I would need to work at a depth of psychic pain completely unfamiliar to me—fathoms below where I had once considered myself to be "done." If not now, though, said my fear, perhaps not ever. Slowly, then, I heaved myself to my task—which this time around was not about doing more therapy; it was about me finding me in places no one else could go. Hollis, again:

> There is a thought, a recurrent fantasy, perhaps, that the purpose of life is to achieve happiness. After all, the Constitution of the United States promises 'life, liberty, and the pursuit of happiness'[2]

> Jung has argued with this myth, as follows. 'Suffering is not an illness; it is the normal counterpole to happiness.' Our goal is not happiness, which is evanescent and impossible to sustain; it is meaning which broadens us and carries us toward our destiny.[3]

Chapter one

I began by collecting my questions: Who am I really? Why do I suffer still? What gives me pleasure? What shreds my heart and makes me grieve? Why, at the most astonishing times, does my heart refuse grief altogether? Where lie my deepest, truest feelings—and why those? Do I care enough to do this work? Is there a *reason* to care? Does anyone else care? Is it meaning I'm missing, or something I don't yet know how to name?

Exploring them one at a time, I could find only half-answers to any of them, because the elusive central meaning of my existence belonged at the heart of them all. I could know what gave meaning *to* my life, but not the meaning *of* my life. For example, I loved my children more than I could measure, but I never confused my love for them with a belief that they were the central meaning of my life. Doing so, I knew, would put our relationships at risk. I spent many years being the sole caregiver of my mother, whose greatest unconscious need had been to turn her entire life over to me for safekeeping. Feeling stuck in a role with no exits for what seemed like an eternity, I was determined that my own children would never repeat my experience. I surrendered them to their lives each time it seemed appropriate—or, as with one child, when it was not my decision to make. They knew they meant the world to me, so I taught them what I believed: "Your lives are yours to make and should always come before mine." It was a pretty radical teaching at the time, yet I believe it was and still is the best I will ever do for them.

What else . . . I hadn't loved my parents deeply since my childhood, intuiting at a young age the necessity to protect myself from them, so little positive meaning had survived my parent-child relationship. In my thirties, I made a self-induced foray into organized religion, motivated by an intense need to search for the "larger meaning of my life." It failed utterly to change my outlook, and I crashed back to earth like a rocket out of fuel. I had always cherished the love and companionship of friends and believed that they would add meaning to my life for as long as we lived. Yet, while friends can enhance my life, they cannot give that other kind of meaning that supports and sustains a life when "the dark nights of the soul" begin to have their way. What does one do when faced with those great estrangements— the death of a friend or the loss of a child, existential loneliness or terminal illness, or a depression that hovers over a psyche like death itself? These were circumstances I imagined could break a person apart unless one's inner

What do you mean?

strength was tough and enduring. So how was I to seek this glorious "meaning," so far beyond my ken? When hope had been my talisman, I could fully imagine finding my way to it. Was it "merely" hope to think I could overcome my suffering—or was hope the essential prerequisite for success, I wondered? But when hope began to die, I began to question whether I had believed so deeply in my quest for meaning because it was at least *something* to believe in.

My mind had refused to read or write anything more than a shopping list for months. Not to find pleasure in doing these things that had always brought me so much delight was a frightening prospect, at first—until even fright became no more than a yawn. Those lifelong pleasures had once meant so much to me; they had inspired my imagination, fed my curiosity, filled so many of my needs for self-expression. Gone now. Could I resurrect enough wit to do the work ahead? It was crucial to make my life matter to me again: I had to try. So I picked up my books, committed my brain to taking instruction, and daily recorded my thoughts. I *read*—almost exclusively in psychology (where I met Jung and Hollis and many other gifted teachers), and then, in a seamless and natural transition, I found myself reading extensively in the spiritual wisdom of the ages. I made no intellectual or deliberate decisions about whom and what to read; I simply moved in whichever direction my healing took me and at whatever pace my mind would allow. Picking through the notes and bibliographies of one book would set me on the trail of a dozen more wherein I found the wise minds and teaching hearts who counseled me through my confusions. Digging deep into their treasure began a process of renewing my energy and ordering my mind, of lifting the gloom and resurrecting hope that I might finally "beat this rap." And I wrote—to nurse my flatlined feelings back to life. First I wrote the hard, heavy words that image despair and anger and self-pity. Later, with a lighter hand, I wrote about my awakening desires, future possibilities, and the growing optimism that was signaling my recovery. Just so, I persisted on my journey of no certain end—head down, mind open, and absorbing as much as I could, given my circumstances. I was trusting the process, but warily—trying not to count the days or predict any outcomes—carefully keeping in mind T. S. Eliot's cogent counsel to "wait without hope, for hope would be hope for the wrong thing."[4]

Chapter one

But I was healing, and I knew that my healing was *structural*. No longer a facsimile of myself, playing all of my parts in daily life again, I became increasingly aware of a psyche transforming itself, creating changes in a process so subtle I could define them only after the fact. One day I noticed that I was smiling effortlessly: such a simple thing. Another day I joined some of my office mates for lunch: a big thing. The monochromatic tedium of a world seen through the screen of depression was gone; my world was dancing again, bright with color. My body parts were animating—eyes brighter, hands flying, body loose and graceful again. I was moving back into the society of others—and into my own society, feeling once again the pleasure of my own company. Then, one day I was simply back altogether, reconstructed from the ground up: happy to be fully living my life rather than merely crawling through its days, grateful to be standing on the far side of hell's dominions. Here's what happened (Hollis again):

> The activity of the psyche is inherently religious. It seeks connection, meaning, transcendence. It is the most profound of paradoxes that we may discover these divine principles less on mountain tops, less in cathedrals, than in swamplands.[5]

By trekking all the way into the "swamp" with my name on it to reclaim the cast-off suffering of the child, and staying long enough in that unseemly place to pick through its ancient, crusted treasures until I found what I was looking for, I discovered the spiritual dimension of my self. There, buried in the pit to which I had consigned the terrifying god of my early years, was the larger meaning of my life—the sacred part of my self that my heart had yearned for and my mind had denied. In time, all of my answers came clear—tumbling out of me like a bucketful of stars upended. I learned that when "happiness" had wandered away from me, it was not its loss that had caused me to suffer, but how little I knew about *authentic* happiness. My depression had been a late, great clue from my unconscious, demanding to be deciphered, and a warning to redefine happiness until I got it right, because only then would I find the "pearl of great price" that splices happiness to meaning and sets a life free. In his autobiography, C. G. Jung says that one's myth—one's personal metaphor acknowledging that there is something more

What do you mean?

profound than the ego-self—strives to be meaningful. Meaning is what sustains us when we suffer; without it we cannot know joy. From the same book:

> Meaninglessness inhibits fullness of life and is therefore equivalent
> to illness. Meaning makes a great many things endurable—perhaps
> everything. No science will ever replace myth, and a myth cannot
> be made of any science. For it is not that "God" is a myth, but that
> myth is the revelation of a divine life in man. It is not we who
> invent myth, rather it speaks to us as a Word of God.[6]

Jung did not literalize God as "other" in his psychology, believing that we carry the God-image ("meaning") within us—if not consciously, then unconsciously. It was Hollis who taught me to see that every depression has a discoverable meaning, that we need only look *in* and go as deep as it takes to find it. In every case, one must ask, "What is the meaning of my depression? "The well with no bottom always has a bottom, but we must swim down there to see it,"[7] Hollis says.

My depression had been an urgent signal to me to wake up and locate my buried "myth"—to twist, drag, tear, or tease it out of the wordless dark of my unconscious and into the light of my mind, there to find and experience its value to my existence. Today, I have deeper access to the meaning that makes "a great many things endurable—perhaps everything" when considering the state of the world today. I think of it as the *ground* of my being; home base for spirit; the sturdy, familiar inner place of peace I could only imagine when I was wandering through my hells and hanging on for dear life. I have to believe there are more congenial ways to research and rescue one's meaning than by crawling through the fog of a depression. It's worth whatever it takes, though, because, as Hollis says:

> During this struggle we move from the fantasy of permanent
> happiness, or shame at not achieving it, to what is perhaps the
> greatest gift—the knowledge that we can live without happiness,
> but not without meaning.[8]

Because I've never met the god whose hand I could hold or that I was convinced would or should save *my* troubled soul before anyone else's, my

Chapter one

God turned out to be a concept: ineffable, paradoxical, a *symbol* of my meaning. But I have long considered that my life—all life—is miraculous, a gift in every way sacred. Why? Because for as long as I can remember I have felt a responsibility to attend to my life: it's as simple as that. There were times I was at a loss to attend to it well, yet it has always been clear to me that I should at least try. Peter Kingsley expresses it well, I think. "As human beings we've been given something divine, meaning something intensely mysterious and real, and we can't hand it back."[9] Because the feeling has never left me or changed even a little, I don't question its dictum. I didn't question it even when I was having trouble doing life at all, because it feels right to me—organic, born of some intuition too deeply hidden to locate. It has led me through the black dark of many a midnight, when I was not conscious of its Good Samaritan work until years later. I believe that intuition is a big player in the "divine" life within all of us.

I learned a couple of things really well in my times of trouble. One is that without a clear perception of my deepest meaning, I am simply a body with an unconscious, unattended brain that generates a never-ending stream of thoughts that act me out, move me around, stop me short, and start me up again when morning comes. Thoughts are seldom "whole"—they are unremitting, unregenerate, unreflective, and usually going nowhere in every direction. Have you ever noticed that? A thought is not worth much to me until I grab it out of the flow of its stream, sit it down, focus on its intention, determine its value, make out its meaning (therefore, my meaning), and then put it to some good purpose. When I am not consciously connected to my deepest meaning, I am nothing, incomplete and lost in an unanchored chaos of mostly random thoughts. I must always "go below" to keep life meaningful. The universal energy of which I am a small but critical mass requires me to spend time reflecting a truer reality from a different dimension of my self every day, and that would be when "spirit"—the essential meaning of my life—resides alongside a mind at peace.

So there it was: the central, structural, comforting, evergreen, big-time meaning I was so depressed about not having by midlife had been, all along, my life itself. I just hadn't finished enough of its lessons—hadn't gone deeply enough into self-discovery to even ask the right questions. The questions I noodle today *have* no answers: What is the source of "essential meaning"?

What do you mean?

Where does it start, and does it ever end? Is it God? Emptiness? Universe? Spirit? How about intuition—or truth? I'd settle for that one; I always did like it best. I confound myself with these questions, but I ask them anyway because they lead me without fail into the deeper meanings of meaning—not by way of my intellect, but in awe and wonder, as an open-minded innocent who lives surrendered to life just as it is. How can I watch the sun sink into the sea and not be completely amazed? And how can I be a quasi-divine human being—a little wise and a lot curious—and not noodle the "God" questions? The unknown has always been worthy of speculation; it is, after all, our only eternally fascinating mystery. The human mind, so impressively imaginative and inventive, has been studying clues to its origins and scratching its collective head since the beginning of time and still has not resolved its biggest, most burning question. But have you ever thought about what we would do with the answer? How uninspired by life we might be without our mystery? Creation is the only "whodunit" in all of the universe in which the chief suspect is never caught out, the only "absolute certainty" we have been chasing since our minds learned how to chase—so profound is our need to prove its identity, wrap up the mystery, and pronounce the case closed. Inside that paradox lie tantalizing clues to the meaning of life—for all of us, in all our billions, one, by one, by one. That's breathtaking, isn't it?

Chapter one

two

Success as other than it seems

> One day a student was in the hall at Sokoji when Suzuki
> Roshi approached him. "Just to be alive is enough," Suzuki
> said, and with that, he turned around and walked away.

—Shunryu Suzuki

My *dictionary*[1] *defines* "success" in five different
ways, one of them being, "*succès d'estime*: an achievement that
wins critical respect, but not popular success." This kind won't
earn you money, fame, power, or prestige, but it will give you
deep personal satisfaction and a reason to celebrate quietly. I've had
a few of those, but only one that blazes comet-like, and it was,
in fact, so difficult to achieve I believe I will need no other—at
least *this* time around—to justify my existence. At a cost I often
thought was unreasonable, even unbearable, I did finally overcome
a conflict that had me in chains until I was twenty and continued to
test the limits of my endurance for nearly a lifetime. I snatched
my victory from defeat just in time, which was not long before
my mother's death. I say "victory" because there were times,
especially toward the end, when I was sure I would "lose it" with
her—that for once I would shout my truth out loud to her—and

live to regret it forever. Yes, too often toward the end of her life I brushed close enough to rage to set it afire, and only my deeply rooted fear of the awful consequences pulled me back and saved us both. She would have been devastated. I would have slain my soul. No one, not even those who knew me best, had ever guessed the truth.

I arrived on the planet to an uncertain welcome—as an unexpected pregnancy, one more mouth to feed—in a small family of non-successes in the time of the Great Depression, when losing a job or a fortune or hope was not uncommon—just a sign of the times. However, my father's failures had little to do with the plight of the general population; although he was a hardworking, well-intentioned man, he was plagued by an addiction to gambling. Several nights a week, he came home to exchange his blue denim shipping clerk's shirt for the only suit he owned and ride a streetcar for over an hour to a crummy little outskirt town, where playing poker and losing money was legal entertainment. If he came home late and roused us from sleep with a sack full of hamburgers and fries, we knew he had won. If he returned early, silent and sad-faced, it meant he was broke. I was too young to feel angry, so I felt bad for him—and for me, because I knew he was too sad to feel better about how much I loved him. Try as he would to unhook his addiction from his desire to succeed some other way, his iron-jawed resolve to "give up the damned cards" would always give way to magical thinking—the recurring certainty that lures anyone who is addicted back to his obsession: "*This* time things will be different," is what they say. His widowed mother, whom he felt obligated to support and who lived with us, was similarly addicted; she added to his troubles by betting on the horses. My mother, his wife, was more child than woman for reasons made understandable by her childhood. She was also clinically depressed for years at a time, finding no will to achieve anything even close to success in her roles as wife and mother. A sister, fifteen months my senior, completes the small family roster and describes the psychological environment in which I was forming a searing desire to achieve some success so outstanding it would attract the whole world's amazed attention. My quest would begin, I had decided, as soon as my acne was gone and I looked old enough to get a job. C. G. Jung's observations ring loud and clear and very much concordant with my early years:

Chapter two

> Nothing exerts a stronger psychic effect upon the human envi-
> ronment, and especially upon children, than the life which the
> parents have not lived. . . . That is to say, the children are driven
> unconsciously in a direction that is intended to compensate for
> everything that was left unfulfilled in the lives of their parents. . . .
> The psychic health of the adult individual, who in childhood
> was a mere particle revolving in a rotary system, demands that he
> should himself become the center of a new system.[2]

I wanted out of my childhood as soon as I could think. And I wanted *my* life to count! I was terrified that my future life might resemble the lives of my parents, which I perceived as "utterly failed," so it was fear that fueled my grandiose commitment to become not just different from them but *hugely* different. There would never be money for college, of course, so high school graduation was my calculated start date to begin my real life. I was eight years old when I vowed that within minutes of receiving my diploma I would have already shed the cap and gown, said my "see-ya-laters," and marched resolutely north from the house and family I hadn't chosen. Traveling light with my few belongings, I would be out of there—gone lickety-split into the world of my dreams.

What would my *real* life look like? I was expert at escaping into lives I read of in books, but I had trouble imagining a world different from my every-day, hardscrabble, hang-in-there existence. Then, at the magic age of eleven, schoolwork and the movies came to my rescue. Motion pictures were afford-able entertainment for everyone in those days, so I drew from that vast largesse all the images I needed for painting a picture of my future: I would cultivate just the right persona (worldly), the perfect lifestyle and wardrobe (urbane, simple, and chic), and a good-paying career (secretary). But that would be only the beginning—then up the corporate ladder to a glass-enclosed corner office. How easy it was with my big hopes and dreams to make the wildly assumptive leap and actually believe I could reproduce my life from what I saw on those fabulous silver screens. There had to have been millions of us depression kids suspending disbelief in the magical dark of movie houses to live an hour or two in some other life than the one waiting for us outside.

Success as other than it seems

As soon as possible, I set about acquiring the practical knowledge I would need. In my world, for girls who did not go beyond high school, a limited number of business courses was available: shorthand, typing, business correspondence, and basic bookkeeping. Never mind; the movies said that with those skills and (thank you, God) a pretty face, I could get my foot in the door of an advertising agency on Madison Avenue, rent a single apartment, feed and clothe myself, maybe meet the man I had not yet thought to dream up, and live successfully ever after. Well, I could do all of that! Just let me in the door and I'll take it from there, is what I would promise them—and then go straight to the top.

So, the willing and determined student (me) made excellent grades, ceremoniously received her diploma, tore off her cap and gown, and—you can't guess what happened. My truly extraordinary future, scheduled for years to begin its rollout on that fateful day, was put on hold. Instead, I was out looking for the first paying job I could find to support myself and my mother in a place of our own, while she—having just filed for divorce from my father—waited the requisite year to marry another man. It was a move so bold it made her physically ill, so "Would you, please, honey, just for awhile?" she asked me. I felt sick, too—not to mention amazed, even hurt, that she would ask so much of me. Why couldn't the groom-to-be finance his lady-in-waiting? I wanted to ask, but I didn't because I was taught not to sass my elders. It was a long year, foreshadowing big chunks of my life to come by revealing the depth of her reliance on me (my sister had married and was gone) for a whole lot more than merely paying the rent. She sought constant reassurance that she had done the right thing when she left my father, for example, hoping aloud again and again that she hadn't done the wrong thing when she asked me to support her—"I *didn't*, did I, honey?" Yes! You absolutely did do the wrong thing, I might have said, but I was not yet ready (enough my own person, that is) to tell her my true feelings. Anyway, the year would soon be over and my life would finally begin— that was all I wanted to think about. Well, I was hardly finished with my mother. Many years later I was still resisting the *fact* of her. From a journal entry . . .

> To Mother (the letter I will never send):
> . . . My fantasy is that if I could flash-freeze our mother-
> daughter principle, pull it out of the long time warp of our history

Chapter two

and hold its concrete, three-dimensional mystery in my hand long enough to probe its appalling complexity, our riddle would decode and yield up my Nirvana. If I could somehow describe you to myself in words so nuanced I would have pinned your essence—or if I could paint your perfect likeness, the faded grays and umbers that shadow your dispirited features and your tiny, crooked frame . . . what then? If I could probe your mind, freeze-frame an interpretation of you that fits all of our complex scenarios, maybe then all of my shifting and conflicted notions about what is or is not right, or appropriate, or permissible between mother and daughter would—detonated in one holy moment of clarity—yield a simple set of instructions from which I could glean the "what to do" and the "how to behave" with you. Maybe then, I could even step briskly and confidently away from you—away from the awesome power of your reaching, radiating needs—and stand forever separate and outside and unconfused about where you and I begin and end and all would become bearable. Because in those moments when I am wandering around in our relationship and feeling too old to be so utterly lost, it would help to have some definition of you that is not a moving target; to have some perfect point of reference around which to summon my paralysis and direct my cornered feelings. Or do I find fault because I'm unable to make all of your pieces fit some description of you that would allow me to love you?

Survival, plain and simple, was the real and much narrower focus of my life for a long time following what was to have been my day of liberation. Before I occupied the corporate offices that finally separated my childhood circumstances from the start of a long and productive career, my biggest "success" had been to endure the long delay in getting started. It took that year and some fraction of the next to wave my mother off to her new life. I traded two more years in the Women's Marine Corps for the educational benefits, which sent me to college for two more years when I finished my term of service. And

Success as other than it seems

by the time I finally stumbled onto and into the career of my choice, I had wakened—had walked out of my childhood movie. And I was reevaluating the meaning of success from my own perspective, going deeper, evolving strands of my thinking—perhaps learning better *how* to think is more accurate.

Maybe I had run into enough walls on the way to my dream to smack me sensible, or maybe I had simply grown mature enough to question what "success" really meant to me. Because after I had finished apprenticing and gone down a few miles of the corporate road, I was not so eager to climb—at least not *their* way—the ladder that gets you the kind of success almost everyone on the planet seems to covet: the attainment of wealth, favor, or eminence. Observing all around me how many "peripheral" skills were required to get to the top, I understood right away that I was not equipped with the battle gear it takes to win that war. The race to the top— subtle and ruthless; the politics of favoritism, promotion, and pay; the sly injustices of sexism, ageism, racism—the whole construct for making it to the top ran counter to my every instinct. It felt wrong. How was it possible that mean-spiritedness and self-aggrandizement as qualities of character or corporate policy could ever lead to success? In his matchless style of admo- nition, J. Krishnamurti warned how easily competition can expose traits of our lesser nature: "The man goes to the office where he is brutal and ambi- tious, greedy; then he comes home and he says, 'Darling, how lovely you are.'"[3] Much more sternly, he also said:

> Everyone says that he must make his way through life; each one is
> out for himself, whether in the name of business, religion or the
> country. You want to become famous, and so does your neighbour,
> and so does his neighbour; and so it is with everyone from the
> highest to the lowest in the land. Thus we build a society based
> on ambition, envy and acquisitiveness, in which each man is the
> enemy of another; and you are "educated" to conform to this
> disintegrating society, to fit into its vicious frame.[4]

There will always be souls more acutely ambitious and politically adept than I am to play the wealth, favor, and eminence game; some will even manage to keep their souls intact. Yet I think myself lucky never to have been seriously driven by raw ambition. More luck, I'm sure, is that I was simply not cunning or quick enough to compete on their "acutely ambitious" level—yet I was able to win past them many times in my own style. I was a conservative, cool-beauty introvert, after all—and we just don't do "aggressive." So it was not long after I entered the world of the seriously working that I lost my desire to woo "the world's amazed attention" and was content to make all the big and little efforts needed to prove my competence and increase my value in the workplace. It was success enough for me to earn the genuine respect my work received wherever I went and pay that has never been less and often more than adequate for my needs. Into the bargain I learned that my life didn't have to be hugely different from my parents' lives to be different enough, nor did it have to be "hugely" successful—as long as I was defining and achieving success that satisfied my soul.

⌘

Twenty years into their marriage, my mother's second husband died. It fell to me to supplant his "fathering" ways with the (still) child-woman. I moved her close to me and resumed the caretaking role he had once lifted from me—forever, I had hoped—for fifteen long years. Depending on how she is perceived, a child at any age can be unduly demanding, and I found her personality unchanged in that regard. But far more difficult than taming my impatience with her fretful ways was my having to sacrifice freedom and solitude, which had become in the intervening years as precious to me as the air I breathed. So it wasn't long before I felt again the old childhood resentments—more sharply than ever because I was fully conscious now of how and why I carried them. Were it not for my work and the society of a few creative and like-minded others, the constraints she placed on my limited inventory of pleasures would have taken a toll greater than I want to think about. Even so, as the years marched by I began to lose hope for reclaiming the future I was (once again) waiting to call my own.

From "the letter I will never send:"

Success as other than it seems

Fearing as I do to speak out loud, naked with resentments and uneasy in the uncertainty of my own perceptions of you (so many others see you so differently!), I would give all to find some higher ground above the drowning pool from which to address your needs, from which to separate the you and the me in our relationship and impugn neither one. From a distance I could decipher the kaleidoscopic miscellany of desires you deliver to me in tongues: words that give me permission, silences that take it away. Your tremulous petitions for this and that, the crumpled and cranky discontent of you when they are not what you want after all, might become sensible had I some distance from you. Given room to observe, I could perhaps translate those fleet, dark ignitions of memory in the back of your old eyes which speak of ancient fears in a terribly deprived child and of the pain buried deep in your halting, arthritic gait; memories transposed over the span of your long age from "what was" long ago to your chronic refusal of "what is" now, when nothing is ever quite right. If I stood at some reasonable distance, perhaps I could, with just the right words, fill up the awkward, white-sound silences that come between us—when, wordless, you are begging me with your eyes to make sense of your needs and I, blind, am trying to decode them. Oh, Mother, your timorous, controlling ways. If you could only look into your own eyes and behold the soft steel of your willful inertia and the nearly total state of fretting obsession you have become! If you could only behold yourself . . . would it make a difference?

My history with my mother inspired me to keep a vigil over my children's inalienable rights as human beings. I had much to learn about parenting and learned most of it through trial and error, but experience taught me that there are certain things to which every kid in the world is entitled: a sense of themselves as unique and separate; a sense that they are loved deeply, but in no way "owned" by their parents in exchange for the nurture incumbent on parents to provide; finally, when they are ripe enough to drop from the family tree-house, their most important entitlement—personal freedom—is theirs for life. My part was to prepare them for taking their

Chapter two

leave from me by listening to their minds and hearts, teaching them all that I knew, and convincing them that freedom comes with a couple of caveats: to take unto themselves total responsibility for their lives—first and always to and for themselves, then to whatever and whomever they chose to love, honor, cherish, or respect.

You might guess that holding on to my viewpoint was sometimes more complicated than my desire allowed: there were plenty of times I "got in their faces"—and in the way of my own best intentions to allow them to think for themselves, to make time and room in my life for their mistakes, and to applaud them often for just being alive and brightening my day. Hardest of all was keeping my hands off their "inalienable rights" when they were hurting—especially as they grew older and began to experience the kind of pain that goes deep and stays long. When I was tempted to move in on them with too much concern or too much to say, I would pick up my pen and bear witness to their angst and loss of innocence by journaling, as I had done long ago when I was suffering the pain of growing up. Mostly I wrote to remind myself that what I had learned in the time between my painful experiences and theirs was of critical importance to all of us; that while my instinct even today is to rush to relieve them of their hurt any way I can, I could, in fact, do no better than to monitor their process lovingly and attentively, to wait in the wings with a pair of skilled and willing arms to hold them close if necessary—and if invited. Can there be any pain more extreme for a parent than knowing we each must suffer in order to grow? Can there be anything more difficult than comprehending the paradox that becomes the parent's only recourse: she must set both child and parent free; she must sacrifice her desire to alleviate her children's pain and permit them their holy rites of independent passage into adulthood. I wrote:

> I am inclined to surrender to the paradox and to hope—the only
> action in my arsenal at the end of the day—that intuition will
> continue to serve me as a sort of divine prod, instructing me in
> its gentle, wordless way when I persist in a need to hold them too
> close or love them too much—reminding me to hover over them
> from a distance with great intelligence and to take extreme care

Success as other than it seems

with how (or whether) I mitigate life's dangers for them. More than everything else do I venerate with all my heart and mind their right to live free of my "mothering ways" in that private, awesome space wherein lies their soul.

I wrote slowly, carefully, and frequently during those years, pressing my mind to be exact, with my best and truest thinking, reaching back into memory again and again to verify my reasons for holding to a principle born in me because so little consideration was given to my rights as a child. I was burning into words precisely what I believed I owed my children: a certain kind of love so willing to guarantee us freedom from needing each other too much that it might take years for them to pluck out the principle of the thing. I was writing "for my eyes only," of course—so as to never forget what I believed. Just to have persisted in remembering I count as another one of those big "little life successes" that are privately worth the world to me.

It is significant that my perception of my mother was mine alone; to all others in her world she was consistently remarked as being delightful to know: sweet, good-natured, and lovable. She was not two people, being someone different with me than she was with others, nor was she dishonest or conniving with me. She was simply *unconscious*: hidden and protected from accountability in the chrysalis of childlike innocence from which she unconsciously refused to emerge. She would have been the last to know, and appalled to think, that she was using me in the same way she had used her husbands; we greased the skids of a life she had never mastered. How many times did she absolve herself in words of gratitude to me for making possible a life she couldn't imagine living without me! If she had crowded my life with her problems, she had done so unwittingly, and so both her problems and the rest of her life were mine to sort out *wittingly*. And were I to display impatience, or break the silence that subsumed my helplessness, she would react as she had done all her life—as someone will who has never resolved a severely traumatic childhood—by withdrawing into another depression.

Chapter two

My challenge with her had always been the same: to accept my reality and do no conscious harm to her, nor to myself, because were I to not succeed in enduring her lovingly (or something close to that), I might one day be scooping up the pieces of her shattered psyche. I did not always feel up to the challenge:

> Ghostly hopes to live a separately identified life scamper down life's shortening corridors for the daughter growing older. I ask myself the essential question: if she has looked to me for too much, have I tried too hard and too long to please her? And I see that my own complicity renders any answer to my question irrelevant. I can't talk the talk again, Mother; I can't sit your little-girl self on my lap and hold her in my arms and try to persuade her—gently, to spare her too-tender feelings—that life is not a protective womb and that your needs are not as great as you perceive them to be. No, not again—not when my own need is to cry out that it is a mother's responsibility, one of the most precious gifts she can give to her child, to endure her own life, to contain her own pain, to take no child for granted in reward for having birthed her. The devil is not in the details of your deprivation, Mother; the devil perches in the hole at your core and supports your infernal need to fill the hollow. Reaching out to me for relief from uneasiness is your holy grail, Mother, and our dance of death—the dance that goes on until one of us calls it done. It is clear to me this curious need of yours to live your days in the past of your anxious childhood will not abate but endure ever more obstinately as you move closer to the edge of your time. So I shuffle along with you, drop-dead tired of the dance and powerless to get off the dance floor.

So bitter in silence are my pitiful words—keening to come up off the page and be heard! I read them now and weep, remembering our separate burdens. I went back into therapy, hoping to find some new and larger perspective to keep my resolve secure from blowing us sky-high. A remarkably

Success as other than it seems

creative and gifted therapist gave me better than I'd asked for: genuine compassion for my circumstances and some good old-fashioned mothering for the first time in my life. The "child inside," who had lived too much in deference to her parents' needs, was given a full share of close attention and permitted to cry a full measure of tears. Then he taught me how to heal the child's heart by loving her and to detach from unrealistic expectations of the mother-who-was-not. Six months later I had learned to divert much of my psychic energy away from my mother and focus on my own inner needs. I can't say she noticed a difference in me, because I had always played my part convincingly, but I felt the difference as, each day, I was better able to walk the path of least resistance with her. I could not choose to "not be there" for her; *that* decision had been made a long time ago at the level of soul. So my work was to reperceive my "freedom" in a context broad enough to include her, because I knew the freedom I had won and lost from her twice before—though I cherished thoughts of it still—might not come my way again. Acceptance was my only option, the only key to my success, so I began to practice the art of it every day. My resolve was not tested too long: less than a year later she had a massive stroke and died.

Your imagination will do better than my words to describe how I felt at the close of our long relationship. Society—the whole world—says so many things about "mother" that I never experienced about my own; yet, I had always understood that she was lost in the world, asking only that someone—anyone—take her by the hand. My conflict, and biggest torment, was that I felt compassion for her in her circumstances, and at the same time I resented her refusal to reject her fears, if only a little, and step outside the self-imposed walls of her tiny life. Gone now were all my conflicts, traveling with her at the speed of light into the universe. What I remember most about the day she died is the feeling of lightness that drifted all through me, softening my spine, saturating the crannies of my consciousness, sweeping my mind clear—like oxygen, or a cool breeze, or a long, deep exhale of relief, giving me permission to loosen up and let go now, all the way.

I took some days off to honor the event that had suddenly ended our long relationship and to reflect on the enormity of the impact her death would have on me—surely as enormous as the impact her life had made.

Chapter two

What I returned home with was revelatory and conclusive: all along I had been serving the meaning of both our lives by serving hers. Because I had not "given the child away" (as her father had done when her mother died), I could quietly declare success on two counts: for having done the human, caring thing and provided a safe way for her to live and die; and for respecting my soul's instruction from beginning to end. I have wondered since how we are able to do these things—stay true to ourselves even under profound duress. My best guess is that we have an instinct, a propensity, a need to love—and to respect love as the fundamental principle of life itself. Yes, love can succumb or lie fallow in the heart if too much is asked of it. How much is too much is a question only one of us at a time can answer. I am convinced now that choosing to love, if only just enough to keep our humanity intact, is our soul's instinct to survive. To have done that, however imperfectly, enabled me to redeem from my mother the only gift she had to give me: my freedom with impunity. Gently, gently, so as not to offend her, I closed the book on us . . .

> We played our parts, the two of us; we danced the dance. And
> your departure was, after all, exactly on time—just in time for me
> to complete the lesson your life had always had in store for me.

The next day, just before her casket was lowered, I placed a small card on it bearing these words written by a Zen monk centuries ago:

> *Suffering pain . . . not her who*
> *hath finished her journey,*
> *who is free from grief,*
> *who is emancipated in all ways*
> *and whose knots are unloosed.*

There is not room in the dictionary to define success completely, because we could all add a dozen to Merriam-Webster's five separate entries. And how we define it for ourselves will always matter most, because success of any size is uniquely (perhaps only) meaningful to the one who strives to achieve it. My own successes, the ones I savor privately and that please me deeply, continue to be small, cumulative, personal, and of little interest to anyone else. One by itself was never the point: all together, though, I like the story they tell about my character. I doubt I would trade even one of my successes for all of anyone else's. Over time, I developed my own criteria for success using only those that are valuable and meaningful to me—declining to judge my success (and my worth) using the "one size fits all" standard for the general population: rip-roaring success. I have to ask, who but me can judge if I have succeeded with a thing unless they know exactly what I'm trying to achieve, how I rate its importance, and the depth or shortfall of my satisfaction with my result? Who but me, unless you have it on my authority, can dare to say I am a failure—or a success? To clarify my point, who but me knows I am striving this very day to plumb the elusive subtleties of just being? Diligently, mindfully, in the present moment, and fully aware I may never achieve my aim, I practice just being, nonetheless, and count each day that I achieve my goal a truly impressive success. It is helpful to the task when I keep in mind the poet Rilke's words about being totally open to whatever comes next: "to have patience with everything unresolved in your heart and to try to love the questions themselves . . . [l]ive the questions now. Perhaps then, someday far in the future, you will gradually, without even noticing it, live your way into the answer."[5] I am persuaded by them to keep trying—to add yet another "win" to my collection of little, meaningful successes.

Had my original idea of success—meaning fame, financial security, power and plenty—become all-consuming, I would have been off the mark by miles for creating the better story I had in me to live. I'm not looking for any more "comet-like" successes, take my word for it—one of those is enough in a lifetime. But I mean to keep having those little ones, if I can. William James said everything about the success to which I aspire:

> I am done with great things and big plans, great institutions and
> big success. I am for those tiny, invisible loving human forces that
> work from individual to individual, creeping through the crannies

of the world like so many rootlets, or like the capillary oozing of water, which, if given time, will render the hardest monuments of human pride.[6]

To live simply, to grow in humility, to honor the gift of my life, just *to be*: those are the prizes my eyes are on today. They are the most difficult to win, but there are no others today about which I feel truly passionate, and a day in which I've had any success at all in feeling genuine joy and gratitude for just being alive is a day like no other—worth every effort I make to deserve my life.

three

Life's labor, mindfully

> I have been thinking how easy it is to dissolve into
> fragments among the ten thousand things—how only
> work can hold one together—work outer, work inner—
> work that is the incarnation of one's own inner truth—a
> building of something, within and without. . . . This is
> the way till death.
>
> —Helen M. Luke

Upon reflection, I seem to have always been "about"
work. Nothing new there; the great majority of our species has
always been about work; from the time of the hunters and gath-
erers to the space station and cyber-world engineers of today,
nearly everyone—unless they are rich as Croesus or too physically
or mentally impaired—has worked or will work the greater part
of their lives. Working in exchange for the coin of the realm
was the way I fed, housed, and clothed myself, and I assumed
that my motive was the great reason for *everyone's* labor. Later I
learned there are other reasons to work, often layered and subtle
and just as important. I know people who work without pay or
simply work in preference to not working, from some inner need

to be creative, constructive, or of service to others. I learned, too, that work can often be unrewarding and hard to bear—often begrudged when efforts put forth are not equaled by compensation or personal satisfaction received. But for those who are more fortunate, the workplace often serves as a kind of "life school," which was my experience. In the workplace I refined my ability to socialize and learned the value of teamwork. I learned to discriminate between personal and collective values and how to improve my skills for better pay. Best of all was my discovery of the personal pleasure I derived from doing my work well. Observing my peers over time taught me that if I took my work seriously and did my best, I would gain self-confidence and—if it mattered enough—financial independence. But the most obvious and enduring lesson about the workplace was one I picked up in a matter of weeks: my *attitude* mattered to everyone. My perception of my work and myself in relationship to it illustrated who I was, revealing to those around me whether and how much I valued them, the quality and integrity of my work, and myself. I understood right away that I would be measured for the rest of my working life—as are we all—by my attitude. So, given my hard and humble beginnings and being in need of every kind of opportunity, it was lucky for me that I considered work a *good* thing right from the start.

Between the ages of six and twenty-three, I was already "working" with the singular purpose of making money and discovering in the process the nearly desperate determination I possessed. Whether I was picking beans in a field as a kid, waiting tables after school to pay for my room and board, or carhopping to buy my first set of wheels, I loved to work. For one thing, the money I earned bought me what I wanted or needed and would otherwise have had to do without. More important than the money, though, was that working made me feel powerful and independent—and it challenged me; whatever I worked at, my goal was to achieve a personal best. My mind was set on being the fastest bean picker in the field, on becoming the preeminent waitress on staff, and on hooking more food trays onto more car doors than any other carhop on the lot. Working made me feel grown up, on my way out of childhood and into a life of my own. However false my sense of security was in those years, I was convinced that all I needed to prove my worth and survive anything was a respectable job.

Life's labor, mindfully

At age six I was hawking lemonade to buy penny candy or ice cream bars from the Good Humor truck; only a decade later my work was funding necessities—clothing, school tuition and books, food and rent in support of my mother, and, when I finally arrived at that life of my own, in support of me. Then, when I was twenty-three, I found the job that became the career that not only finished growing me up *really*, but revealed who I could become. Eventually, it provided me with enough financial freedom to make some important decisions: my ability to support my children and myself, for example, allowed me to end a marriage that was no longer viable. Had I not stumbled into that job exactly when I did—and had I not been invited to work for the only person I have ever known who offered just what I needed to thrive—I would have lived a totally different life.

Behind the walls of a low-slung, radically modern structure built mostly of glass, there worked a congenial group of architects, master planners, and interior designers with whom I felt immediately at home. I had applied for a lesser position just to get into the place and was happy to wait inside for something more challenging. Who cared how long it took? I'd been in love with the art and artistry of architecture since I was a teenager, so I was thrilled to death just to be in its milieu. And I could not have been more certain that this was the time, the place, and the vocation for which I'd been waiting—the one that would roll out the future I had dreamed about since I was a child so eager to leave home. The firm's creative director was one of two partners who owned the company—the one with the remarkable talent, good looks, and an eye for beautiful women. Before long, I was interviewed—first by the office manager, then by him—to replace his executive secretary (she was beautiful, of course), who was trading her job at the office for a different set of pleasures: marriage and motherhood. He must have hoped I would have the right stuff, but seemed perfectly willing to hire first and evaluate my limitations later. I knew it was the pretty face that got the job. I also knew I was qualified to do the work and that his offer was a rare opportunity to prove myself in a profession that could hold my interest while I learned everything it could teach me. I accepted eagerly. Our relationship was complicated within a week.

Framed photos on the wall behind his drafting table told me that he was married and had children not much younger than I, yet he flirted with me

Chapter three

in the subtle, decidedly experienced ways that came as naturally to him as did his breezy air of self-assurance. I was newly married—flattered by the extraprofessional attention and unwilling to take it seriously. When I easily exceeded his expectations of my capability for the job, he began to teach me about his profession. It was his talent as a teacher—his incredibly conceptual mind and broadly educated intellect, the depth of his creative imagination and his worldliness—that I found seductive in the extreme. He was old enough to be my father—and in so many ways the father any young woman who felt deprived of one would long to have as a substitute—and my attraction to him was both intellectually complete and psychologically bewildering. From the outset, our relationship was restrained and gracious, but just beneath a deceptive surface calm there bubbled a hash of ambiguous feelings—mine *and* his—that soon had me uneasy with feelings I could not shake off. It was a long time before I could see through the fog of my unconscious emotions, flush out the right from the real in them, and reach enough clarity to articulate my conclusions—first to myself, and then (when I found the courage) to him. Hesitant as I was to declare myself, I knew I must set us both straight, and if he refused to accept the truth of my conclusions, I would have to leave.

Oh, how long I struggled to put names and reasons to feelings I was experiencing in his presence for the first time ever, and how I feared the possibility that naming them would jeopardize my dream to forge a strong, whole, independent self in a career that could, among other things, finally define me. I was young, inexperienced in the ways of the heart in spite of my marriage, and because my psyche was still fragile from the patched cracks of my childhood, I needed this perfect opportunity to heal and mature into all I imagined I could be. But I could not bear feeling so troubled, and so I resolved to search myself for as long as it took to find out why. It took nearly two years—one uneasy day after another—to sort it all out and see that there was only one solution to a problem it would take two of us to fix. According to Jungian analyst James Hollis:

> Guilt sits like a large black bird on the shoulders of most of us.
> Jung's concept of the shadow reminds us all of our participation

Life's labor, mindfully

in the forbidden, our egotism, our narcissism and cowardice. . . . Thus, part of the legitimate development of the individual is the appropriate acknowledgment of guilt, which is to say the accep-tance of responsibility for the consequences of one's choice, how-ever unconscious one was at the time.[1] . . . It may be that at first one may not legitimately understand the harm done, but when such recognition is available, then consciousness must acknowl-edge that yes, I did that, caused that, am responsible for that.[2]

At first I did not understand "the harm done." I hadn't done anything wrong, so why did I feel guilt? We worked together so closely that I was intuiting his wishes for something more than a professional relationship—that's why! He did not speak of them, but they were thick in the air. Because I was in the orbit of his personality the greater part of most days, I became adept at seeing through his persona and into his private thoughts. I was "read-ing" his feelings, sensing his expectations, going behind his compliments to decipher the reasons he placed me so often at his side—even as I uncon-sciously denied them! I felt my conflict long before I understood what it was: I was an observant, passive, and unwilling participant on one level of our relationship—the part that was "thick in the air." Yet there I was—the eager, fully engaged, more-than-willing student, sitting opposite him and radiating my desire to learn everything he could teach me.

For the first time I experienced guilt as something layered and compli-cated, and it confused every part of my life—my marriage, my work, and my sense of myself as a good person. In some indecipherable way I felt wrong even to be in his presence, reluctantly paying witness to his unspoken re-quests of me, even as I hoped with all my heart he would fill *my* need for an interested "father" and career guide. There was my conflict: what we wanted from one another was a tradeoff I knew I could never make yet unconsciously felt I *should* make in order to be "fair" to him. Had he been reading me and misinterpreting my confusion? Was he waiting me out in hope that I would eventually yield to the obvious? Or, perhaps he wanted me to stand up and declare what the hell I *did* want so that we could end this game and get on with the work! When I finally unraveled the full extent of my naïveté, I screwed up my courage and scheduled a time on his calendar for us to talk.

It could have been my gamble to lose. After all, this was during the 1950s, before the feminist movement had begun to rock the cradle of change for gender parity and employment rights in the workplace, and while I wanted that job desperately (viewing it rather dramatically as the key to my entire future), he held all the power. But it never came to that; all it needed was for me to communicate what I understood to be his feelings for me and that I could not, for reasons I named, reciprocate them. He said he understood, conceded my case, and thanked me for expressing my concerns. Our meeting concluded; my troubles were ended. By that time we had developed a deep respect for one another because we shared a common desire to achieve excellence in our work; we also thoroughly enjoyed our roles as teacher and student. By focusing on what we did well as a team, working together became effortless and highly productive. When I knew him much better, I realized that the potential for losing my job had not been nearly so great as my anxiety had construed it to be. I thought, too, that he could not have modeled "interested father" nearly as well as the interested friend and mentor he eventually became. I worked with him before, between, and after the births of my three children—for more than twenty-two years.

I got the best of the deal. At the end of my first two years with the firm, his partnership split in two over irreconcilable policy differences. I, along with three architects loyal to his creative vision, moved with him to a different location, set up offices, and started a new practice from the ground up. It was an extraordinary opportunity for me—the gift of a lifetime! My responsibility was to put in place the administrative infrastructure. Had he presented it to me that way my knees would have buckled; fortunately, there was no time to think beyond what needed doing each day—and so I dived in, triaging our needs, working each of them through to completion. I hired administrative staff, requested vendor bids, purchased supplies and equipment, established relationships with legal accounting and part-time personnel firms, and vetted their contracts. I designed an office-wide communications system, researched and wrote job descriptions and office policy manuals— whatever it took to get all the wheels turning to support the professionals.

Life's labor, mindfully

34

It was a unique time in my life. Only by concentrating on everything new I was learning—grateful to think it would keep me in demand and financially secure for the rest of my working life—did I get through that year. It was the kind of baptism by fire I hoped to go through only once.

Meanwhile, my mentor hired and trained the professional team, marketed his firm to potential clients, and contracted for engineering, master planning, and interior design talent. Ever the teacher, his door was always open to senior staff for counseling and support. I flourished under his tutelage—happy to be challenged, exhausted at the end of every day. If I sometimes felt out of my depth, he urged me on: "Trust yourself, you can *do* this," he would say, reminding me that he was always "right next door." Less than a year had passed when word got around about his new digs and the projects began to roll in. I was twenty-six years old and sinking roots fast into a career as an administrative professional. Any similar career climb might have taken twenty years to orchestrate and been only half as interesting; it is certain I would not have had the kind of generous support, tutelage, and deep trust that he placed in me. Was it timing, instinct, or synchronicity? I will always call it the miracle that set both my lives—inner and outer—in motion.

CRS

The children, though—what about the children? you might ask. A working mother is conflicted. Period. She wears conflict like a hair shirt that scrapes her heart and mind a hundred times a day. She might feel a *little* less conflict if she and her kids absolutely adore the caregiver. She might feel a *little* less guilt if she has no choice but to work and leave them every day. She might feel a *little* better if her husband is a rare one who can work at home and has proven that he can care for them well. Otherwise, she bleeds the drip . . . drip . . . drip . . . of her bloody conflict from the minute she leaves them in the morning until she is back through the door at night calling out their names, her arms open and hungry to hold them close and appease her guilt. That's the truth, straight up. I felt it the day I returned to work after my first child was born, and I felt it every day thereafter for the next six years, when the third child arrived. Then, the house filled to its eaves with noise

Chapter three

and disorder, I took a four-year sabbatical from work. We—the children and I—needed some quality time to develop and express the full range of our feelings for one another, time for them to cement their trust in my total availability. I needed to live in one world for a while—to focus on each growing, lovable one of them, and on all of us together as a family. I needed to peel off my hair shirt and give conflict a rest, to watch them grow hour by hour and feel the joy of my love and devotion to them for whole days and weeks at a time. I needed all of that just as much as I would need, again and again, to attend to my own personal growth, challenging myself intellectually and creatively to produce interesting, excellent work out in the world. In a nutshell, I needed it all.

Whether or not she has a choice to work outside the home, when a woman becomes a mother, she *must* make a trade; hopefully it is the one that will cost her least. What more can I say? I have wondered whether women have more needs than men, but I think it does little good to generalize about what calls for an individual response to individual circumstances. Maybe some women—maybe many women—need more *diversity*. I've not met the man who clamored to stay at home and develop a set of skills with his children that would make him a better parent; but I've known many mothers who, sooner or later, chose to work in the world in order to make themselves a "larger" person—and therefore perhaps a better parent. I didn't have to work until the divorce, though my contributions to the family bank account certainly improved our lifestyle. But working made me happy, enlarged my identity, and strengthened my ego. The workplace is where I found interesting and like-minded others and where I learned to take on the challenges that helped me to grow: the work provided the grist that I milled into greater love for my life.

I also wanted children to love and cherish and from whom to learn. I wanted to atone for my parents' unconscious sins of omission with my sister and me by giving to my children the childhood I didn't have—the one with quality time and love intelligently applied. I wanted to guide my children with care and thoughtfulness through their developing years and to teach them the value of honesty, truth, and integrity as they worked their way through a full course of education—more, if they wanted more. But I didn't

Life's labor, mindfully

want to give up a truly meaningful part of my life to give them theirs; I wanted all of us to have a life. I fully believed it was in the roundness of my self-sufficiency—my emotional and financial health and independence—that we would all flourish, and to the extent (given my several human limitations) that we all did thrive, I was right.

The working mother conflict will be around as long as there is human life on the planet, because there is no help for a mother's instinct to take seriously her child's need for her, wherever she is. Yet, there is no reason for others to judge the quality of her child care because she works in the world—no reason to question women who choose to add a multiplicity of interesting accomplishments to the sacred work of parenting. Willing to risk repercussions, I knew long before I was a mother that I wouldn't follow the conventional wisdom of my time about child raising, yet I'm as certain today as ever that I—and my children—would have lived a life much poorer in every respect had I not worked both inside and outside the home. I take no credit—or blame—for daring to differ with the majority of mothers and fathers who thought differently then; I was merely following, as I had always done, the voice that leads from within. I examined my circumstances, weighed our collective needs against the probable costs, made my decisions, and lived my life. That will sound easier than it was, of course, yet I have never regretted my choice to "have it all"—or as close to "all" as I could get. My choice was mine to make and would be unacceptable to a great many women, even today. It has always been a comfort to me to believe that we all have a right—I would say a responsibility—to live life "my way."

And then, years and years later, there was more work to do. "One of the signal events of what I have called the middle passage is the recognition that having achieved one's goals, one still hungers for the inexpressible,"[2] Hollis says, speaking of the "midlife crisis." He is saying that the work we assumed would keep us engaged and satisfied indefinitely often does not, referring to a time in life when our selves and our senses have given and received the most we can reasonably expect from the years—usually decades—

Chapter three

we devoted to the workplace. It is a time when many of us feel a growing need to transit out of one kind of life into another because working in the world no longer "works." When I left the architectural firm I took my skills with me into some famously wonderful companies, being careful always to choose a setting in which I was deeply interested. I worked with CEOs and executive committees and boards of directors in the film industry, in communications and journalism, in corporate public affairs, and, for the last dozen years of my paid employment, in the soul-satisfying world of non-profits. My "executive assistant" title assured there was little business under the corporate sun I would not in some way be involved with—that was half the fun. Always, though, the most pleasurable parts of my days were spent writing—brochures, newsletters, press releases, speeches, articles, proposals, reports, and analyses—so various in kind that I was never bored and, as ever, still found myself challenged to do my best. What a great ride, my work in the world! I loved everything about it.

Then, on one otherwise quite ordinary morning, I woke up—and I was "done." I mean, *done.* Once or twice I had felt small tugs at the corner of my mind, urging me to consider some new thing. But I never took them seriously. "Not yet, I still need the income," I'd think, or, "No, no, no, what on earth would I do all day?" Yet, on the morning of the day I swear I never saw coming, a world I knew intimately—had mastered, loved, and lived in for as long as I could remember—had simply stopped mid-turn, never to turn again. Too stunned to grieve, I could only conclude that having picked and shoveled for its riches the whole length of my career, I had finally extracted every last bit of treasure the working world could yield. What now? I gave notice. I hired my replacement—and then I jumped off that moving train as naked as a baby, leaving on board a lifetime of rich and verdant abundance which, in a span of hours, had dried up to desert. Having assumed I had some good years left to go, I was surprised again when I landed in the middle of a psychological nowhere and could not imagine when or how—or whether—my life would ever take root again. I knew only that not too long before my work had been more than enough to keep me happy and soon after that it was not nearly enough. I must have asked myself a thousand times: *what is happening to me?* I didn't hear back right away that in fact I was

Life's labor, mindfully

"hungering for the inexpressible," but those words did in time become the overarching answer to questions so new I didn't know how to ask them.

⟠

"When one sees someone still obsessed with 'success' in the second half of life, then one is encountering a non-reflective ego,"[3] Hollis says—noting that while ambition may be necessary in the first half of life,

> in the second half of life we are invited to leave ambition behind, as well as a preoccupation with self-esteem. . . . Then what, one may reasonably ask, is one to do in the second half of life? What does one serve if not ambition?[4]

What, indeed? With the exception of some interim work at home for my last employer, my days were completely unscheduled for the first time in memory. Yet, so uncomfortable was I to be at loose ends in a luxury of daylight hours, the first thing I did was to schedule my time! First breakfast, newspapers, then two hours for "serious" reading, a light lunch, preferably out-of-doors (this was L.A., after all), and journal writing until four o'clock. After four, I was saved from the yawning abyss of my never-ending freedom by reading mail, paying bills, running errands, and evenings as usual. I was off the train, but I couldn't stop moving. It occurred to me I might become bored or lonely, two possibilities I refused to contemplate.

With worldly ambition behind me and devoid of a single idea about what new thing I should do, writing soon became again the best part of my day. I wrote mainly to assuage my feelings of aimless wandering, burrowing into my psyche to make sense of my recent revolt against a world that was already receding from memory and leaving canyons of empty space. What was the underlying significance of that truly courageous—or perhaps foolish, certainly radical—decision to disconnect forever from the habits and professional comforts of nearly a lifetime? I persuaded myself I had not been foolish to end a career from which all ambition and passion had vanished. But had I been precipitous? Maybe I had bolted too soon from a patch of garden-variety boredom that would have run its course. Still, I felt no tug to return to my former life; "deprogrammed" was how I felt, disoriented by the sight of my empty desk.

My writing produced no answers, but it gave me two important insights. For several years prior to her death, I was aware that, if and when I were to be released from the responsibility of caring for my mother, I would inherit a windfall of personal freedom that would transport me to something akin to total happiness. Yet, until my freedom was a fact, I would need to continue to work to pay for a not-small number of expenses incurred each month for her care. Psychologically, then, I couldn't afford not to love my work—one does not often hang out consciously with more psychic pain than is necessary, especially when there is no way to predict its end. My mother died suddenly and unexpectedly—opening space in my psyche to experience simultaneously not only my freedom, but the equally sudden death of my need to—and interest in—working in the world. In time I would discover what else besides "happiness" had been waiting on my freedom: the prospect of a whole new life—but I would need to plumb my depths to find it.

I realized, too, that I was writing to find "commonsense" reasons to explain an action triggered at a deeper level of my psyche, where logic does not abide. It was too soon for me to know that an interior process was already underway, pacing itself and needing nothing from me—yet. I could only wait. I floundered around for a while "practicing waiting"—something so new it was often painful to endure. Some months later, though, I began to trust that by simply living my quiet, eventless days one at a time, I would in some way be taught how to inhabit my brand new egoless "I." Recalling other major life changes I had managed to survive well enough—marriages, motherhood and divorce, a couple of major crises, and one very painful loss—I accepted that I was once more merely in transition, and though I couldn't yet find my center or describe my purpose, I began to love my new life. I stopped scheduling my time and started walking the beach any time I felt like it.

Life's labor, mindfully

James Hollis again:

> One is called to live one's values in the world, quite apart from
> the likelihood of success, validation or self-aggrandizement. The
> embodiment of one's vocation, the calling to be a person of value
> in the world, is arguably the chief task of the second half of life.[5]

My life passed back and forth in review for over a year as I walked those beaches, rolling out my history all the way from then to now for one final look. I had made my amends wherever needed years ago and resolved every negative perception I could hunt down in my psyche to make more room for lightness in my being. Having learned through years of therapy to forgive my "failings," to see them finally not as failings but as lessons for the road ahead, I found little in my past to judge harshly this time around. So I rolled it up—released my history to the universe, to infinity—to God, if God had an interest. I was ready then to turn my undivided attention to "the chief task of the second half of life"—the inner work of completion that measures "a person of value in the world."

Like the multitude of others who face trying circumstances in childhood, I got an early start on life-crisis management, which is a big part of the inner work of coming to self-awareness. Even so, it has taken time—a whole lifetime (and one is never "finished")—to quietly reflect on the ten thousand things I needed to know about myself in order to enlarge my consciousness. I believe that if I had not made the effort, I would be of limited value to myself or anyone else today. What helped me to respect the importance of my effort were certain memories from childhood. I grew up in a virtual laboratory of depressed and neurotic family members and had a surplus of opportunities to observe the workings of their troubled unconscious minds; they all seemed unable or unwilling to do the inner work that might have repaid them with optimism and a happier life. They were all gone before I knew enough to forgive them, I'm sorry to say, because they, more than anyone or anything else, "inspired" my earliest efforts to get at the truth of myself and find my value.

There is no tangible measurement for the psychological and spiritual wealth that accrues to a life lived consciously. Yet it took two marriages—where one

Chapter three

might have sufficed had I been more conscious—before I knew that some-one as truly introverted as I am would have a rough go sustaining a working partnership if married to someone as truly extroverted as were both of my husbands. We might have taken turns—one time going out on the town with plenty of friends in tow, the next time staying home by ourselves to quietly and separately read a book—but after awhile, I didn't want to take turns—nor did they. That one fundamental difference between us—though there were others, of course—was enough all by itself to cause my marriages to fail. An introvert concentrates and evaluates experience inwardly and gains most of her nurture there, where she feels most at home. The extrovert thrives "out there" in the objective world and will not feel "at home" for long without the stimulation he gets from the group. You could say, then, that my hus-bands and I virtually lived in two different worlds. Years later, when I knew enough to reflect on those relationships in depth, I had to face the awkward truth that both of those men were more accommodating to our differences than I ever had been. Each of us suffered: perhaps they suffered a little less because they were more adaptable. Living without adequate amounts of solitude—needing more of it, I think, than any marriage could reasonably sustain unless both partners are introverts—I finally became too unhappy to stay in the relationships. Had I known this simple truth about myself earlier, would I have married either one of them? Would I have ever married? The questions are moot, but the point is surely not lost: my lack of awareness at that time about the basic nature of my own personality was the cause of a lot of unhappiness. And so it goes in the world. A few early mandatory psych classes for every teenager in the family might be helpful—don't you think?

That is just one example of the relevance of self-awareness to a hugely important life decision made (twice!) by me in ignorance, and just a drop in the bucket of the inner work that begged to be done—the sooner the better, if I were to become a person of value to myself and to important others in my life. And how does one become self-aware? Slowly, I found out—a little at a time, forever! I paraphrase here some words I read a long time ago about consciousness that captured my rapt attention: if I don't know who I am, I am little more than a body with a head autonomously churning out a continuous stream of fleeting and unrelated thoughts. I took the words to

Life's labor, mindfully

mean that one must stop and think, reflect, question, mull over, and chew on whatever comes up that puts a dent in self-complacency, and that by doing so one gains self knowledge and becomes of value in the world. When you think about it, consciousness certainly has its advantages. For example, if I can respond satisfactorily to your questions—and my own—about what I think and how I feel about myself, it is safe to say I can be in a healthy, loving relationship with someone. I am at a severe disadvantage in making good decisions about my life if I can't name my strong points and my limitations (or my personality type!) or if I don't know my tolerances for someone else's characteristics. It helps to know what gives meaning to my life, how much and how well I am able to love, and whether I know how to communicate love and respect and gratitude—and my negative feelings, as well. I have another leg up on decision making when I have a set of personal values by which I am guided in all matters, great and small. And if I know exactly to whom and what I have chosen to hold myself responsible, I will have no trouble making commitments that I can honor. And, and, and . . . but you have the idea now.

Considering all the obstacles that stood in the way of my coming to awareness, I believe that I am now psychologically pretty healthy; even so, there are some things that will never delete from my hard drive. On a spiritual level, I know enough about God now to use the word "ineffable," instead, and to realize that I can know nothing about God, even as I continue to feel an ineffable presence in my life. And if I were asked today, "Have you become a person of value in the world yet?" I would dare to say "yes," but would *not* dare to overstate my value, which will always be limited by the work I have yet to do. Ego has no part in inner work; the more conscious I become, the more I understand that on one level of our being we are all the same. Humility is the big prize for self-awareness; it takes me out of competition and jumps me three levels higher in happiness just to be alive.

My instinct to jump off the ego train was not precipitous; it was a symptom of my need to locate a deeper level of my being; I have no doubt about that today. The time was ripe to shift my focus inward and look for new life. Walking the metaphorical beach whenever I was moved to do so was the beginning of my learning how *to be*—a direct path to my sacred inner

Chapter three

self, where I go to be with my soul and the peace that can lift the harrowing weight of the world off my heart. I am consistently amazed at the spiritual largesse that waits for me in that deeper dimension of the self. Attending to my life contemplatively, by simply paying witness to whomever or whatever is before me in the moment—peeling away the layers of shallow and obsolete head chatter to make room for a deep and well-considered consciousness—is more than enough in a day to keep me spiritually familiar.

As I write, my closest friend is in danger of dying, diagnosed less than a week ago with inoperable lung cancer. There will be nothing to distract me today from experiencing the profound effect on my life that even the possibility of her death is having. There is nothing as important to me as reflecting deeply on our twenty-nine-year relationship and how much it has meant to me and feeling the poignancy of everything we've shared, in good times and bad—and wondering if perhaps this is the beginning of the saddest and most awesomely beautiful time of all. I will take all the time I need to consciously linger on the intricate and exquisite ways I have come to love her—and to feel the raw pain in my throat when I think how much her children would miss her should she not survive her disease. I will break from my writing—the only thing I do now—to be with her, fully present in the moment, as she begins to make a new and important journey into the mystery of unknowing. I will practice dying right along with her as she moves through the days, in her typically classy way, responding fearlessly to whatever will be—and hope to improve on my own less-talented ways by watching her. I will reflect on how rich I am just because she exists on the planet, so that I can love her better now than ever before. As often and as long as I need to, I will sit on my bench by the sea and think of her and feel increasing gratitude for the sun and the moon, for the planet I call home, for the genius of our humanity—and the shadows that stalk our humanity—all parts of the life that "is what it is." More than anything, I'll be grateful for having known her for even a day. I know how to do this now—to go inside and do the deep inner work that will complete the cycle of my lifetime.

Life's labor, mindfully

Helen M. Luke:

> There is only one "work" now—the finding of that rhythm, that
> flowing in, flowing out, in the minute particulars of every day.[6]

It is impossible to think of my life without its long history of work in
the world, or without regard to the impressive range of its core influence
on my personal development. Working increased both the heft of an ego
dangerously slight in size and the vibrato of a personality initially way too
tenuous and somber. During my apprenticing years, I could palpably feel
my work saving my life, stitching together old torn-up feelings, settling down
anxiety, nailing my existence to a platform of solid purpose. The workplace
served as both context and crucible in which the "I" of me could evolve
while no fewer than three life constructions were maturing simultaneously:
the professional life, to which I gave my all and got so much in return; the
life of my psyche, so much in need of a healthy makeover; and the emerging
creative life of a writer. I grew up and grew strong during the years I worked:
I *was* my work until I could be more than it. Work was the metaphor for
life itself, until, finally fully alive, I could feel my blood course and hear my
heart beating whole and healthy.

But that was then. Now I am more than ever inclined to continue my
long habit of writing on the deep and personal inner-work level with which
I have become so intimately familiar and comfortable, gently probing the
mysteries of the universal self with the inner eye that sees poetry, the inner
ear that hears silence, and the heart that sings for no apparent reason. There
I roam for hours at a time, searching for words to describe things that are
indescribable. When a need *to be* takes me inside, I try to go with an open
mind and a willingness to radically change my worldview—which is as it
should be. It is my season to be radical, my time of life to be willing—my best
and last chance to complete myself.

Turn, turn, turn: "To everything there is a season, and a time to every
purpose under heaven" (Ecclesiastes 3:1). There have been many days in my
life I would have gladly traded for better ones—but never a season.

Chapter three

four

Relationships

Anything but Easy

[H]uman relationship is one of the most radical, basic,
essential things we have to find out about, because from
that we may find out for ourselves what love is, what
love really is, not what we have made of it .

—J. Krishnamurti

They were a classic "beautiful couple," though
only recently conferred the title—less than a year before this story
begins, as I remember it. She had just moved in with him—she
thinking they would become engaged immediately, he thinking
they would know in a year or two if their love was strong enough
to commit to marriage. They had not yet discussed their separate
assumptions—not enough, anyway, and certainly not definitively.
But they were in love and what could go wrong? And so they
began to argue about those separate assumptions almost as soon
as she was unpacked. One of those two beautiful, then thirty-
something people is a child of mine. Out for a long run on a
Sunday afternoon in a direction away from what had morphed
into their marathon quarrel, he stopped by my place

unannounced. He was pretty distraught, so we talked for quite a while. At his request, I invited her over after he left and made tea while she told her side of things—which was considerably dissimilar to his, as you might guess. Then *we* talked for quite a while. I said the same things to both of them— that they had just given birth to a relationship that, like any "newborn," would need a lot of tender, loving care to survive; that the relationship would not carry their angry arguments for long and might buckle under the burden; how important it was for them to communicate and conciliate— things like that. I trembled to think how accountable I was for my words, but I needn't have—words were too cool to survive the heat in their emotions. She threatened to move out. He acquiesced to the engagement. They married, honeymooned, bought and furnished a home, and got to know each other better. The separation came less than two years later, then the divorce. Another couple of years went by while they suffered hurt and anger from what they believed the other had done to them, and then sorrow and remorse when they finally owned up to their separate stuff. Let's say they learned a lot about themselves: if they did so too late to resurrect the marriage, clearly it was soon enough for both of them to do better in the next relationship. I suffered with them at an appropriate distance, knowing from similar experiences that coming to consciousness about relationship—or anything else important in life—can be tough, painful, and time-consuming. I could only hope they would discover that coming awake is also incredibly freeing and *necessary* if we mean to live a truly meaningful life.

I, too, was thirty-something when I faced a deplorable lack of self-knowledge, and one of its ranking consequences was my inability to successfully connect in relationship for lack of an educated, objective view of myself. I have only to recall the two most important decisions of my early-to-midlife adulthood: one was to marry the first time—I was twenty-three, we divorced fourteen years later; the other was to marry a second time—and then think better of my decision five years later. My marriages are perfect examples of the way two people meet, fall into rapture, and project commendably upbeat expectations for a long and happy relationship. Not right away, but soon enough in both marriages, we were projecting reasons to blame each other when our individual needs and expectations went unmet—

Chapter four

and we did it *sub rosa*, for how could we say to each other what we couldn't sensibly describe to ourselves—or, more to the point, how could we face that we were each a part of our problem? Eventually we fell out of love and into disillusionment, the way so many couples do. Hope dies. Divorce follows. I never really understood how either marriage came to an end, but I adamantly defended myself against any blame for their failure—as did they. We walked through the years asleep—both of us, both times—chock-a-block with ignorance and with self-knowledge years away. It is common knowledge that most couples who divorce bring one marriage to a close only to repeat the whole unconscious process. Why would I do that, I wondered when the second one ended—how could I have twice managed to marry "the wrong man"? It took several years of serious probing to uncover the "wrong woman" who lived with those men, barely aware of herself in too many ways that really counted. It hardly matters that she intuited, long before meeting either one of them, that she was out of her depths in relationship. Aniela Jaffé says:

> The experience of meaning—which is what, ultimately, life is about—is by no means equivalent to non-suffering; yet the resilience of the self-aware and self-transforming consciousness can fortify us against the perils of the irrational and the rational, against the world within and the world without.[1]

Not many years into the first marriage, I was so certain I needed help that I made a commitment—and was actually eager—to undergo psychotherapy. It was a watershed decision that initiated a series of remarkable changes—better said, a continuing process of change—in a psyche that was crying out for change all the way to its core. At the time, I was responsibly—if somewhat mechanically—meeting the obligations of wife, mother, and working professional, yet, I could not name *me*. By looking for me, I hoped to locate some unifying purpose to my life—to find my center, wherein my several separate identities could hook up and ground me as a whole and happy individual. Therapy did in fact become my road to a conscious life, but it was not a walk in the park. Whatever I might have imagined, I found no quick and

Relationships: anything but easy

brilliant shortcuts for saving that first marriage—or the next one. It was a long, transformative process, I mean to say, and frequently painful. Fortunately, tiny precursors pointing to an increasingly better life-in-progress showed up almost immediately for me and became the good enough incentive to continue doing the work.

It was never in dispute that I needed rescuing from the drowning pool of my childhood. The therapist made his assessment early and easily and confirmed my own long-standing sense of things. Pretty soon came the hard part—bringing up to consciousness the fears and angers of a child still locked into an intricate system of defenses she had erected to prevent all further intrusions of pain. The system had once served to keep a fragile psyche afloat, but my defenses had mutated with time into full-blown neuroses unfitting to my later age and circumstances and damaging to my relationships. I had somehow pulled and patched together enough of an adult persona to navigate my days persuasively by acting as if all was right in my world and making a good appearance. But now—though I might excel in my work, mother my children with care, and "invent" a relationship with my husband that seemed to work on its surface—I was running out of appearances and exhausted from contriving an identity I could only guess was me.

The therapist quickly observed that I hadn't yet acknowledged the child still wandering around in my unconscious in search of attention. She would have been in my way, you see, giving the lie to my carefully constructed pretense of self-sufficiency. So she went along with me to the wedding. And whom might he have brought, I wondered? But never mind that—our plan was to sail through it all; we would steer through the best and the worst of times in our marriage on the deep supportive seas of our incredible love. Helen Luke:

> It doesn't mean you can do without relationship: very much the
> opposite. But you recognize that relationship cannot happen until
> you are separate. Otherwise it is just a mixup in the unconscious
> of two people. You have to be separate in order to unite, because
> uniting means two unique things that meet. Not two fuzzy things—
> that merge![2]

Chapter four

You can see the cracks in the construction here: I hand over to him my responsibility for the little girl, unaware that she and I lack the wherewithal to take on so complex a relationship as marriage without running into serious trouble. For starters, can you imagine that inept and uneasy child in a 1950s marriage bed when I tell you that I am a virgin on our wedding night? Blithely unaware of her, I have not a concern in the world on our wedding day; he has professed his love often and convincingly and I harbor no doubts that we will live happily ever after. Consciously, I vow in my heart to do everything it takes to make him happy (whatever I might have meant by that), because he is perfect and I adore him. So there we were, standing at the altar: "two fuzzy things"—merging. My memory of us is poignant. We were Lancelot and Guinevere, romantically projecting and superimposing our fairytale love and impossible ideals on a couple of inexperienced, wannabe grown-ups and not one *bona fide* between us for making a marriage last. It worked for a few years, then less and less, and in the end—hurt, saddened, exhausted from trying, but still pretty much clueless—we separated out our marbles from *this* pile of unrealistic expectations and went bravely on to pick up the next game. And right there—at that very point—my lesson *might* have been learned—and wasn't.

Prior to both marriages, I fell madly in love with my husbands-to-be. In each instance I was swept away, so uniquely excellent were they in every respect. My feelings of love and good fortune were complete—why on earth would I question them? I was drunk with love, delirious to have found a perfect mate. This was doubly true of the second marriage, when a windfall second chance at marital bliss for both of us was almost too marvelous to take in. (Does it sound like I had learned much about choosing a partner for life yet—or more like the same old magical thinking?) The first time was for the lesson, you'd think. So, when alarms began to sound the second time, why had I ignored them? Why had I not stopped to contemplate—not even for a day—how "iffy" were our chances of survival in that marriage? Here's why: because the still-needy child in me had leapt ahead of my better instinct to be cautious—and because for some of us the mills of the gods grind enlightenment *slowly*. So my lesson had waited for me until now, when for the first time I sensed my life whooshing through the neck of time's hourglass. Thoroughly chastened by a second divorce, I set aside all thoughts of relationship, intimate or otherwise, and redoubled my efforts to come awake.

Marie-Louise von Franz:

> Just as we tend to assume that the world is as we see it, we naively suppose that people are as we imagine them to be. In this latter case, unfortunately, there is no scientific test that would prove the discrepancy between perception and reality. Although the possibility of gross deception is infinitely greater [with people] than in our perception of the physical world, we still go on naively projecting our own psychology into our fellow human beings. In this way everyone creates for himself a series of more or less imaginary relationships based essentially on projection.[3]

I understood then that I could go on making "more or less imaginary relationships based essentially on projection," or I could step off the blind horse of my persisting ignorance, dive deeper inside to find what else about me there was to discover, and hope one day to grasp and take responsibility for every mistake that belonged to me. It was a formidable task and took several years to accomplish, but I did that. I took back all of the impossible expectations I had once placed on two husbands and on the state of marriage itself, examining with great care and scrupulous honesty one false notion at a time until I could identify their causes in me and fully understand my contributions to relationships that had touched so many lives in my world—and failed. At the same time, I took hold of my little girl with the growing consciousness of an adult woman, grew her up, and integrated her with the rest of me. When I had done all of that, I could think I knew who I was; I had found my center and was traveling in the direction of "whole and happy." And I knew at least this much about relationship and could say on my own authority: any significant partnership between two people requires from each of them enough mature and consistent self-awareness and self-sufficiency to preclude a need to ask—from the other or the relationship—more than either can bear; otherwise, all is lost—or soon will be.

Chapter four

But what is "projection," apart from being something we all do unconsciously that is the cause of some of our most egregious mistakes—especially when we are in close relationships with others? Helen Luke says about projection:

> And you don't do it deliberately. It just happens. Projection is the way you see everything that is unconscious in yourself. If you didn't have that projection, you'd never see it. You wouldn't even know you had it.[4]

In therapy, I found projection chief among the different principles of psychological behavior to understand. I didn't want to believe that I projected my dark side willy-nilly onto my children or my husbands or my friends. It wasn't difficult to see how my children projected their fears and fantasies and other broad inaccuracies onto their parents; I observed firsthand how they overreacted with their siblings and schoolmates—hating one, adoring another—for reasons having little to do with whomever had inspired so exaggerated a response. But it was difficult to grasp how I could project my thoughts and feelings about you *onto you*, and then assume it was the truth about you! It was hard to accept that "it just happens." I thought myself a terrible dunce to be so unaware, and was not at all happy to think I had no control over behavior that was dangerous to me and everyone in my proximity. When I studied it, though, I could see that every first impression I have of a place, an object, or a person is a projection that comes from within me and which I perceive as the reality outside of me. When I finally grasped the principle of projection, I could use it to my advantage. Now, even if I don't project deliberately I am aware that I do it and that my projection is not an accurate measurement of *anything*. If I meet someone for the first time and involuntarily size them up—identify, compare, and categorize *them as I see and think them to be* and then conclude I know that person—unless I catch myself in that act of projection, I have just created a fiction of someone I don't even begin to know. I learned the hard way that it is only when my mind is clear of my own thoughts and fully open to learning about someone else—which takes time, no matter how brief or long our "encounter"—can I begin to know a person. According to C. G. Jung:

Relationships: anything but easy

> A man who is unconscious of himself acts in a blind, instinctive
> way and is in addition fooled by all the illusions that arise when
> he sees everything that he is not conscious of in himself coming to
> meet him from outside as projections upon his neighbor.[5]

Much more serious, often devastating, are projections we make in close, constant, and important relationships. There was a time in my first marriage when I assumed that my husband cared less for his family than his career; he proved as much because he spent so much time away from home. I wouldn't have done that had I been in his place—so there was my proof. Did I *talk* to him about it? No—because "it" was merely an amorphous, quasi-conscious, and unhappy sense of things, floating just under the radar of my awareness and spreading like an oil slick. I also assumed that he thought himself in some way superior to me because he participated so much less in the care of our children than I did. It was obvious he considered everything concerning the children to be my responsibility—a woman's responsibility—though I worked outside the home just as he did. Yet, later, in my second marriage, I determined all by myself, of course, that Husband Two behaved imprudently with my children—he was too harsh with them, insensitive to their feelings—so I insisted that he leave all the parenting to me!

With these and a hundred more examples I later suffered the sometimes humiliating truth about myself in relationships—of how I projected irrational fears and anger onto two different men, mostly without the benefit of their input. If I did voice a grievance, it was expressed as a fact, something I knew was true, so would not in my heart reconsider. Had any one of us possessed enough self-knowledge to convincingly articulate who we were and what we wanted, we might have withdrawn our projections; we might have found ourselves truly interested to know more about the other *from* the other. Then, fully respecting our separate standpoints, our hearts and minds might have met willingly, more often, and with growing affection. Uniting in relationship, we might have extended our marriage a day at a time.

Even today I'm not entirely certain why I married the second time, but I do know that my reasons were plainer than the glorified ones I professed at the time. I suspect it was mostly about sex to begin with—all about learning

Chapter four

the art and pleasures of skillful lovemaking, which I had been too astonished and reticent to engage in the first time around. But sex by itself—sex *as* marriage—was a diet both too rich and too lean to overcome the differences in our personalities and was finally just sex. My mistake, that marriage—though there were many lessons I took away from it to examine. It took a heap of work to separate myself from the men in my marriages and become accountable for my actions. Were some of my assumptions about either man correct? Well, that was irrelevant; it was *too late* for us to work on relationship together. More relevant, and the whole point of learning to know myself separately from others, was for me to study *me*. And I did. Over time, I was able to take back projections from all of my relationships, locating their origins in my family of birth, learning reasons for my defenses against what was once but no longer so, then following the threads of my neuroses all the way to and through my relationships. Only then did I acquire enough self-awareness to prevent doing any more serious harm to myself and to others who were (and are) close to me. Krishnamurti says:

> As long as we do not understand individual relationship, we cannot have a peaceful society. Since our relationship is based on possessive love, we have to become aware, in ourselves, of its birth, its causes, its action. In becoming deeply aware of the process of possessiveness with its violence, fears, its reactions, there comes an understanding that is whole, complete. This understanding alone frees thought from dependence and possessiveness. It is within oneself that harmony in relationship can be found, not in another nor in the environment.[6]

So it is not relationship that changed over the years, but I who changed in a long process of coming awake to live better in my relationships. I learned to be mindful in them, to persist in evaluating them until I had no reason to doubt their worth, and especially to revere them. Any relationship I have valued enough to take seriously has been the greatest proving ground for my growth, providing plenty of opportunities to "collide" and learn more while the bruises healed. If the relationship recovered, it was because we

Relationships: anything but easy

had sunk enough healthy roots to protect us against whatever was left of our pathology. Even so, it was in relationships that did *not* recover that I did my hardest work and learned the most, and when they were over I never once thought of them as a waste of my time. The understanding I gleaned from utterly failed relationships paid me back every time with more depth and quality to my sense of myself. That remains true today—and must surely be true of every person who works at self-awareness. Krishnamurti again:

> Self-knowledge is from moment to moment in daily conduct . . .
> and without that self-knowledge there is no right thinking. You
> have no basis for right thinking if you do not know what you are.
> You cannot know yourself in abstraction, in ideology. You can
> know yourself only in relationship in your daily life.[7]

As awareness heightened, I became more selective about my relationships, taking time to reflect and assess with all honesty whether the relationship would accommodate my values and my needs—and whether I could provide reciprocity. Important relationships require an awesome investment of time and energy, caring and loving, patience and persistence—so I became mindful about keeping them to a number that allowed time to fully enjoy and explore them. I came to believe I owed relationships complete honesty and thoughtful attention, and to expect the same in return. If just that much becomes the grounds for its growth—and if the relationship is not asked to fix what only two individuals can put right—separately first, and then together—it will grow *naturally*. Push it too hard or too often and it will fall down dead, I've learned—take it for granted and it's as good as gone.

I learned to accept my limitations in relationships, as well—to remain clear-headed about certain principles of mine which for the sake of my hard-won self I would never again compromise. My limitations might not be acceptable to someone else (nor theirs to me), so our relationship might never get started or might need to come to an end. Since I have chosen to live my life as close to *my* truth as I can get, choosing to opt out of a relationship that isn't working requires me to be courageous and responsible enough to break the connection. Whichever is called for—choosing to nurture one's healthy, mutually aware relationships or choosing to back away from those no longer meaningful—each provides a powerful way to maximize happiness or minimize suffering. I agree with the Buddhists that, although suffering is systemic in our species, I have caused much of mine by clinging, desiring, expecting, denying, and giving away my power or responsibility—in brief, by stubbornly refusing life on its terms. I will not say that it was easy, but it was possible for me to "unmake" most of my suffering—to peel away the layers of dis-ease no longer appropriate to my life and to seek new perceptions of things. As Jaffé says:

> Man possesses a consciousness that not only perceives and reacts to what it experiences, but is aware of perceiving and understands what it is experiencing. It has the faculty of reflection and insight, and, through its recognition of the outer and inner world, of self-extension and self-transformation.[8]

Becoming enlightened is work for a lifetime; it goes on as long as one believes that self-awareness is the way for meaning to enter a life. Still, it is possible—easy, in fact—to fall asleep and lose our mind again and yet again. Seven years ago, that child of mine and his wife ended their marriage. Neither has married again, though now they both appear to be "seriously" interested in someone else. They are friends today, I think because it's hard to forget the part of a relationship that once carried genuine meaning—and because it's not too big a reach to believe they plucked their friendship off the heap of feelings that died, choosing to keep a thing of value alive. I'll make a guess—or say a prayer—about both of them now in their travels with someone new: they are wide awake and reviewing everything they ever learned about being in relationships.

I began to measure my respect for self-awareness by my increasing desire to have more of it, because it made my life so much larger and more meaningful. That has been especially true of my relationships. I am much improved by the ease, the honesty, and the extraordinary depth of feeling they concentrate in me today. Relationships keep me prosperous with good-natured feeling and open to the power of love in my life.

Relationships: anything but easy

five

Friendship

The Best of All the 'Ships

> We all long to fly from loneliness to "togetherness,"
> but the only real cure for loneliness is to accept the
> "aloneness" of the spirit, and then, to our astonishment,
> real relatedness, real friendship will come to our
> doorstep, wherever we may be.

—Helen Luke

Friendships do not necessarily begin in the
workplace or in social encounters and are not always assured
in married or unmarried relationships, or even—sometimes
especially—in family relationships. But friendship is not just de-
sirable, it is acutely necessary for getting through life's rough-and-
tumble. Friendship is one of the two or three things that finally
shake out and remain truly important in a life—or as a life.

Each time I read Sidney Creaghan's *Letter Written by the
Sea*, I admire again how gracefully she has transmuted feeling
into words, and then, when I parse the words for their meanings
and metaphors, I think, oh, *yes*—this poet describes true friendship better than anyone else. She begins:

I want to say the word friend to you.
I want to tell you I know what it means.
Something uncomplicated and simple
something unusual, struck while alone
sitting in the surprised voice silence brings.[1]

True friendship ("Something uncomplicated and simple / something un-usual") is a gift of extraordinary value, so I think it is even more extraordinary that I count four true friends about whom I might have written similar words had I talent equal to the poet's—or had it even occurred to me words could be found for feelings so rare. Four of them!—and one other with whom I think friendship might achieve "true" status if current trends prevail and we all live long enough. It does take time to harvest this kind of friendship—years, at least—and an absence of self-conscious meddling between the seed and the flower, because it will or it may not become extraordinary. My experience has been that, while I might feel a strong con-nection to someone as early as our first meeting, true friendship has had to process along in the dark like a well-kept secret into that future day when— "in the surprised voice silence brings"—it has become itself. It is not unlike the process that completes a fine wine, which, when it has reached that rare complexity it was groomed to achieve, slips smoothly over the taste buds and into the bloodstream, exploding the whole course of its way in a soft rush of pure enjoyment. It reaches its peak unannounced and is transformed in a split, unanticipated second. True friendship, in a delicate shift to some new meaning that suddenly bears fresh consideration, peaks and "emerges" the same way. I have combed the long years of these special friendships many times looking for, and not finding, words to do them justice. I congratulate the poet.

It seems to me that four-possibly-five is a breathtaking number of these friendships to have gathered in a single lifetime—a huge gift of privilege to be walking with through time. One of them is the friend I wrote about in an earlier chapter who had just been diagnosed with cancer. She survived two rounds of chemotherapy, one surgery, and three more rounds of chemo, and her latest scans present no evidence of cancer. She's doing well and looks great, but she is changed, of course; she perceives almost every aspect of her life differently, discriminating especially closely between what's important and what's not. I'm not surprised. What a boon to those of us close to her and privileged to have watched and felt the power of her courage and grace under fire. So, if neither of us falls off a truck or out of a plane, we will have more time yet for this friendship that was just blessed again by a generous and willing universe. A few months ago it was hard to dispel my urge to feel grief about a loss that, while only potential, seemed both possible and imminent. All my fears were scattered by such breezy good news—and by my gratitude, which is a huge and beautiful thing.

Marie-Louise von Franz, a Jungian scholar and depth psychologist, and C. G. Jung himself come closest to describing my sense of true friendship:

> Each person gathers around him his own "soul family," a group
> of people not created by accident or mere egoistic motivation
> but rather through a deeper, more essential spiritual interest of
> concern: reciprocal individuation. . . . [T]his kind of relationship
> . . . has something strictly objective, strangely transpersonal about
> it. It gives rise to a feeling of immediate, timeless "being together."
> . . . In this world created by the Self [Jung's term for the God
> Image archetype in the collective psyche] we meet all those many
> to whom we belong, whose hearts we touch; here [she quotes Jung]
> "there is no distance, but immediate presence."[2]

Of my four true friends, two are men and two are women; in that order, the length of our friendships in years is fifteen, eighteen, twenty-three, and fifty-three. They don't all carry the same or even the sum of characteristics I include in my definition of true friendship, but they all come close. I will not pretend to speak for them about our friendship, though I doubt they would be far off my mark were they also to describe it. Here is the somewhat poetic center around which I believe most of our thoughts and feelings would congregate . . .

Foremost, there is a lasting quality to the relationship, which is by now so much a given it has become the very spaciousness in which we roam

Chapter five

through each other's lives—in and out, to and from, now and then, or hardly ever. That one fact is always unobtrusively present in our consciousness and goes largely unremarked by us—but it lends enormous comfort to our friendship and has important implications. It certifies that our friendship has been fully tested; we have kicked away the crucible in which friendship was formed and are now and forever close kin. Our training wheels came off after we had skinned and sliced and processed ourselves long enough to be rendered thoroughly acceptable—welcome any time to each other's company. We did not one day decide that our relationship was special—because friendship ripens slowly, as I've said, until somewhere in time it turns a corner and "becomes itself" and is lasting.

Over the years, we have paid witness to each other's lives by sharing most of the best and worst of our individual trials and circumstances—celebrating outcomes that were good, or good enough, or better than expected; at other times, feeling helpless to do more than listen attentively, we could only rummage around in our souls trying to find something more of ourselves to give. No matter what, though, we come when called. And if at times it would be easy to judge the other about something we would have done differently or better, in sustained acts of generosity we do not, because we know from experience that to be human is to be vulnerable, is to make mistakes, is to suffer—and to cause the "slings and arrows of outrageous fortune" to rain on our own selves from time to time. No, it inheres in these friendships to remain respectfully neutral on every ground but caring—our caring is spontaneous, trustworthy, and plentiful. Our love for one another is not so much unconditional as fully accepting of the conditions that each of us, imperfect, brings to the friendship.

We are often serious together, though not deadly serious—we laugh at ourselves a lot—but we do talk about our "world on the brink" in a way to coax out the universal truths. Pushing our minds and our imaginations to "see" the bigger picture, we probe our commonality with the rest of our species and try to take heart from the many who have so much courage and try so hard to overcome the sense that humanity is helpless in an exploding universe. Spontaneously, intuitively, or consciously, we manage to take conversation to a depth that will reveal something new and make us more

Friendship: the best of all the 'ships

awake. We listen well, we talk by taking turns and—what a treasure this is—we are completely at ease in the silence that is apt to fall between turns, giving us time to think privately. And since we are so often seeking answers to unanswerable things, "God"—who has long since been located and identified by us with our separate metaphors and is the operating spiritual principle in our lives—walks in and out of our conversations easily and often and is always welcome. My friends and I talk politics, too, because we are spiritually and politically aligned, which is less a matter of luck, I think, than our deep heart-and-mind compatibility. What best defines my true friendship relationships, though, is how we come together—not in the neediness which expects to be fed, but with a healthy human desire to connect and to share the awesome gift that is life itself. If all goes well, I expect we will connect and share again at the end, too; for sure I'd like them around when my time comes, because these friends will know exactly how to celebrate our parting—and that would be, in the same spirit we have celebrated our friendship all the years on the way to parting.

We have widely differing personalities and characteristics, my friends and I. We disagree because we are idiosyncratic, but our differences make no difference to the friendship because our worldviews are nearly identical. My sense of us is that we value life in all ways alike. Looking past the world "out there" and into ourselves, we meet in the same bedrock reality that both includes and transcends all differences as mutual, reciprocating friends. Even so, it is natural to us—and an instinctive necessity—to remain at all times our separate, unfettered selves when we meet there; in that way we are free to tell of ourselves truly, offering each to the other our uniqueness as well as our similarity. And, always to my surprise, there comes the inevitable "accidental" fallout from these friendships: as I see and enjoy in my friends all of the most lovable qualities that I myself possess, they are having the same experience. As a result, I can simultaneously affirm, forgive, and appreciate both my friends and myself—which tells me that it is through our friendships I have come to love myself. True friends are more than companions, more than student to each other's teacher—more than all these words have tried to say. If I had to, I would exchange all else in my life for just one of these true friendships. Which leads me to wonder why other relationships—marriages,

Chapter five

for example—are so often so very problematical. Krishnamurti said a couple of chapters ago:

> Since our relationship is based on possessive love, we have to become aware, in ourselves, of its birth, its causes, its action. . . . It is in oneself that harmony in relationship can be found, not in another.[3]

It is not at all unusual to find possessive love in families—between a man and his wife, between unmarried partners, between parents and children, just as a start. Perhaps too simply described in too short a space, I'm going to say that possession is all about position and power in families: the parent "owns" and wields power over the child, and the child, in sibling rivalry, for example, wants with all his heart to possess the total love of each parent. Where possession exists between couples, it shows up in gender-role differences and sexual relations, each partner unconsciously "owning" the other ("my man" and "my woman"), especially in sexual matters, where a price can be paid as often for an innocent flirtation as for having an affair. True friendship will not support possession, so power and position are not germane, and if sex were to be introduced to this friendship it would change its nature: it might fall into possessive ways and might come to an end. I see it that sex belongs somewhere else—maybe everywhere else—but not in true friendship. It is the one dynamic too highly charged and too often irrational to integrate with the deeper, separately reflective calm so characteristic of relations between true friends. I can say from experience how perilous it is to think that one's own true friendship will be the exception to this: first goes the friendship, and soon after that, *all* is lost.

Can there be no friendship in marriage, then? I will say yes, but cautiously, because I've known only three such friendships, and because it will be a different kind of friendship than I've been describing: more complex. True friends do not usually live together and share responsibility for children or for keeping a common household. Leading separate lives, friends are free to come together at will, to exchange their best aspects, and then to leave. At least in theory, couples, married or not, form a full-blown partnership—two

Friendship: the best of all the 'ships

people who live and work and relate to each other most days of the year and who ideally possess strong self-images, maturity in thought and action, and above-average communication skills. They operate as a team, each assuming a fair and thoroughly considered share of the overall responsibility. If you don't know many "ideal" couples, you probably know many who (like most people) married before they knew much, if anything at all, about living together in harmony as partners and friends. Certainly I was one of those who understood none of the enormous implications of being married. At twenty-three, I had only the romantic idea of marriage; I could see only as far as that perfectly planned day when my beloved and I—celebrant, smiling, king and queen for a day—would be duly historicized from several different angles "on camera" making a solemn commitment to be together forever.

At twenty-three I had no idea yet who I was, and had no skills for life beyond those I had developed for my own psychological survival. That alone could explain how we failed to construct the underpinnings—the bones and guts and love and friendship—needed to support the relationship. We did not, as it turned out, weather or win the long slow ripening of a friendship strong enough to float—or save—a marriage. We had some good years "growing up" together, and we bonded around the children—awestruck by the miracle as we learned together to diaper, feed, and walk the floor with a brand new baby. But it was not a bond that tested our mettle, it was not convincing enough to secure our original vows of intention when the rains came—and then stayed. We never learned to partner; we did our thinking separately and failed to communicate what we thought, so our friendship was too fragile to hold together. It served us well enough at first, when everything was new and brightly lit, but a dozen children would not have forged the kind of deeply fixed togetherness that allows one to know the other one, to forgive mistakes—and gives full, conscious support to the concept of partnership. I was not yet self-sufficient when I married—in no way ready to begin a meaningful relationship. "It is in oneself that harmony in relationship can be found, not in another," Krishnamurti taught. My self—even at the end of the marriage—was still a dream trying to wake up.

Since a lasting marriage is affected by—at a minimum—the family and religious backgrounds from two childhoods and by the ages, degrees of

Chapter five

maturity, personality differences, and life and learning experiences of both participants, in a world of perfect people all of these factors would have been carefully considered *before* marriage. Yet, I have come to believe with my whole heart and mind that the most important influence on any relationship is how well an individual knows her or himself, because self-knowledge is the great preventive for self-inflicted heartache and the best—often the only—defense against everything that stands in the way of friendship and partnership for a long and happy marriage. I have known a great many like myself who—married, but not yet ripe on the vine—have found themselves dramatically short on ability to create a deep and meaningful relationship in marriage. I know only three couples with children who not only kept their vows to remain together, but were in each case also able to forge a close and enduring friendship. In some year of the first decade of their marriage, one of those couples had to first survive a searing, over-the-top emotional "brawl" initiated by the wife when she found out her husband was having an affair with a married friend of theirs. It was painful to behold his wife's response to so great a personal affront: she went *wild*—shrieking and moaning by turns, her psyche doubled over in the anguish of betrayal. Then, when anger took over from hurt, she went smashing and crashing around their house like a feral animal. He was penitent, but she was crushed and exhausted—mind, body, and bone. We all gave that marriage about two more seconds of life. It took months, maybe years, for all the fractures in their relationship to heal, but the miracle happened: the marriage recovered, their friendship was born again. Their love was stronger than anyone—even they—would have believed possible until it was tested *in extremis.* So there is the proof: it *is* possible for friendship to develop, grab hold, and persist in a marital relationship; even so, I think the odds in favor of it are not great. Unmarried couples without children have less to bind them but fewer stresses, most likely, so who can guess if their chances for staying together are better or worse? Meanwhile, I've read about several unions entered into at midlife as a result of an already developed friendship that seem to be faring quite well.

My true friendships have outlived two marriages of several years each, yet not once have they caused me to struggle against the gradual loss of comity and good will that I experienced in marriage; quite to the contrary, my

Friendship: the best of all the 'ships

friendships only deepen as the years go by. Why are the dynamics of the two relationships so different? I could say it is because my true friends and I don't live together, are not under contract to share the countless quotidian burdens of a shared life, and are not obliged to resolve the differing gender, sexual, or spiritual inclinations that couples must resolve in order to keep their partnership tethered to a long view. Or I could say it's because individual personalities, perceptions, and expectations are often discovered to be starkly different in two people only after their knot is tied to a legal, moral, and psychological commitment. All of that would be true, I believe. But I could also say that my husbands and I simply drifted apart—that at some time in the marriage we failed to notice that we were traveling in different directions to separate destinations—and that would also be true. But what is closer to truth is that the dynamics of a marriage with children and the dynamics of the true friendship I have been describing will not relate; one can juxtapose the two relationships but not compare them.

For example, for fifteen to twenty years after the birth of the first child, a marriage with children is in many ways a daily grind. There is no time to respect individual boundaries, which are crossed without thought a dozen or more times a day. Task-loaded and action-oriented, this marriage is stressed to the max with coming, going, and doing, leaving precious little time to reflect on its status and update its mission statement. I don't remember ever asking either of my husbands, "So, how are we doing with this marriage? No, *really*, what do you think?" Whereas friendship encounters are not only occasional, but also immediate, to reiterate Jung: timeless in nature and content, expansive, and engaging. They deal exclusively with the sharing of two lives, usually in an unhurried setting away from the world at large, always and rightly perceived as a treasured opportunity to peel away personas, exhale, get down, and get real. So it seems to me that the time-honored expectations and stressors that define a marriage with children can bear no practical resemblance to a true friendship relationship: the two are like apples to oranges, or bears to berries. Where true friendship does abide in marriage, it will be between two people who have always known and honored friendship *first*, is my guess; they will have possessed much wisdom early— they will be rare and exceptional people.

Chapter five

Besides *true* friendship, there are many other kinds. A long time ago, when my days and years were longer and my life had no visible horizons, friendships were formed without much conscious thinking; I didn't selectively choose my friends and I didn't weigh their worth. They just "happened," at special times around special needs. First, there were the kids in the neighborhood with whom I played jacks and kick-the-can and hopscotch. When I started junior high school, my friends were more specialized and I had favorites—we slept overnight at each other's houses, cooked batches of fudge before bedtime, wore each other's clothes to school. There were the friends who shared my interests, like roller skating and tap dancing and practicing left-hand boogie riffs on one friend's piano until her mother went starkers and withdrew my favorite privilege. When I started high school my friends were mostly books—the one safe and saving escape from an incorrigible case of shyness induced by a spectacular case of acne. Post-acne, I formed friendships with boys and then men—and then with other new wives and other new mothers, and with a couple of wonderful women with whom I bared my soul's woes and listened to theirs. There were also friends at the office, my children's friends, retreat friends and support group friends, and others. A few of my friendships today are sustained by a common bond, like those I enjoy in the fellowship of Alcoholics Anonymous; others are casual—like some of the folks in my little town. I count as an important and meaningful friend one talented psychologist with whom I finished therapy finally, and I am as much friend as mother today with two of my children. Many of my friendships had by their nature a limited life expectancy—they served a common purpose that ended, or one of us moved on or away, and so the friendship drifted into history and sometimes out of memory. All of my friendships have added to my life and enriched me—even the ones that flared and fizzled and left me to sort out their lessons. But the kind of friendship that has always meant the most to me and makes my life exceptional in every way is the one I call true friendship.

Friendship: the best of all the 'ships

But there is a special relationship whose story begs me to tell it. It is with my first "ex" and his extraordinary wife, and it's worth the telling because of its immense contribution to my life and happiness. I call it my "post-first-marriage friendship," because I've not seen or heard from the second "ex" since the day we legally parted company. First ex is the father of all of my children, and what is most unusual about our friendship today is that it would not have happened without *her*—his present wife. The story goes like this . . .

We began the painful process of our divorce and quickly established two households; the children stayed with me. We each had a stash of resentments to justify blaming the other, but we agreed to keep our mouths zipped in front of the children and spare them any more misery than they already suffered and perceived to be unbearable. Since we were hardly without temptation to play the usual "his fault–her fault" game, our vow of verbal chastity was not always easy to keep. But we did our best and after a while, when most of our collective hurt, anger, and wounded pride had abated, we managed to serve up some pretty convincing courtesy inside the circles of our ex-nuclear family and friends. And when enough time and distance from the divorce made it clear that we had done the right thing after all, we even came to think well of one another again. However, in that brave new world of maturing divorced singles who were exceedingly quick to form new relationships, we did not engage in any "extended family" picnics—oh, no: he didn't like my choice of partners, and I didn't like his. So for our kids—and a few million others now being looked after by double sets of divorced caretakers—there were for the next half-dozen years or so two Christmas trees and far too many presents, and of course two Thanksgiving dinners.

Now when those partners—whom we eventually married and divorced—had made a mighty try and served their time, I gave serious thought to my now-somewhat-parlous history of relationships and decided to take myself out of competition. He, on the other hand, had the nerve and the courage and the optimism to persist until he got it right—and he finally did get it exactly right. So he married her—that really remarkable woman who, in her infinite wisdom and bone-bred exuberance not only allowed, but *insisted* that every member of our newly configured family enjoy the love and friend-

Chapter five

ship of every other member simultaneously. And so we began a habit of gathering around one Christmas dinner table and only one Thanksgiving turkey: "Whose house this year, yours or mine?" We were all enhanced over time, like a great *pot-au-feu* that simmers year-round, steeping richness and substance. "Come on down!" That's how she was. Is. And he stood on the welcome mat right beside her. Her penchant to include is so authentic and so rare one is unsure whether to believe it, even as the love in her wide-open heart extends to and acknowledges everyone in her sight line. It didn't happen overnight, of course: we all had to shift gears and come to believe. But she was there first—as the catalyst—as the outrageous, unconventional, and totally generous "leave no child or ex-wife behind" free spirit who kept us all together in relationship. Her decision to take on his whole family tree completely stood on its head the age-old convention that banishes every ex-wife to hell. "Be gone, ignorance," is her cry to those so lacking in civility. It was not long before she and I were quite congenially collaborating on the Mother Project with my kids/her stepkids—combining our intelligence on mothering matters large and small as though they had been *our* kids forever. He was right to have kept looking for her. They are still—more than twenty years later—the most perfectly aligned partnership I have ever known.

Now you know how he and I became special friends—for the first time, really. It was she who linked us again to our original bond of love and respect for our children by inviting me into their home as an integral part of the family. To that opening he and I added our mutual regard for his beautiful wife and her huge no-boundaries mind. Had she been less special, I don't think he and I would have forged a relationship that was more than the merely civil one we enjoyed otherwise. We were able to bring to our new friendship all of the maturity we had harvested separately in the years until he married her. The years between gave a long and comfortable distance to our ancient unhappy "then" and eased the way for us to begin again. While I can barely remember the details of "then," I can recall vividly how little I had to offer as a partner in true partnership. I'm going to guess that some of the wisdom we managed to acquire separately in those interim years rescued our original mutual attraction, which was the recognition of something of lasting value in the other. The recognition came too late to save a marriage, yet

Friendship: the best of all the 'ships

was somehow held in waiting for her—who then salvaged *us* for the better-fitting and finally authentic friendship we enjoy today. Dear Her: "Thank you." She is a rare and special beauty and a wonderful friend.

❧

If you're like me, there is not room enough in your psyche or time enough in your life to embrace every kind of friendship effectively. I had to become clearer, more realistic than I used to be about how to spend time in friendship. Friendships do differ, both in content and kind, and so today I consciously choose to be with someone who is, from my point of view, interesting—someone from whom I can learn and to whom I can give my honesty and trust, my promise to listen attentively, and my willingness to tell the truth. This would be, too, someone who enjoys exploring a subject of common interest—something of value, please, and with enough pith in it to chew on later. My introversion has never required a great number of friends, but depth in a relationship seems to be a real requirement; penetrating the surface of things is, without a doubt, my greatest pleasure. We must suit ourselves, is something I believe passionately now that I have reached the time in my life when the road is narrowing and I can see my own horizon. Accordingly, it feels right—even necessary—that I shun every small extravagance of time to better use it with my true friends. Weaving in and out of a process of mutual storytelling rich in detail and complexity, we work the threads of our friendship into a kind of Aubusson tapestry "portrait" that, by reflecting our features, becomes itself over time. Creaghan ends her poem:

> I would like to chisel friend from an oak's heart
> expose the rings of longing and nourishment . . .
> create a new matrix of devotion
> courageous enough to remain alone
> yet kind enough to be a friend.[4]

❧

Chapter five

Surely you've heard or read this along the way: To keep something of value, one must surrender it completely. This says to me that true friendship—something of great value to me—insures the freedom of its two constituents in order to preserve the friendship. Obligations do not attach to this kind of friendship because demands are never made of it. Free and separate, two friends lend their sovereign selves to a mix of deeply meaningful similarities that yields a friendship needing nothing more to complete itself—not even the frequency of physical presence, because friendship sustains intimacy by living in the heart. True friendship is to me spiritual and psychological and emotional treasure—the most meaningful kind of relationship I have ever experienced. Over time I have learned to love my friends actively—sensing their presence within me, feeling the grace of our connectedness—so that now they are integral, vital parts of my separate self. I touch my heart and say, "Hello, friend," and there she is! Or there he is—as real and constant and alive to my consciousness as when we meet—not nearly so often—in "reality."

six

How much do I owe?

When one does "the next and most necessary thing
without fuss and with conviction one is always doing
something meaningful and intended by fate. . . . But
simple things are always the most difficult.

—Aniela Jaffé

Have you ever asked who or what "God" is? Listen
to the writer and poet Annie Dillard in her book *Holy the Firm*:

Every day is a god, each day is a god, and holiness
holds forth in time. . . . I wake in a god. I wake in arms
holding my quilt, holding me as best they can inside
my quilt. . . . Today's god rises, his long eyes flecked in
clouds. He flings his arms, spreading colors; he arches,
cupping sky in his belly; he vaults, vaulting and spread,
holding all and spread on me like skin.[1]

There are many metaphors for God, but I like hers best
of all. I like thinking that the minute I open my eyes and fill
them with the new day, I am—like everything I see in it—an
inextricable part of the day, in and a part of God "spread on
me like skin," because that confirms to me cleanly and clearly to

whom or what I am responsible. When she wrote her book, Annie Dillard's god/days wakened her in Puget Sound, where she describes them cavorting geographically:

> The day is real; the sky clicks securely in place over the mountains, locks round the islands, snaps slap on the bay. Air fits flush on farm roofs; it rises inside the doors of barns and rubs at yellow barn windows. Air clicks up my hand cloven into fingers and wells in my ears' holes, whole and entire. I call it simplicity. . . . I toss the cat. I stand and smooth the quilt. "Oh," I cry, "Oh!"[2]

Oh, the joyous, god-given day, everything in its place, including just enough room for me. Her metaphor allows me to imagine that God is indeed real, clicking in the days and their inhabitants for all eternity, filling up the crannies of our planet with the requirements of each of its species. I can imagine that each god/day is a god/gift over which I have no right of refusal; hence I, too, am real when I wake, already meaningful, and by implication my work is to carry a measure of the total responsibility for each day. And what would that be exactly? I asked—and answered—the question many different ways until I had one I liked that worked for me, and then I threw away the question. Fundamentally, my responsibility is to myself, because while I am only one among multitudes who inhabit the day, I am only my part of the day—so I have limited responsibility to it and limited power over it.

Not all god/days are felicitous, of course, and "responsibility" is many-layered. Making notes for this chapter today, I sit on a public bench I lay claim to because I am so often and happily occupying its seat. My bench faces the whole of the Pacific Ocean, or so it appears, and a horizon that splits the double infinities of sky and sea into two shades of blue, each made more fabulous by the brilliance of the sun. It is easy—here, today—to warm my body and meditate my psyche in conscious awareness of the god/spirit I also lay claim to. It's easy to feel clear, clean, and certain about my share of the day's responsibility because I wrestled long and deliberatively to define it. But when I leave my bench and go home, later to see and hear the news of the day, night will have fallen and I will think again—as I have done for over five years—about the dark underbelly of the beautiful day where reside the *shadows* of our gods, their gods and ours, who are warring and killing, like unto like. My heart will chill in the mayhem I observe on a small screen that spares me only a short physical distance from dark red and still warm blood spilling out of bodies—theirs and ours—ripped into parts and flung on the ground. Then comes, always, my separate share of the unshakable anxiety that hovers vague and insistent over us all, over the entire planet I'd guess, on these seemingly endless god/dark nights.

I listen to the screen, to the thousand million words from those "in the know" shoveling crises and calamity into my ears, and wonder how many others are discovering a personal limit to their tolerance for the intolerable. Do they, like I, wish it were not so easy to *feel* the enormity of the story telling itself behind the screen that gives us so much access to pain? Or does anyone even watch "the war" anymore—how long *can* we watch without falling over, soul-dead? I reflect again on the one thing I know for certain about every war story since man began: The gods are us—those are our shadows dancing on the walls of our ignorance, sliding under the doors of our reasoning minds to sell us our own hidden agendas. It is *we*—some of us, some of them—whose shadows demand the appalling sacrifice of blood to validate a just and righteous cause that each righteous side claims at any cost. With a hand over my mouth, I sit mesmerized by the day's carnage—so repetitious now as to no longer seem outrageous—wailing without sound in an agony of knowing that once more it has all gone terribly wrong. Later, lying awake in the shadows of my night, I will question as I always do whether—and in what ways—I, too, am culpable, and whether my view of personal responsibility can possibly be as clear and cogent as it seemed on the sunny side of this god/day.

If all goes well, I will wake in the morning feeling more certain than ever that my responsibilities in this life—to others, the world, the universe—are real but limited, requiring only that I speak my self in her naked truth and act accordingly. To all those who are living the nightmare of war, who literally and figuratively will never know morning again—the raging disaffected, the homeless, the émigrés, the chronically shocked and awed, and especially those who mourn their wounded or maimed or the loss and love of those

Chapter six

whom they once held close (*the children!*) before they were shot, bombed, burned, or blasted out of their last day on earth—I feel deeply responsible to say out loud what is silently in my mind all of these days and nights: "Were these things up to me, this would not be happening; you would not be grieving these things." The feeling response to those who suffer comes easily, of course—it is instinctive with most of us when or if we look in their direction. More to the point is how do we respond to the appalling insult of unnecessary suffering? My responsibility was to consider the implications of war and then to honor my point of view appropriately; yet, while the decision was not mine to make and I feel no personal guilt—I am not relieved. My "innocence" in no way lessens my grief as this recalcitrant "wild child" of a war grows older and no wiser.

I could write a letter to the editor addressing "Those in the Know." I would begin it this way: "While I feel somewhat disadvantaged debating minds far more studied in the arts of geopolitics, statesmanship, and warfare; nevertheless, I wish to present my simple case on your page." Were the editor to publish my letter, and were those "in the know" to read it and respond, I wonder how much thought they would give to it. "Too simple," I can imagine they would say, then, in a somewhat scolding tone, they might explain to me that "the issues at stake are so far-flung and require decisions so tooled and complex that it's possible—and understandable, of course— that you are not able to apprehend the scope of our problems." Forgivable, too, they might say, is "the inability of the general public to appreciate the difficulty of our work and the intricate planning and calibrated responses with which we deal every day in a virtual maelstrom of shifting unknowns." Finally, they would assure me that "the best minds—the most experienced scholars, politicians, diplomats, and warriors in this country and beyond— have been pressed into service and are doing everything possible to address your concerns. We appreciate your interest, etc."

I would not be "assured," of course, because, as I would have said in my letter to "Those in the Know" via the editor: "There is another view, a different reasoning, which runs counter to yours, and it is not mine alone. There are millions who share my concerns. It is a worldview—larger than yours, you might agree—that says in principle: Human life is more important—

How much do I owe?

is more sacred, unassailable, and inviolable—than any common cause that involves war. It says, too, that because the means to destroy mankind are ubiquitously available, no matter what the reasoning about the substance and worth of the cause you undertake, it is faulty reasoning that commits a collective decision to pay for war with innocent lives and populations of heartbroken, downcast survivors." I would have ended my pithy little letter like this: "I ask you not to dismiss my view as being too simple, but to think of it as a clear and straightforward statement of principled fact. And I would ask that you and your colleagues—who are, as you noted, 'the best minds in the country and beyond'—seriously deliberate whether it is not life itself (using your own as the first example) which ranks highest in value among civilized peoples; and that being so, should it not be your first consideration before every decision you make? Thank you very much, etc."

Whether or not I agree with "Those in the Know," the moment is largely their responsibility. They chose—after we the people chose them—to lead us through a war and its consequences that will ultimately either rest lightly on their minds or swarm their consciences like a nest of hornets. I didn't send a letter to the editor, but I count it as a responsibility I shirked indefensibly, because expressing my fury "out loud" would have been the right thing to do for *myself*—and now my moment has passed. Important collective decisions are made every day in which an individual may not, therefore does not, personally participate, making it easy for us to believe that, because the power of one is so frequently attenuated to zero, we are free to blow off the issues and ride helpless in the results. Objectively, in my country at least, I can do a few things to be politically responsible. I can examine the issues, stay alert to their implications, telephone or e-mail my government—and I can vote my choices from a ballot of imperfect people and hope that my choices will join with enough like-minded others to win the day. I think all of these things are my responsibility and I mostly do them; even so, my personal influence in the world remains remarkably limited. Or so it seemed to me, until . . .

I was in my thirties, spinning way too many plates in the air and trying my best to answer a question that haunted me daily: to whom, to what, and exactly where do my unbelievably too many responsibilities lie? I separated

Chapter six

them into categories: what I owed to my marriage, my children, my family, and the in-laws; to myself—my academic interests, my career, the boss, and my coworkers; my friends, of course, and what about the voting drives, community volunteer work, the children's schools—and, hey, how about a day off? The more I resisted the call of so many obligations, the more guilt I felt about saying no to even one of them—yet there was just not enough of me to go around and the price I paid for doing too much was to take no real joy in doing anything. My body came to my rescue, faltering and then sputtering to a stop in that admirable warning way the body will force an answer to a problem. I did what mothers do when it's possible: I put my career on hold for a while. As my body recouped, I had time to seriously think about responsibility—not as a word tied to a generality having little to do with me, but as a uniquely personal psychological conflict whose unconscious cause was affecting both my body and my mind every day of my life. The two big questions needing answers: why did my sense of responsibility drive me so hard, and why was guilt so much a part of being driven? Not surprisingly, the answers had their roots in my childhood (briefly, too much expected of a child too young to refuse), which meant I had to recalibrate an unconscious perception of responsibility that was not only outdated, but was flawed to begin with. When I finally connected my present physical "rebellion" to the child who knew only that she must not rebel but rather conform to the expectations of an unreasoning parent, I was then free to define my responsibilities to the world—and myself—as I saw them.

It seems to me that it is good for all when, after a time, a sense of responsibility no longer embodies the parental—or conventional—voice of authority and becomes our own thoughtful voice, meant for our ears only. Responsibility is a choice made and accepted by me on my terms, because my life circumstances are unique. That's how I think about it now, and whenever I practice this point of view it works for me. It seems reasonable to me that I am ultimately accountable to only myself for every choice I make to either accept or reject responsibility—a bit of thinking that adds precious hours to my days and welcome relief to the life of my mind. Once having acknowledged the sources of the guilt I carried for saying no, I refused thereafter to surrender my sovereign right to decline any responsibility, including all of

How much do I owe?

those traditional ones "writ in stone." On the other hand, I have kept my vow to commit myself to only those choices that feel right to me—or necessary (which makes them right)—and to approach my commitments eagerly and do my best with them, thus making my contributions meaningful to everyone concerned. You might guess that where my commitments inconvenienced others, I did not make them in a vacuum. I shared my intentions, took comments, and measured the good I could bring as a matter of courtesy—yet I considered the final decision mine to make, and were there to be consequences, they would be mine to suffer.

I think responsibility must always start and in a certain sense end with me because it takes its shape from my private considerations, all of which have been reflected and tested through years of life experience and trial and error and transmuted into my very own treasury of personal principles that daily guide my life. How seriously, how much, and how well I take on my share of responsibility for each god/day I am given—just my portion, just enough to keep me fully engaged—gives that much meaning to my life. I can't work your corner of the day and you can't work mine, yet working the day separately unites us one and all, and together we create and reflect back to ourselves the world in all of its dimensions. How much do I, we, what we do, and how we do it matter? I like to say that if enough of us—no need for a majority—work our share of the day responsibly and give it a personal best, we spin with the planet into infinity. If we don't, the planet spins on without us because we self-destruct. Our species will be outta here—done in, slam-dunked, knocked off by the biggest, baddest war of them all, is my guess—bringing the known world to its history-making conclusion, or more accurately: its history-ending tragedy. That's how much I believe that being responsible to ourselves in our god/days matters. (*Factoid:* Without our species, the planet regenerates in a New York minute.)

Testing, tweaking, altering my thinking about personal responsibility over the years, I gradually took ownership of my own imperative, which became to use only my criteria for choosing to what and to whom I am responsible. Do I have room and time for this? Is my interest authentic? Can I describe my responsibility exactly? Do I have something of value to give here—enough talent to do what needs doing well? Do I feel mentally and emotionally invested

Chapter six

in the outcome? Finally, the principles of my thinking had become part of who I am simply because they worked for me. Until now I have never debated or discussed my theory on the subject because living the rather solitary life of a writer whose only aim is to speak the truth of her life to herself, there is nobody at home to rebut me! Even so, if my thoughts differ from the way others think about responsibility, I am satisfied mine have merit for me since all these years later I remain peacefully untroubled by them. As soon as I could think beyond responsibility in vague, general terms and begin to shape its meaning within the context of my own life, I had a way to measure my personal power—and considerable influence—in the world. Today I see both my responsibilities and my influence as the individually limited, co-equivalent attributes of a life lived consciously—wholly contained in the individual, yet contributing and extending literally into the universe and infinity. By withdrawing my bewildered gaze from "out there" and looking back to myself for answers, I found the locus of my life—the center from which I attempt to live all parts of myself to the impressive power of only one.

My wisdom was least when I needed it most. Finding my way through the thickets of parental responsibility was a slow and erratic business, a thousand trials and almost as many errors. On the way to developing authenticity in my role as parent, I made some pretty grave mistakes with my kids. I think the worst of them was overplaying what I dimly surmised were my God-inspired rights of authority over them. My unartful errors were grave enough to ignite more anger, rebellion, and even heartache than necessary during the years we lived together. Yet, unskilled and jejune though I was, I was also well intentioned, and at least two of my three children must have sensed that because they never booted me from my job for very long. My era's sagacious Dr. Spock notwithstanding, we and the other marrieds-with-family whose close company we kept at the time ate a lot of crow as we time and again demonstrated our ineptitude as authority figures. Even so, our children grew up, moved out, and somehow acquired the enormous generosity to forgive most—though never all—of our mistakes. And we

How much do I owe?

forgave ourselves pretty much, though it is easy to recall how "green" and unschooled I felt during some of the more turbulent years of their teens; as late as today I am able to feel some "compassionate remorse" for how much I lacked in wisdom at the time.

When the children were young, the oldest not yet seven or eight years old, parenting them seemed anything but rocket science. Ten thousand things a day presented themselves to be done, and I responded to all of them with hardly a thought—more intuitively, I'd say, learning as I went along like most parents do. I did my best, never perfectly, but I *loved* my kids and being responsible for them gave me deep satisfaction. Then, suddenly they were older, curious and eager to extend their minds and bodies beyond the constricting years of early childhood; and just as suddenly the time was upon me to "outfit" their hearts and minds for a larger world filled with things brand new to me: cultural punk, a coarser morality, free-wheeling behavior—in short, a world far more risky (even a little sinister) than anything I had experienced at their ages. A single parent by that time, I felt my responsibilities as something huge—suddenly a whole *lot* like rocket science; it kept me anxious and uncertain for years. Spinning like a top through a roadrunner cartoon, feet-wheels whrrrring and out of my depth, I tightened up and began to fret. Where to begin and what to teach them? How to pull them away from their cliff edges, steer them clear of temptation—how to save them! Oh dear and oh dear and O my God! I examined every new sign of anything at all that looked like it might be trouble, talked to every parent I knew or chanced to meet in a checkout line, and searched everywhere for the *Complete Dr. Spock on Teenagers* that he must have forgotten to write. Eventually I wore myself out, surrendered to "overwhelm" and my obsession to get "this parenting thing" perfect, and copped to the obvious: Pull back, Mama—and breathe. A little late in the game, but finally the beginning of some wisdom—ask any parent you know about that.

I fussed through their teens with high purpose, assuming my rights of control just like every other socially adapted head-of-household of my generation (I wanted so much to believe I was all grown up and could parent them well), only to discover much later where I had gone wrong. In assuming too much responsibility for their well-being—control was their name for it—I did dam-

Chapter six

age. I obstructed them—walked all over their budding sensibilities more than was necessary, I think now. The rest of my mistake was having too little trust in myself—my fundamentally decent values and character. Had I been striving less for perfection with my parenting, I might have loved them more perfectly. I might have thought that by modeling my own good-enough perceptions of things we could learn *together* and that with our shared love serving as bond and mainstay we would navigate the choppy waters of adolescence (mine and theirs) just fine. How wise Emerson was when he wrote, "Trust thyself: every heart vibrates to that iron string."[3] But it takes a long time for some of us to become wise, or to feel as strong and durable as iron.

We all survived, of course—they survived me and I survived myself, but there were times when a couple of us bled a lot over my reasoning and judgments, being as they were sometimes too hard on them and sometimes too easy. Many years went by before I connected my anxiety about parenting my teenagers to my own teens, when, lacking direction from either of my parents, I was left to pretty much fake a self that would get me through those years on my own. So, of course I was going to over-teach my kids. I found out soon enough that even with the best of intentions, a paucity of healthy life experience and a plenitude of ignorance does not substitute for a little wisdom and competence. In an overreaction to all that had gone missing in my own early life, I felt that my most essential responsibility was to ensure that my children would arrive at the doors of their adulthood chockfull of love, intelligence, and independent thinking—taking joy in their matchless individuality. So it was my perception of my responsibility to them—the unconscious, unrealistic, and somewhat romantic notion that somehow I (though I knew no others who did so) was meant to clear every obstacle on the road each child chose to travel to his and her separate, stunning future that drove my "mission impossible."

⁂

If there is a particular responsibility I wish I had been more conscious of when my children were growing up, it is how urgently they needed me to guide them through the shoals of society's rules and influences on the young

80

and vulnerable and to teach them when to think against the grain of our culture's mores. The Indian philosopher J. Krishnamurti completely rejected the materialistic values lived by most of the modern world. He abhorred the all-pervading cradle-to-grave stress that society places on competition—in sports, education, commerce, politics, physical beauty, the corporate ladder-climb in pursuit of wealth, power, title, property, and prestige—and to which our youth are introduced at an astonishingly early age. He believed that the unreflected values of our time serve to starve or divert our better human inclinations for practicing love, compassion, and creativity. And he was not a bit shy about placing responsibility for society's collective values at the feet of the individual, nondiscriminating, "well-intentioned" parent. I was startled to read this in *Total Freedom*, a book of his teachings:

> Most parents, unfortunately, think they are responsible for their
> children and their sense of responsibility takes the form of telling
> them what they should do and what they should not do, what they
> should become and what they should not become. The parents
> want their children to have a secure position in society. What they
> call responsibility is part of that respectability they worship . . . they
> are concerned only with becoming a perfect bourgeois. When [parents] prepare their children to fit into society they are perpetuating
> war, conflict, brutality. Do you call that care and love? Really to care
> is to care as you would for a tree or a plant, studying its needs, the
> best soil for it, looking after it with gentleness and tenderness—but
> when you prepare your children to fit into society you are preparing
> them to be killed. If you loved your children you would have no war.[4]

These are words of great wisdom, I believe. What I took from them I cherish still, and I mourn a little even today that I hadn't the benefit of his insight in time to better hone my skills for parenting. I understood his message to mean that my fundamental responsibility to my children was, and would always be, to live my own life deliberately true to myself, setting an example they might accept or reject, in part or in full, and always at their pace, never mine. That is, in fact, even when I was unaware of it, the most and best I have ever done for them. My only power over their lives was my proximity to them as I lived and modeled my own life every day. Of course any parent, conscious or unconscious, has the negative power to threaten, manipulate, physically harm, or psychically destroy a child. A power too often exerted in the world, it is destructive of relationship and murderous to the meaning of every life. But I speak here of a parent's power for good. When I was able to fully embrace the concept that my first responsibility is always to myself—to make good, thoughtful choices, to take actions born of motives that are clear, clean, and sound, to make certain that each personal principle I speak out, act out, or act upon is honest and integral with who I am—then I could believe that all that is best about me will follow from me and in one way or another do its powerful work. Good spreads and goes far; like sonar it pulses and sounds through eternity, influencing powerfully far beyond the span of the body's lifetime.

When I say my first responsibility is always to myself, I am at the heart of the matter and the center of my thinking about what or how much I owe to everyone else. You might be asking, What about my husband, or partner, or lover—my ailing mother, my best friend? What about the child who is being physically or verbally abused as I stand watching in some checkout line and my whole psyche is writhing in disgust? I would answer this way: I am always the first beneficiary of my benefaction. When I make a choice to be responsible to or for any person, idea or cause, even then I am making it first of all to please myself. When my heart and mind and instinct instruct me to jump in here and take this on, I jump first to honor my own life, rightly intuiting that to deny my inclination to give the gift of myself at a moment I feel is critical is to do something *against* myself. I would cheat my soul on a day that will never recur and forfeit my share of the day's joy for not making a small but important difference to the whole world. Staying alert in my days, sweeping my corner mindfully: as I see it, this is what earns me my place in Dillard's god/day. Beyond that, to give meaning to responsible action measures my worth and my power into infinity with exquisite precision.

In a perfect world I would live fully awake and take my full portion of responsibility for each and every day. I would dive into the art and science of my life and try to elaborate, even if only a little, on however much I

How much do I owe?

already own of psychological health, humility, and wisdom in order to give it away wherever it's needed. I would live always alert to the irrepressible dogfish ego—ready in a flash to snatch back my meager stores of precious humility from ego's rapacious grab for power—power over *you* is ego's usual gambit, control over your share of the day. I would cultivate consciousness, work ahead of the curve as a witness of this wild and wonderful and woe-be-unto-us world we all live in separately together. In the way each drop of dew reflects the moon simultaneously, I am the world—and every day would turn my full attention to it. I needn't say that the world and I are not perfect, yet I deeply believe that if I do nothing more with my days than seek to improve my own humanity, I will have lived a hero's life. I would bet the universe that my personal efforts are measurable and, extending the principle, that when I am counted in with all the other heroes in the day who make similar efforts, my efforts are measurable exponentially as the collective effort that keeps our world afloat in consciousness. I like to think that the intention behind our self-serving, world-serving acts of responsibility skims, then drops like a pebble into the ponds of the cosmos. It makes great sense to me that when my efforts merge with one of the countless far-flung streams of small heroic efforts generated here on planet earth, the best of me is registering both in and outside of time to make a meaningful difference.

∞

Recently I wrote to a friend several years younger than I who had just returned from a trip to India. Settling into being home again and making compari-sons between the two countries, he was having trouble feeling "too much in the world" in ways he felt helpless to remedy in our whirling-dervish culture. I wrote, in part:

> Somewhere along our march of time, nature kicks in with her infinite wisdom to suggest that we get some distance from our self-inflicted, over-full lives—that we do what it takes for one person, each in his own way, to achieve a peace that will abide in you with constancy. Age works an attitude adjustment and begins to believe

Chapter six

that peace and compassion and "giving back" are the only real imperatives. Take heart, dear friend. Life gets wiser every day because it gets shorter every day, and the resulting perspective saves us by the temple bell!

From best to worst, the gods are us—that is a metaphorical fact. Eschewing the god of war, I search, soul in hand, for the gods who will act responsibly in our world, since my only power—limited, but compelling—appears to be choosing *which* of the gods I will honor.

seven

The happiest people I know raise a glass half full

> Within the soul from its primordial beginnings there
> has been a desire for light and an irrepressible urge to rise
> out of the primal darkness. . . . [It] is the same today as it
> has been for countless millions of years. The longing for
> light is the longing for consciousness.
>
> —C. G. Jung

Damn! Who can think happiness? For the past three weeks I have felt as unhappy as I have ever been. Nerve pain: sporadically severe. I can only hope—it's not guaranteed—that I will be improved soon with a couple of injections. Please pray with me; cortisone has worked before and with any luck it will do its magic again. But even as I hold tight to my hope, happiness is a long, ironic stretch for my mind today, as hurt sweeps clean all memory of a body that was once pain-free, requiring nothing—much less a syringe full of magic—to just do its thing, unnoticed and uncomplaining. I've tried every way I know to take the high ground here, but I am humbled by my failure to sustain even the smallest measure of acceptance; equanimity is out the window. I'm surprised that I fail, having always thought I would do well with it when the time came, and there were clues that it surely would. When I entered what I supposed was the last trimester of my life, I made a statistically probable assumption that my aging body would sooner or later find itself "on the rack" and actually took up a practice of bearing pain. Clever of me to have thought of the idea early, was my thought way back then; like banking money for one's old age, I would learn how to manage my mind around pain. I would make all of those spiritual and psychological mind-body connections I had been studying for so many years and learn to control pain—to render it bearable with meditation and my oh-so-enlightened perspective. I picked a master on the subject from my personal library and proceeded to reread all of Stephen Levine's remarkable books on pain and conscious dying, including *A Year to Live,* in which he counsels the willing to study pain by

> opening to illness. Each time you get a cold or the flu, use it as
> an opportunity to soften around the unpleasant and investigate
> how resistance turns pain into suffering, the unpleasant into the
> unbearable. Notice how discomfort attracts grief. Watch the shad-
> ows gather in the aching body. Hear them mutter in complaint
> and self-pity. Pity arises from meeting pain with fear. Compassion
> comes when you meet it with love. . . . We have been conditioned
> to withdraw our awareness from the unpleasant. Break that
> imprinting![1]

Easy to *say!* All right, resisting pain is counterproductive—and I concede that pandering to self-pity does nothing to lessen pain's misery. But I've yet to find enough love in my cupboard to give to this kind of pain, which my mind is ready and willing to call unbearable. Could it be I have not practiced enough? It's a fact that I haven't been sick in bed for the usual reasons—the flu, a bad case of shingles or *E. coli,* a fractured collarbone, or a broken spirit—in a dog's age, so there have been few opportunities to meditate on the deep and recurring kind of grief I feel today. Now, having given my best effort to Levine's first-rate advice to meditate in real time—when the pain is on and pulsating—I'm folding my cards. Not for a nanosecond will my

The happiest people I know raise a glass half full

efforts alone overcome so much discomfort; the deafening scream of an inflamed sciatic nerve does not, will never, compare to any sickbed I have ever occupied—and that settles *that*. And worse than the pain is my humiliation: so far, I have failed every test to halt a descent into morbid self-pity, so I cry and curse a lot—which is so unlike me! Defeated, I am holed up at home, sparing those who would offer me condolences, sparing myself from those who would say, astonished (and disbelieving): "Surely you jest—you've never looked better!" So here I sit, feeling cranky as hell while I process my testiness on a word machine that may not give a damn how much I hurt but won't tell me to stop whining, either. For the first time in my life, I am absolutely certain that real happiness is nothing more or less than the absence of too much physical pain.

◌◦

One week later I am exhaling the longest breath in recorded history. My thanks to those who prayed: I am better by miles. The shots "took" almost immediately, and today I sit in giddy reunion with my sense of well-being—neurologically pain-free, equanimity restored, and mind set to address a half-full glass and the happiest people I know. Allow me first, though, to give you a context for the word "happy"—what it means to me, because you might define the word differently and my "happiest people" might not be whom you are expecting to meet.

For me, happiness began as tiny seeds of potential, producing fruit that ripened in its own time in the rich loam of my personal experiences, painful and otherwise, and a slow-growing hoard of personal wisdom. Scanning my history to locate some of its memorable bright-light moments, I see happiness in my early years as intervals of joyful anticipation of some new beginning—times when I cherished magical, made-up reasons to believe that some burning desire of mine would soon be gratified. In truth, I think this was not really happiness yet—merely fleeting little fits of pleasure generated by hope and a fierce will to have what I wanted—please, God, just this once! For instance, as a young girl I ran to meet my father's streetcar at the end of his every workday, filled with joy to think I would have him all to myself as we walked the two long blocks back to our house. And every day, I was disappointed. If my father felt any joy to find me waiting just for him, it was never apparent. Disembarking from the trolley, an empty lunch pail in one hand, a rolled-up newspaper tucked under his arm, his face inevitably projected the thousand and one concerns which I took from his mood were dark and troubling things I dared not ask him to share with me. So—again inevitably—we would walk the two blocks home in silence, each of us alone, while my too-high hope morphed into an ache and a yearning for a moment that had once again passed us by. Maybe tomorrow, or some "next" time, I would think to myself—whereupon I would fire up another burning desire to accommodate my loss and stoke it with anticipation to keep my hope alive. I should note about these burning desires of mine that I was way short of psychological maturity and way long on untutored ignorance—the innocent not-knowing of a child that persisted, along with her desires, long after the child had become "woman." Too bad, because that pattern of perceptions and reactions that became so stuck in childhood—the happy anticipatory moments, quickly dissipated by unmet expectations, followed by feelings of disappointment—became an albatross too weighty to hang on relationships, sinking first one marriage and then another. But then came the "work," and the long metamorphosis that would change the whole shape of my life and thinking and finally locate a happiness better fitting the child-become-woman.

There is nothing extraordinary about my "happiness" history, unless you count how late it got its start. Nothing leaps off the pages of my life and shouts, "Happy at last!" There were no fabulous blowout events, no life-changing lotto numbers, and no five-star satoris that ushered in "happiness." What was extraordinary was the process that brought me to it. If at first I lacked tools to break out of the unconscious neurotic expectations that held me in thrall, I eventually acquired them and began my transition to a different perspective about happiness itself. When I began the slow surrender of the child's stubborn insistence to have happiness her way (no longer possible, of course), and commenced exploring a whole new concept of happiness with my newly tutored and awakening mind, my day was won. I could finally discern the difference between life's small pleasures, which are by their nature momentary, and a *state* of happiness—the sense of "okayness" about life and myself that is not too much to expect—a state that becomes

The happiest people I know raise a glass half full

and then stays. This is the low-simmering process of discovery that permeates a psyche one tiny revelation at a time; it infuses the personality, changing it imperceptibly until it is changed radically, and exposes the expanding consciousness to the subtler, truer nature of happiness.

My early perceptions of happiness derived from inadequate parenting and the collective deprivations common to many families emerging from the Great Depression. Too young to protect myself against the circumstances, my responses to the world were confused and equivocal, wobbly imitations of my peers' ideas about everything, including happiness. Yet, as my persistent, searching self bumped along through the years making mistakes and learning my lessons, I began to have credible intimations of a separate self at my core and to recognize that my "I" had needs and desires often remarkably different than those advertised by the collective "we." In the argot of C. G. Jung's psychology, I was "individuating"—authenticating my ego, finally looking to myself to define and create the happiness I was beginning to experience. Cracking, shedding, stepping out of my too-many, too-delicate skins, I was ultimately clear-minded and ego-strong enough to forge a future with right results. It took a decade to clear the biggest hurdles in my path and nearly a lifetime to distance the child who viewed her world "through a glass darkly" from who I am today—loving life just as it is, wishing for nothing more. Only time could temper, compress, and recalibrate what needed fixing in me and reveal my happiness as a different point of view and a new state of mind.

It seems to me that happiness percolates in us on different levels at different times, ranging all the way from "sensual" or "fleeting" on a surface level to emanations of quiet joy from the deep place of soul. What causes happiness can vary radically from one person to the next, but to know why I am happy—to know what works for and against who I uniquely am so that I can make the right choices to stay happy—is crucial when life's inevitable conflicts beg to be resolved. Experience tells me that the more conscious I am, the fewer conditions happiness requires. Even so, there are conditions.

I've found four cardinal contingencies on which my state of well-being depends. Each is separate and inconclusive when considered by itself, but when all four conditions are met, integrated, and working on my behalf, they are the platform on which my happiness rests, the essential psychic props that catalyze and inform my sense of my world as being quite wonderful, thank you. Yet, should any one of them become compromised enough to upset this perfect but delicate balance, it's possible that happiness would lose its name for me. These conditions are happiness as the absence of psychic pain; happiness as the ability to give and receive love; happiness as (and in) solitude; and happiness as the absence of physical pain. I'll take them in turn:

Happiness as the absence of psychic pain. Short-term and recurring, or long-term and persistent, psychic pain can chew up happiness and spit out the dispirited remains faster than a heart can beat. Where suffering resides and finds no easy or frequent exit, there is no potion with enough magic to crack a face into a smile; the will is useless, the spirit refuses. A psyche can wither from too much pain in the same way an afflicted body limb will shrivel without its supply of blood. Happiness shuns altogether a mind in mourning or a spirit in depression, so there will be no holding on to happiness unless—in deference to the malevolent power of psychic pain—we can somehow cut it off at the pass. And who among us has not had, does not still have, some degree of psychic pain to conquer—and reconquer? From T. S. Eliot's "East Coker:"

> Shall I say it again? In order to arrive there,
> To arrive where you are, to get from where you are not,
>> You must go by a way wherein there is no ecstasy.
> In order to arrive at what you do not know
>> You must go by a way which is the way of ignorance.
> In order to possess what you do not possess
>> You must go by way of dispossession.
> In order to arrive at what you are not
>> You must go through the way in which you are not.
> And what you do not know is the only thing you know
> And what you own is what you do not own
> And where you are is where you are not.[2]

How Eliot's words still resonate with me: I understand their meaning as perfectly reflecting a time in my thirties when I had just begun the hard

The happiest people I know raise a glass half full

work of bringing to consciousness that sorry lot of fractured psychology I was still hanging on to from my childhood. Shouldering the Sisyphean work of psyche's reconstruction, I too went "by a way wherein there is no ecstasy in order to arrive" at what I needed to know. If you've ever spent time in psychotherapy, you know it is everything except ecstasy! I resisted Eliot's every metaphor at first reading—then finally surrendered to them as being perfectly fitting. His words conveyed a sweet and knowing recognition of my plight and gave me wonderful comfort all through the daunting process that was slowly knitting self-awareness to the "the way of ignorance" in a search to "possess what you do not possess." Eventually I won my prize—and what is more, a cache of extravagant treasure: a psyche free of its chronic pain and a splendor of relief at the death of who I once had been but was no longer.

Happiness as the ability to give and receive love: For many years, my ability to love intimately and profoundly—and to be loved in return—was more a wordy abstraction than the real thing. I fell into love's extravagant bliss for the first time when I became a mother. It is a way of loving that from its beginning was more real than anything else about me—the root of my very being. A mother's love is deeply nuanced, often plunging to depths that never reach bottom; yet, I discovered about myself that my ability to love as a mother was exclusive of my ability to love well otherwise. Like others I've met, I used the word "love" too frequently and without skill, applying the term indiscriminately where it didn't belong because I had never studied its meaning for precision. "I love you," we say nonchalantly, unimportantly, as a verbal arabesque lightly flung, and as the words breeze by catch-if-you-can, the word *love* is stripped of the promise and commitment and gravitas it wanted to convey. I love to dance and I love the color blue and I love the way you look—but what is the love we feel? What do you feel deep inside yourself when you say the word *love* out loud and from your heart? I have been head over heels "in love" twice, only to discover each time that what I mistakenly thought was love that would last couldn't go deep enough to embrace the sacrifices that true love—love larger than I had ever experienced—is willing to make for the greater good of a relationship. I found out soon enough that love in marriage is complex; it must overcome romance—and "the ten thousand things"—to survive the natural wear and tear on years of togetherness.

Chapter seven

Every morning, I jumped out of bed, pulled on my persona, and went forth on the day to meet every one of my responsibilities to the best of my ability. That was not love. That was the child *earning* love—giving her all in order to be loved. I didn't know what was not in me to ask: If I wasn't in a loving relationship with myself, how could I deeply love anyone else? How could I not be inadequate to, and even be mystified by, the kind of love that was trying to come my way? No, I would not be "adequate" in love's presence until much later, not until I had learned its requirements of me and how to conjugate its multiple meanings—certainly not until I understood that prerequisite to developing an ability to love is having *been* loved—as a child—deeply and profoundly.

And so that became my work: climbing back through the years and layers of a patched-together personality to find my "original face," as the Buddhists say it, to find that small, vital, unsullied body who was love itself—reaching for affection and willing to return it a thousand times over to whomever would mirror her longing to be loved. I found her, of course—and what a find! It was the original face of a perfectly beautiful child—so dear, and so infinitely lovable. Since finding her, it is my custom to image her often with my mind's eye and imbibe her presence. I imagine her playing alone, absorbed and content, or with a friend in all the sweetness of sharing. When I look into the soft, open petal of her face and our eyes connect, I return her eager smile, take her hands, hold her close, and feel her joy. Her willingness to love is organic; her responsiveness when love is returned is as predictable as a sunrise. My heart feels full and protective of her—the treasure who, even in my darkest moments, was always me. She clamored for my care and affection for too many years, but her needs were too many when added to my own. So I shunned her, believing I had more urgent problems to solve, which is a truth that breaks my heart every time I think of it. Today I see her with the loving eyes of a mother, care for her as I do my own children—deeply, profoundly, forevermore.

Learning to love and value myself as someone perfect in my own broken-ness enabled me to love others *as* myself—and to comprehend how others could love and appreciate me. At some point I really "got it" that we are all eminently lovable, or could be—that we all have an original instinct to give and receive love in all of its nurturing shapes and ways. Without that

The happiest people I know raise a glass half full

precious exchange of love with others in my life today, happiness would quickly lose meaning for me and "God" would be impossible to locate. To honor every act of love in my life in conscious awareness—those made by me and those that come my way—sets the precedent for my happiness. If the clear perception of love's importance to my life were not always in my mind, I could sicken and die, along with my original soul.

Happiness as and in solitude: The life of a solitary is not for everyone and it is not my intention here to make a case for or against it, especially since statistics show that most people in these United States choose being in a long-term relationship over living in solitude by at least three to one. Others are happiest living in a relationship that permits time for solitude in a balance configured to suit their needs. The smallest number, of which I am one, are almost always introverted, loner types; we wend our ways to solitary lifestyles eventually, if not immediately, in a process of discovering that solitude is where we are most comfortable, most creative, and feel most ourselves. I came to it by midlife, settling into my preference for solitude with more and more certainty as I became aware of strong inner imperatives to live the lifestyle and I found the courage to honor my conviction. Anthony Storr says in the introduction to his book *Solitude: A Return to the Self*:

> Love and friendship are, of course, an important part of what makes life worthwhile. But they are not the only source of happiness. Moreover, human beings change and develop as life goes on. In old age, human relationships often become less important. . . . In any case, there is always an element of uncertainty in interpersonal relationships which should preclude them from being idealized as an absolute, or seen as constituting the only path toward personal fulfillment. It may be our idealization of interpersonal relationships in the West that causes marriage, supposedly the most intimate tie, to be so unstable. If we did not look to marriage as the principal source of happiness, fewer marriages would end in tears.[3]

Storr notes that some psychological probabilities for negative isolating tendencies do exist for some in early childhood. But when he describes a healthy child's ability to be alone in a positive sense, he says, "The capacity to be alone thus becomes linked with self-discovery and self-realization; with becoming aware of one's deepest needs, feelings, and impulses."[4] This describes my young self, too, as I discovered in therapy. During all the years I labored for self-discovery, my inner need to write and reflect in solitude increasingly influenced my outer lifestyle. Eventually the two were melded, resolving a conflict that had pulled me two different ways since I was a teenager: Was I to satisfy the conventional call to live "wedded" to someone for as long as that was an option, or might I live alone with the freedom and the time to acknowledge and pursue my deeper self on a faster track? It seems I was meant to travel one road until there appeared the crossroad that would take me "home"—my good luck, for I can't imagine life without my children.

So, for me solitude was an evolutionary process. I feared it in my very young years because I was too frequently left alone. Yet, by the age of seven I was craving it—pleading to be excused from the family's ritual Sunday movie outings. Finally persuaded, they left me alone with my books, my journal writing, and the delicious pleasure of two or three hours in silent retreat. Storr refers to these "seeds of solitary interests" as noticeably present in some from their earliest years, which was certainly true of me—foretelling, had I understood the signs, some key characteristics of who I was to become. Much of my life to its midpoint was filled with anything but solitude, of course, as I lived my several vocations—marriage, motherhood, and a long span of years working in service to a career. All of them required good-to-better and best social skills and I soon learned to "extravert" with the best of them when necessary. There are times, too, when introverts feel the need to spend time in society with others—a need every solitary ignores at their peril, though "society" might be only one other person and time spent together no more than an hour or two. Truly, my happiest and most authentic self is home alone, reading, writing, or meditating, as close to soul and silence as I can get. "The creative person," writes Storr,

> is constantly seeking to discover himself, to remodel his own identity,
> and to find meaning in the universe through what he creates. He
> finds this a valuable integrating process which, like meditation or

The happiest people I know raise a glass half full

prayer, has little to do with other people, but which has its own separate validity. His most significant moments are those in which he attains some new insight, or makes some new discovery, and these moments are chiefly, if not invariably, those in which he is alone.[5]

The time I spend with my bright and lively children (extroverts all) is always keenly anticipated and absolutely essential to my happiness—the manna that sustains my soul, warms my heart, and feeds every cell in my body. Their beauty hurts my eyes and makes me wish time would stop so we could live this moment forever. Only when I am with them do joy and sorrow fuse and catch in my throat to remind me: time will end, the "moments" will stop. A few hours later, though—I have to say it—I am filled up on the fruits of our shared love and meaningful exchanges and feel a tug to "go home"—to be alone. My friends are immensely tolerant of me; my children still find my ways a bit "peculiar," I think, but we are all patient and loving of one another. Ask anyone who lives alone happily and they will tell you they must be their own best friend and have an ability to be alone without feeling lonely. I guard against the danger of pushing my limits with solitude, though; as with any style of living, mine, too, needs tuning and tweaking to stay in balance. There are quite a few like me in the small town where I live and we know who we are; we have recognizable traits in common, the most respected one being that we are friendly when we meet up, but never, ever garrulous; we let each other go and move on. To the unpracticed eye, I think it must seem that we who choose solitude live terribly quiet and minimalist lives—all burrowed into our introversion and a good book as we mostly are. Yet, it is so rich a life from my point of view. How crucial it is for each of us to become who we are and live as ourselves! I will say on behalf of any others who would truly claim the name, though: being a solitary is absolutely essential to our sense of well-being.

Now to finish my thoughts on happiness as the absence of physical pain—by which I mean not the "background noise" discomfort which I have learned to tolerate well enough, but chronic, unrelenting pain in a degree of intensity that has yet to seriously test my mettle. I have done all I can do in the present by acknowledging the possibility of that kind of pain in my future, so I simply wait now in awareness for what life will bring to me. While waiting, I pray for all earthlings everywhere that none of us will meet with too much pain—whatever "too much" means to each of us. My recent joust with sciatic nerve pain was a watershed experience, though, from which I gleaned this one probable certainty: I am not one who could sustain anything close to equanimity were I to suffer that same pain for more than a few days without benefit of effective and prolonged relief. I would resist taking drugs—but for how long, I wonder?

Should I ever have need, there exists in my country incomparable, state-of-the-art pharmacology replete with every kind of mind-bending "designer drug" solution to serious suffering from any and every cause. I foresee that at the very least I could always be made more comfortable, and at most—reaching an absolute end of my tolerance for pain—I would be given an option to "trip" to a new reality. If I took that option, I would be more or less removed from the state of conscious awareness I have worked a lifetime to achieve—even as I might feel gratitude for having the option to take! A few years ago, I paid witness to a process of pain *in extremis* when a friend came to terms with death as a result of cancer. She was a beautiful, energetic, bright-as-a-butterfly midlifer determined to squeeze every last clock-tick of consciousness from whatever time was left before the disease turned off her lights. The pain advanced slowly and steadily, as did the medication she was given to ease it, and in a few short weeks she died—free of pain, full of the morphine that became her only surcease, and *in absentia* for her death. That last assumption is only a reasonable guess, because who can know such things? I truly believe in conscious dying—it is definitely the way I want to go, so I took time to reflect on a burning question about my own death: Would not being conscious at life's final crossroad be my worst-case scenario? I was quick to decide that I can't answer that question yet, not until I get to my own time and circumstance. Even so, it's not hard for me to imagine that were I in a situation similar to my friend's when the end is imminent, all of my passionate intellectual commitment to conscious dying might dissolve like sugar in a cup of hot tea. As I write these words, I cleave to my hope

The happiest people I know raise a glass half full

that I will leave my body with enough mental clarity to experience some unimaginable out-of-body transition to who-knows-what—were there to be one.
In the present, where I mostly spend my time in a state of nonmedicated
awareness, life is chanting a peaceful *Ommmmm* . . .

There are four definitions of happiness in the eleventh edition of *Merriam-
Webster's Collegiate Dictionary*: (1) good fortune, prosperity; (2) a state of
well-being and contentment; (3) a pleasurable or satisfying experience; (4)
felicity, aptness. Only the second definition gives me a chance for happiness
when all others fail, so I will name a state of well-being and contentment as
my happiness of choice and make it the context for describing those whom
I say are, hands down, the happiest people I know.

They are all graced—in the sense that they feel favored or blessed; in their
wildest dreams, they would not have thought they could feel so much gratitude just to be alive. I generalize when I say "all"—of course no two people
are exactly alike; nevertheless, I speak nothing but the truth here. They are
grateful—as in "there but for the grace of God go I." Gratitude is what sparks
their energy—gets them up in the morning, gets them through every day,
and even visits their dreams in the night. Maybe you know one, or some, of
them—maybe you are one of them. If so, you know there's a certain lightness
to their being, an easy, pleasing attitude that tells you right away they will
never adjudicate your peccadilloes; they're apt to know where you're coming from—apt to have been there—but you and your ways are yours to judge.
But, oh, that gratitude! It's the most remarkable thing about them—organic,
pulsing along, as reliable as daybreak and as steady as a heartbeat, no up
highs, no down lows—not anymore. They emanate a diffident, quotidian
humility—not self-deprecating, not deferential, not submissive—more of an
awareness deep in their bones that the whole of humanity is sacred—also
flawed—but derivative of godliness, they think it's not too much to say. They
know as well that happiness is not measured by feats of the ego, but draws
from some other source they feel certain gives us access to the experience.
Accepting and supportive, generous and compassionate, these people are
almost always capable of saying something wise or uplifting—of giving us

Chapter seven

something to think about. They are and do and feel all of this because they are *awake!* Do you wonder what is the cause of so much gratitude? Or how they can sustain an attitude that is almost reverential of the plain, simple fact of a day in which they are alive?

The happiest people I know are found in groups of a dozen or more—sometimes a hundred or more. What links gratitude to their happiness is that every one of them has walked to "the edge of the abyss" and circled its slick and shifting perimeter more times than they care to remember. Most of them would be dead by now had they not survived their potentially worst-case scenario: falling down, falling over, falling *into* the abyss. I'm one of them. One at a time and over and over we share our stories about the abyss. The stories are all different; the abyss is the common denominator, the metaphor for death-by-addiction every one of us has escaped—at least so far. We are people who join hands in the fellowship of Alcoholics Anonymous, gathering in meeting rooms all over the world to share our "experience, strength, and hope" about the times—fearing each would be our last—we stood peering over the dizzying edge of our physical or spiritual death. Then, as we teetered on the brink for the absolute last time, full of heartache and our disease, somehow, in some way, for some reason we will *never* know, we fell backwards instead—into a state of grace as Something greater than our addiction scooped us up with infinite generosity and gave us a chance to rethink our lives.

That energy I tried to describe—energy that is generated by a consistently abiding gratitude for a life that will never again be taken for granted—is what we share in common. This is the great and lasting reason to be happy. Think of it: your very *life*—all but over—then inexplicably returned to you to live again in a continuous and conscious appreciation of its newly discovered value and significance. After that, believe me, we breathe gratitude in and out, in and out—like the pure sweet air of life itself. There is a body of literature about other kinds of "near-death" events in which the survivors tell similar stories about having been immediately transformed by the experience, stunned into a wholly different perspective on life, and left with a profound sense of gratitude for every new day thereafter. That was my experience, too, though "transformation" for us is more often evolutionary than stunning and immediate. What happened to me is no less than a mystery

The happiest people I know raise a glass half full

and a miracle—and deeply humbling. My desire was always to become fear-lessly real, free of my demons and unapologetic. I prayed the same as Rilke when he pleaded at times to be more than he was:

> I want to unfold.
> Let no place in me hold itself closed,
> for where I am closed, I am false.[6]

Part of my miracle was getting everything I prayed for. I can't prove there is a special kind and portion of gratitude that lifts near-death survivors out of their suffering and into "a state of well-being and contentment" (my hap-piness of choice), but I'd bet almost everything I own on the theory. It's true of me—and I hear it from them every time I'm in the meeting rooms with these happiest people I know.

One of the men I married once described "happiness" in words that, though I had never heard them before, seemed as right and familiar as my name: "At best, life is a quiet party." I would add only this about happiness: It is also a glass at least half full of gratitude for the gift that is one's life—I mean the natural, spontaneous, verifiable "birthright" kind of happiness that begins when a baby grabs her toes, squeals with delight, and kicks at the air —thrilling to life with her total being. It can get lost, for some more than once, and it can be recovered—quieter, but intact: just right for me. It may take some luck to hang on to it, though—I have no illusions about the body when it goes to throwing a fit, which it does now and then for reasons all its own and too boring to tell. So I'll raise a glass for all of us, shall I? "Here's to happiness—and the luck of the Irish!"

Chapter seven

eight

Wisdom

What Is It? Who Is It? And More . . .

> When people say I am wise, or a sage, I cannot accept
> it. A man once dipped a hatful of water from a stream.
> What did that amount to? . . . I never think that I am
> the one who must see to it that cherries grow on stalks.
> I stand and behold, admiring what nature can do.
>
> —C. G. Jung

Jung's words, above, evoke the inestimable
humility of a man uneasy with having wisdom ascribed to him,
quite happy enough to merely "behold" wisdom as a "naturally"
emanating influence in his life whose mysterious origins greatly
inspired him. I look in the dictionary for wisdom—*insight,
knowledge, judgment, accumulated learning*—then close the book
and scrub my mind. Wisdom is so much more, or other, than
the word itself. It is immanent, an energy, subtle and profound.
It inheres in our very being, sounding our depths, trolling
for enlightenment, and always on call to the conscious mind.
Wisdom gives an impression it is "out there" somewhere, yet
its source is not to be found. Is it triggered by the mind or the
senses? I hear words that, when strung together just the right

way, sound wise, or I sense a certain "rightness" in my soul that feels like wisdom; yet the science of wisdom remains inexact, debatable, stuck in a mystery it's still trying to solve. T. S. Eliot's so-perfect words from "Little Gidding" describe wisdom as the paradox she is:

> We shall not cease from exploration
> And the end of all our exploring
> Will be to arrive where we started
> And know the place for the first time.[1]

I am awed by wisdom, because though I know it in the sense that I have experienced it, I can never nail it on words. I call my own experiences of wisdom "events"—brief, wholly unexpected, deeply intimate events whose smallest details are magnified and available to total recall. Like holograms, they hang in space outside of time while every dimension of my being comes wide awake, resonating in a crucible of absolute truth and clarity, and I am someone other than my ordinary identity. I do not observe my wisdom event—I *am* the event, and I emerge from it an altered, "wiser" me. Paradoxically, my new insight at once becomes structurally of a piece with the rest of me—whorled into the ongoing, lifelong process of me "becoming." More paradox: I sense my new wisdom as something I have always known—yet how can it be? How can I have always understood a truth I just experienced for the first time? "Of course—of *course*—I *know* that!" is my cry of excitement and gratitude as the event comes to its end.

As I write this, I am remembering in all of its particulars one of wisdom's first "visitations" to me. I was home reading, intensely focused on a book written by a distinguished psychologist whose writing demands close attention. Suddenly, I was so moved by the clarity of a single unconditional truth embedded in one tiny paragraph on the page that I slid to the floor on my knees, sobbing with relief. His words had brought to mind a deeply unsettling question, left over from a divorce, that I had been struggling to bring to closure for nearly a decade. Although the words I read referenced my question only indirectly—even obscurely—their holistic effect on me was that they both answered my question and cleared my mind of it simultaneously. I

Chapter eight

have since unsuccessfully combed through every book I own by that author to find those precious words and reconnect to them. But the truth is, no sooner was my crisis over than everything specific to it left my memory—such is the puzzling nature of these wisdom events: insight seems to "rewrite the hard drive" as it merges seamlessly with my consciousness. Still fresh in memory today, though, is the intensely peaceful quiet of that afternoon as a waning sun streamed through the shutters in pale slats of light laid over the rich reds in the Persian rug where, still on my knees, I contemplated for more than an hour an experience that had just unshackled me from an angst I no longer felt.

I am just as awed today to think that in a mere handful of seconds my whole self was transmuted by a sliver of wisdom so pure, so simple, so perfectly suited to my need that a years-old dilemma was forever vanquished from my psyche. It was truth—unquestionably—and it said, not in words but in a single, sharply convincing flash of feeling, that "to judge oneself or another is *always* to do an injustice." Because this revelation both relieved my mind and confirmed my original intuition of the inherent negativity in judging others, I have wondered if it were not preexisting wisdom—that is, in me all along—that I had only to recognize (when I had become open enough to receive it) as an "Aha!" event. Then again, maybe wisdom is born synchronous with our need for it. My best guess is that wisdom resides in the unconscious until—at some appropriate time and for some good reason—it breaks through to one's awareness. I am certain of only this much: I was changed—and wiser—at the end of wisdom's visit.

Wisdom does its work everywhere—but on the sly: I can observe it, and I can receive it, and for a few split seconds even become one with it, but wisdom's source is always hidden. Three times I studied wisdom's ways in my infant children, yet my studies taught me nothing about its origins. Long before my babies could say "hold me, please," wisdom reached up their arms to me when I came into sight. I *still* wonder how infants know to do that. Long before they could speak their love, they knew how to

Wisdom: what is it? who is it? and more

do it. Still new in the crib, their eyes followed my every move as I tended and cherished them, but when our eyes met and locked in that perfect exchange of love that is impossible to describe, there would come that smile—slow, wide, and tender—eyes fixed and probing mine still as they wordlessly "spoke" their love back to me. I was never *not* amazed, marveling at the wisdom in them that recognized and returned to me what I was feeling for them. And isn't it wisdom that provides the preverbal infant with a language—utterly transparent and universally translatable—to express its all-important "No!" of displeasure? You, too, have seen a baby straighten its legs into ramrods, windmill the air with its arms, scream with its lungs, redden its face, and stream its tears, am I right? How impressive is the wisdom in one so young!

There is, too, the elegance of wisdom's words when, to my complete surprise, they pour off the page to fill my eyes and go for my heart with words shaped into poetic evocations from some deeply creative source inside an author I know only by name and wisdom's special turn of phrase. Wisdom's genius can be found in people of every age who dare to innovate themselves by reaching for the stars in subtle, myriad ways to attain some end they have in mind. Wisdom can be heartbreakingly beautiful when I watch a few easy, unpretentious movements of a body so graceful it says everything about a person; or in a turn of phrase spoken so straight and plain it catches the breath; or in an act of human compassion at just the right time—maybe *just* in time. Nature's wisdom is complete—she who has cycled her seasons into infinity since the beginning of time, influencing beyond our comprehension every sentient organism on the planet—from its birth and growth to its decline, old age and death. Talk about elegant!

Wisdom is all around me when I am awake to my life. It does seem to increase with age and the accumulated experience that frequently redounds to us from the elders—but not always, for we have all met "old souls" of every age. Yet, one has to know wisdom—to have been intimate with it and to have experienced a moment in which wisdom takes you and becomes you—in order to define it; not with words, but as a holographic experience outside of time.

From whence comes wisdom? Stephen Levine says:

Chapter eight

The insights that arise in the wisdom mind are often experienced
as sudden, wordless understandings of how things are. . . . This
level of mind . . . can experience simply being.[2]

A path to wisdom opened in me early out of necessity, I think, shaping
itself almost imperceptibly just beneath my consciousness as a deeply felt
need, an inarticulate longing to locate answers to questions barely formed,
yet already pregnant with importance as pieces of my completion. Books
wise in content do not yield answers to questions not yet or only barely
formed—although reading supported and greatly hastened my search. My
answers came to me one at a time, each in a direct experience of an absolute truth that was born all at once, sunlit and perfectly pitched to expand
my consciousness. I neither willed these events nor imagined them; I knew
them only as a gift of insight that had just changed my life.

So I think words of wisdom are not wisdom itself. The wisdom I claim
as my own is inexplicably evoked as a result of my personal response to
something unusual and unanticipated. Stacked up behind the actual event—
which I might have been "stalking" unconsciously for months or even years—
were perhaps a dozen or so near-miss events anticipating the real deal. There
is "universal" wisdom—words of the wise from other ages so timeless and
meaningful to so many that generations later we still respond to their truth.
Yet I believe the particular wisdom that accrues to us individually is always
a personal experience. It will not transfer from one to another; I must
come to it first-hand—and I will—at a time when I am aching to apprehend a
thing that is uniquely meaningful to me, even if I haven't yet formed words
to express it.

I can compare my wisdom events to Maslow's "peak experiences" as
follows: something *outside* of me strikes a chord that resonates in perfect
harmony with something deep *within* me to produce an insight. I experience
the insight as truth—my truth, god-given and undeniable. Immediately and
seamlessly it will integrate with all else that is me to increase my personal
collection of wisdom. Here's a different metaphor: A wisdom event is a kind
of universal energy exchange between an individual and an unknown source
in a moment when *seeking* and *finding* come together in a flash of intuitive

knowing to provide exactly what is needed to expand one's consciousness. Wisdom happens to me, in and as me—not by me, and though I claim it as mine, it is not mine, of course; wrapped in a great mystery, it is simply entrusted to me to use to good purpose. Again, Stephen Levine:

> There is a difference between wisdom and knowledge. We experience
> a moment of understanding and say, "Ah, that's how it is!" . . .
> The experience of understanding is wisdom.[3]

Now here is where I'm going to call a spade a spade, finally, and say that a wisdom event is not a nano-width different than a "spiritual experience."

Who and where are the wise—and do they teach classes? I've read the books of dozens of wise authors who have mentored, nurtured, and companioned me since the beginning of my questioning. I have met and known many wise people on the road to now; yet only a handful of them have I thought to be terribly wise. I have known women, many of them mothers, in whom the wisdom of the nurturing feminine seemed always to be present and available innately. A few feminists I have known were wise—the ones with honed intelligence and inclusive hearts, and some of them became my friends. Even today I applaud their passion for justice and their wisdom to act on it. If one can generalize (never a great way to make a point but sometimes a way to come close), I believe that the heart-wisdom so often apparent in women is developed and accessible to them early in life, and that the wisdom of the intellect begins to develop and become apparent earlier in men. Each sex is "prejudiced" by its natural tilt and talent in the early years, according to Jung, but he believes that both sexes do better when they consciously develop some opposite-sex wisdom as they mature. I rush to say here that there are untold exceptions to all three of these generalities.

Jung, himself, was a psychologist of remarkable intellect, and he taught many important distinctions between the sexes. I remember one in particular because I am so often met with examples of it in everyday life: he attributed to the feminine gender a natural gift for diffused awareness (think this way: a woman with a toddler under one arm at the same time she is cooking dinner, feeding the dog, and paying bills online). To the masculine gender he

Chapter eight

attributes an equally innate bent for focused consciousness (example: a man viewing a game on television, so intensely focused on details he is unaware that the kitchen stove is on fire). Two separate aptitudes, both accessible to the opposite sex if brought to consciousness and taken seriously. Just as women have made their way into corporate and political life by demonstrating skillful and competitive intellection, so are men in ever increasing numbers evolving their long neglected feminine side by testing themselves on intimacy and as nurturers in and outside the home. Jung's theory is that both sexes win a better understanding of themselves and each other when each acquires a balance of power by becoming proficient across gender lines. I can think of no wisdom more eloquent than this.

Wise men I have known figured no less importantly in my life than my women teachers—often dramatically more so when I needed to learn the specifics of their worlds of business and commerce, pretty much wholly owned by men of that time. I have always thought that the men I viewed as my teachers were truly remarkable. They had many wisdom traits in common—a sensitive, well-developed heart side, expansive minds, generosity of spirit, and a genuine respect for talent and the individual, sex be damned. One man mentored me along a career path that eventually prospered into long-term financial independence. His wisdom was to imagine all that I might become long before I could and to help me develop the personal and professional skills I would need along the way, including, especially, my powers of intellection. A different wise man mentored me psychologically by guiding me through a patch of acute midlife despairing and self-healing. His deep and genuine compassion was always at the ready, reliable and convincing, until my confidence in my future was restored. His wisdom, formed of the most elegant combination of human heart and intellect I ever hope to know, returned "the rest of my life" to me.

The way I satisfied my longings to become whole has always been to explore and study the best minds and biggest hearts I could find. I continue to read the wise ones—always with pleasure and sometimes from need, when I am once again in the crosshairs of an inner conflict. I have cracked open their books—some of them way beyond my intellectual reach—about wisdom of every kind: Eastern, Western, traditional, New Age, collective and individual wisdom, practical, political, psychological, and spiritual—and read a world of words about wisdom. But the wisdom that is unique to an individual—the kind that is recognized and received as a thing already known—comes in a process altogether different from learning *about* wisdom from another. The tool that tills the ground of my psyche to receive wisdom is open-mindedness in all things; keeping a sharp and useful edge on it requires me to practice self-awareness about everything in my day, especially my relationships with others. If only for a few minutes, I will find some time to evaluate whether I am being true to myself—which is to say, whether I am living my life meaningfully—so that, at the end of it (which could be today for all I know) I can leave the life I wanted to live. I take a little more time to reflect on my relationships, reviewing the ways I am both different and the same as the other and how I can refine my respect and sensitivity to both of us: this is never as easy as it sounds. Staying open, though, is what I focus on the most because my experience has been that wisdom seeks the open mind to play with.

So, in my story, the men and women who wrote down in books the wisdom born of their direct experiences greased the skids for me to live some wisdom events of my own. I look to them still, the more so when I am lashed to a problem my own best efforts are helpless to untie. They are my mentors, best friends, tried and true, and dear to my heart. Yet the wise do not *teach* wisdom—they *are* wisdom. Their textbooks may abound with great intelligence and extraordinary insights, but—as with the rest of life—there are no free lunches. My life is the only proving ground where I can qualify my intentions, and where I must suffer the hard lessons that will deliver wisdom that is unique to my story. I remind myself every day: "Come awake!" In enough numbers, the wise will lead the unawake.

There are presently enough years behind me to contrast "then" and "now" with a certain objectivity and I say that "now" we are not doing well in terms of numbers of the wise—not in my country, maybe not in the world. There are no stunning leaders in our societies recalling history, heeding its mistakes, changing our attitudes, opening our eyes, envisioning our future, or guiding us wisely. The mythologist Joseph Campbell announced not long before his death in 1987 that modern society was in a free fall,

Chapter eight

plunging through a threadbare mythology that no longer works into a new myth that is still little more than an indecipherable scrawl. Twenty years later his prescience is present fact. We live in collective chaos, searching for lost order and a deeper meaning to live by and we are split in two—half of us struggling to invent a future we can't yet imagine, the other half desperately clutching the unsupportable shreds of a cultural myth no longer viable. Something workable will doubtless emerge from the split; we can harbor a hope because history supports the probability. But when? We'd like to know because we are greatly troubled about this planet we call home—but we can't know; not yet . . . when the wise ones multiply, is my guess.

They're out there somewhere—"in training," I like to think. Suffering through the hard and confounding life lessons that translate into seriously useful intelligence, they are out there in droves, let us hope—becoming broadly erudite and psychologically whole, exploring all possibilities on their merits, imagining big and creatively, opening their hearts and minds wide. If we're lucky they will offer themselves to the world's societies and then we can welcome them with a great sigh of relief as the wise men and women who will inspire and lead us. As I write this today, too many minds and hearts are anxious, self-protective, and closed—not open, thus wisdom is in short supply. Only openness will save the day—the view that says *Yes!* to life—bring it on, let's take a look and figure things out. The wise people I know practice openness as a permanent mindset because it gets them out on the leading edge and onto some really interesting agendas, and since they are open to everything, everyone listens to them. An open mind is their stock in trade, as is evaluating all problems and every person and thing without bias, embracing and imagining a thing as a whole, then rearranging all of its parts to improve it. It is the wise that view the new and find the good in it and perceive change as opportunity. Because their wisdom is not self-conscious, not driven by ego's need to show itself off (Jung's remarks at the head of this chapter are a great example of an ego beautifully in service to wisdom), I am always struck by their humility—that premier characteristic of our species that attracts happiness ineluctably. I jump at the chance to be anywhere wisdom is; how different the wise ones are from the others who bark at life with an unpremeditated, "No! Not yet! Never!"

Wisdom: what is it? who is it? and more

I owe them big-time, these generous, confident people with their born optimism and egoless audacity, because they contribute so much to society and to me. Surely the best way I can act on my gratitude is to study them, to emulate their manner of openness and inquiry—to stre-e-e-etch my view of the world and add inclusiveness to my thinking. What better than to learn from them how to shout out my own "Yes!" to life and blow open whatever doors in me I'm still taking cover behind? I try because I want what they have, and I think they would respect me for that. They might even treat me as a peer and welcome any contribution I could make in common cause with them—because the truly wise exclude no one. Watch the wise when they are being and doing their wisdom. I remind myself every day: Study them!

Wisdom and conflict in our time . . .

> God, whose law it is that he who learns must suffer. And even
> in our sleep pain that cannot forget, falls drop by drop upon the
> heart, and in our own despite, against our will, comes wisdom to
> us by the awful grace of God.[4]

Has anyone said it better than Aeschylus did all those centuries ago? That there is no peace in a mind where conflict has taken up residence was mine to learn. There were times in my life when I suffered so much psychological conflict that I named my state of mind "black-box paralysis." The "box" was exactly as long, wide, and deep as would closely fit my body with a bit more room to accommodate the decelerating movement of my breathing. A mind in a state of conflict, however, is not the same as a mind with plenty of room to observe and plenty of time to assess a problem that is still only *potentially* a conflict. Jung explains that living as we do in a world of duality—good/evil, order/chaos, love/hate, right/wrong, up/down, matter/spirit—we are faced with a whole slew of "problems" every day that might cause us to feel, as he puts it, "the tension of the opposites." We toss off most of them with barely a thought: size them up, make a decision how best to solve them, take the appropriate action, and *poof*—any tension we might have felt briefly is gone.

But when I am faced with a situation for which no apparent resolution comes quickly to mind—not enough choices, let's say, or many choices but

Chapter eight

none of them acceptable—I immediately feel the old discomfort, the "tension" I'm going to be stuck with until I can resolve my problem. In an all-too-human maneuver, I might make a decision too quickly to get rid of my angst. But Jung suggests it is important to hold the opposites in tension until I find the best solution to my problem—one that is psychologically satisfactory, even if not perfect—because while life is always more or less problematic, taking time to make good decisions, rather than quick ones, is what keeps both the conflict and my angst from returning.

I finally learned how to pull back from my problem, detach my emotions, and observe it from a distance as the way to circumvent the ominous "melt-down of the mind," when conflict degrades into black-box paralysis. Some right solution would always come along eventually—and there were times, too, when a problem would outdate itself, lose its potency, and fade away. My other choice, of course, was to wait for my unconscious to yield up a gift of unexpected wisdom. But what if my conflict is caused by a collective problem—one so big and complex that it involves nations and populations? And what if my perception of the conflict is opposed to powerful others who perceive, and would treat, the problem differently? How can my psyche hold so much tension for so long when "the opposition" renders me all but powerless at the outset? I've been able to do it so far—though not easily, or continuously, or even well—by flying straight into the hurricane's eye—where I have been hunkering down ever since. Krishnamurti says:

> In actuality your consciousness is not yours. It is the rest of
> mankind's, because we all go through the same mill, the same
> endless conflict. When you realize this, not emotionally, not
> as an intellectual concept but as something actual, real, true, then
> you will not kill another human being. You will never kill another,
> either verbally or intellectually, ideologically or physically, because
> then you are killing yourself.[5]

I needn't go far to find a "big and complex" collective problem, need I? The current wars in the Middle East, of course, are affecting at least half of mankind in some way or another. As the insurgent and civil war factions continue unabated to fight their own troops and ours, whole nations—an entire region and its diverse cultures—are degrading faster than sand through an hourglass. Nearly two million people fleeing over their borders; the dead and wounded American troops, civilian workers, Coalition and NATO forces, and countless civilians; the destruction of their countries' land and infrastructure; and the untold damage done to every human psyche fortunate enough to survive physically—these are but a few of the parts of our collective problem that stream out of the chaos and paralysis which now affects all of our psyches, here, there, and elsewhere, too. This is nothing new, historically speaking—nothing new unless you're experiencing it for the first time.

"Whole nations" is a term that breaks down into individuals: you, me, those we cherish, and millions of others. Like you, I am affected by the war in a number of ways that, although not comparable to being in the actual thick of it, nonetheless impinge importantly on my daily life. Though I am in no mortal danger, I experience the war as a dangerous assault on my senses. I have watched carnage, death, and despair right here at home, courtesy of the world's media. At least once a day I hear on my radio the raging helplessness of someone who was just stripped clean of one or two or a whole family of his or her loved ones. I flip a switch at any hour, day or night, and my mind is showered in the politics of a conflict with the potential to become the biggest problem on the planet. The war I have come to know so well is a problem I am personally holding in tension every day—a conflict too huge for one person to resolve and so huge we must each carry a portion of its weight, because just under the radar of all the collective chatter, our personal thoughts and feelings are always in play, with or without our consent. Holding the tension of this war is a lot to ask of anyone; sometimes I'm tempted to opt out of my part of it altogether. But: "In actuality your consciousness is not [just] yours," Krishnamurti says, which means I would be opting out of my own reality. Would it even be possible for me to get the taste of the pain and poverty of wartime out of my mouth? How could I *not* feel the suffering of real people just like me and whole families just like mine? I think about this possibility, too: in a similar war, their land and homes and infrastructure might one day be mine.

I can't opt out—I am too much *of* it. Their misery, now become my misery, has been laid on me for what seems a lifetime and I have no real choice

Chapter eight

but to carry whatever I can bear of that which I construe as a psychological nightmare not of my own making. So—if I can't opt out of the nightmare without denying a huge chunk of my own existence, how does my psyche survive it intact? The question returns to me again and again in my need to be wise and stay objective; it's the question that keeps me inside the hurricane's eye and in the present moment.

Krishnamurti again:

> So how can there be right, true relationship between two people when each one considers his own importance? Self-interest is the beginning of corruption, destruction, whether it be in the politician or the religious man. Self-interest dominates the world and, therefore, there is conflict.[6]

Although the tenor of our currently unsettled times agitates around and through me, I'm confident I have at least enough wisdom to keep my state of mind out of jail—been there, done that, never again. Yet I know that how I deal with personal conflict will greatly influence my outlook and attitude in general. So I protect my hard-earned peace of mind by staying wide of the black box of paralysis and keeping my emotions safely back from the painful abyss that pulls on every heart and mind now carrying the heavy weight of circumstances. Things are what they *are*. I observe them. I live and love the riches of my life while I've got one to live, and I keep in mind that where conflict is, wisdom is not. Like any other survival skill I've had to learn, I know that practice makes all the difference. "Wars have come and gone since the beginning of time; this one is no different," is how I think myself away from the paralyzing effects of falling into "war-mind," and back to a much bigger picture—from here to eternity, I guess you could say. I had the wit to discontinue my cable television service, as well, and now—except for the occasional bird-chirp outside my window—I track the news online in total silence: no bombs in my ears, no blood in my eyes, not even Bach or Brahms are allowed to invade my perfect peace. One bird chirping—that's my limit. I stay literate about how to vote and practice walking—eyes open, steady as she goes—the fine line between my personal conflict, over which

I do have some power, and the collective reality in which I am merely one, mostly powerless, player. In the meantime, I continue to hope that out of the agitating, tension-filled crucible of those two unlikely opposites—war and wisdom—there will come a resolution of the collective conflict to relieve the tension that so many like myself throughout the world are struggling to carry. An army of the wise to lead us to peace comes to mind.

Does wisdom multiply happiness? Yes—and more so as I grow older. But "happiness" is a word, a symbol for a state of mind that is relative to each of us—who we are, what we think, what we want out of life—so personal a perception that the word by itself is almost meaningless. Because so much in my life seemed to challenge my concept of happiness, I had to first "rearrange" my psyche to discover what it meant to me. I went hunting for my bliss—sometimes on hands and knees—in the thickets and cul-de-sacs of my early childhood. Wisdom came to me first so gently as to go nearly unnoticed as I was focusing in and bearing down on what had caused me to get so tangled up in the first place. During the long, slow transformation that changed the framework of my thinking, wisdom seemed to wring itself out of my psychic pain as if by magic. Happiness came in tandem with wisdom, it seems to me—largely in the form of gratitude as the quality of my life continued to improve. It was great to finally dance free in the spaciousness of a mind swept clean of its old constraining shibboleths and unrealistic expectations. It was glorious to walk out of the somber hues of my childhood and find the sun bringing a long, dark time in my life to its final conclusion. As time passed and happiness increased, I was able to revise so much of my "early text" that I could even feel love for my family again—though from a distance dictated by my good sense. I began to think, then, that if it were reasonable to assume that chronic suffering creates a chronic state of unhappiness, it is just as reasonable to think that wisdom creates a state of "chronic transformation" that can—as it did for me—undo suffering and put happiness in its place. Wisdom is a spiritual process, though, not a provable scientific theory—it does not answer the riddle of human suffering that threads organically through a life beginning to end; it will only clear a path to understanding what happiness means to each of us as we seek it separately. C. G. Jung says it begins with the child:

Chapter eight

The child is the beginning and the end. . . . The "child" is all
that is abandoned and exposed and at the same time divinely
powerful; the insignificant, dubious beginning and the triumphal
end. The "eternal child" in man is an indescribable experience,
an incongruity, a handicap, and a divine prerogative; an impon-
derable that determines the ultimate worth or worthlessness
of a personality.[7]

I don't remember how it began, but I do remember that my search for
wisdom was driven by a need to know mysterious, inexpressible things—
things already inside of me unspoken or intuited—that, like certain strains
of music or a poem to which my whole self responds, I experience as a
"voice" speaking directly to me. For many like me, who as children got off to
a wobbly start, there may be some spadework to do before a search can even
begin. I had to speed through my childhood head down and going as fast as
I could to escape all that I hated about it; later on, though, I had to come all
the way back to my beginning and sort through my life stick by stone until
I had located and integrated the child whose task it was to serve me—and I
her—for the rest of our journey together.

So I tell you true, one cannot start out on wisdom's journey without
one's child in tow—from its "insignificant, dubious beginning" to its "triumphal end." When the child I once was and I were finally reconciled—she
now feeling secure in my care and I elated to have her in my life again—we
were poised not only to do the work together that would change our lives
for the better, but to share our newfound love and wisdom all the way to
the end. Would I be wiser today if I had not had so much spadework to do?
Or was it the spadework itself that broke open my psyche so that wisdom
could gain entry? I don't know—but I will guess the latter is closer to how
it worked. What is pertinent to my story is that wisdom was an urgent,
lifesaving need great enough to initiate a continuing process of discovery
that was and is as utterly mysterious as life itself.

Maybe you have heard or read this along the way of your seeking: "When
the student is ready, the teacher appears." Well, how wise is *that*?

Wisdom: what is it? who is it? and more

nine

Growing older

Age Giveth and Taketh Away

You need only claim the events of your life to make
yourself yours. When you truly possess all you have
been and done, which may take some time, you are
fierce with reality. When at last age has assembled
you together, will it not be easy to let it all go—lived,
balanced, over?

—Florida Scott-Maxwell

Stanley Kunitz, one of America's great poets,
was a hundred years old when he died in 2006. Many of the poems
written in his later years reflect the gathered wisdom of his age
in words so beautifully configured they are certain to hold favor
with those "growing older" for hundreds of years to come. "The
poem comes in the form of a blessing—like rapture breaking on the
mind,"[1] he has said about his work. Did he know that his rapture
would break many times—ad infinitum? To all who are "ripe" with
unstated feelings about growing old, know now that words have
been put to them, and you are well spoken for. Written at or about
his seventy-fifth year, here are the beginning lines of "The Layers:"

I have walked through many lives,
some of them my own,
and I am not who I was,
though some principle of being
abides, from which I struggle
not to stray.[2]

So few lines to encapsulate so much life—distilled to an essence at once sparse and rich with untold story. His words held such power for me when I first read them that every circumstance in my past and all of their fateful consequences came immediately to mind, lined up for review and ready to instruct me one more time. At the distance of memory, my life appeared as inviting and harmless as a parade in summer. It's rare that I look back anymore; all the clips and bits of my life experience have been mused smooth, their sharp, pokey edges all rounded and shaved of melodrama—decades of issues dealt with and done. But the poet's words and my enraptured response made me feel as one, and intimate, with him, and they were enticing: "Turn around," they said to me, "roll out your life and look it over—*this* time you can play with it." I hesitated: it was one thing to read a summary of a life sculpted in words of prize-winning poetry—but would my journey read even half so well when exposed to the clarity that time finally brings to scrutiny? Well, if he took the risk . . . so will I.

Is it fair to say that "lives" are also identities? If so, I have "walked through" many lives on the way to this precious present moment, each sporting its own persona, hastily sketched and slapped onto an "identity" I hoped would fix my life. At the same time, sub rosa I was stitching together the bits and pieces of my inner self—building my house by day and its foundation when time permitted. Living two lives at once and one life after another, not all of my personas were going to pan out, of course—though some of them worked like a charm and stuck until they became who I am. A partial list reads: perennial student, journal writer, and aspiring poet; twice a wife, mother of three, lover, and analysand; sister to one, friend to a carefully selected few; career professional, recovering alcoholic, part-time worker, and working writer. Like so many other late bloomers, I would "invent" the role my life

Growing older: age giveth and taketh away

required at the time, learn my lines, and fashion a psychology to convince myself that I could play this part, by God—I could do this life. But the persona business is risky; the learning curve for a wannabe identity is steep because you make it up as you go. Yet, when I reached proficiency and could claim my right to an identity—even when I hit some walls and had to start over with a new one—I rightly thought I was making progress inside and out, and that was the hope that kept me going. To think I have walked through many lives—one or more at a time and always conscious that any one of them could make or break me—leaves me breathless today. Ebbing or flowing, it has always been an intensely meaningful experience, quite wonderful, really, though that is easier said looking back—because it was also anything but easy. But I've got the hang of it now—and the fear is gone. Any past-lives, identities, and personae not kicked overboard by now are permanently fixed and contributing parts of "she who is." For better and worse, I am finally authentic in perpetuity.

⌘

Kunitz, though, was measuring far more than a string of identities dictated by circumstances as he probed his many lives, because even if life appears to be a mostly straight-ahead affair, he made clear when he titled his poem that life is also layered—that within a life we live many lives and all of them are layered, too. I think immediately of times and lives in which my cohabiting heart and mind were calling the shots on several levels. At first glance back, my life looks to be all of a piece, to have grown and spread and deepened rather seamlessly. Yet a closer look reveals how easy it is for me to throw some parameters around specific groups of years and discover differences between them that are startling. It is as though each life-within-a-life describes a time distinctive not only for its central focus, but for a general psychology of thought and the matching perceptions to surround and contain it. Each life had a limited history in which myself and specific others gathered together in a loosely connected "family" of years, bounded by a distinguishable beginning and end. When I think of them today, each was a time I remember mostly for its "mood" and for the quality of life generated by a rather small number of players. Soon, mind and heart were on the move again, slowly exiting one life to slowly enter another—with a different cast of characters and a psychology dramatically dissimilar from the previous one. For example, how unrelated the struggling mind of the young married I once was appears to the serious and more seasoned mind and heart of twenty years later, after "layers" of change, so nuanced and delicate as to go unobserved, had taught wisdom to my mind and made my unforgiving heart soft again.

My lives all had a purpose, I can say, and while some of them overlapped as I "wived" and mothered and worked in the world simultaneously, it is clear in retrospect that each was adding its layers of meaning separately, as well as to the whole, of my life. And through them all, throughout the years, psyche was doing the hard, meticulous work of stitching my lives and layers together to make whole cloth of me—though I shall never be "seamless," nor entirely whole. She stitches me still and without pause, so I had better be done with lamenting yesterday's rips and tears—I had better be living wide awake in the now, instead.

Through one of my lives—my childhood—I more crawled than walked. I named it early: "Life in a Black Box," an impressive number of years in which I suffered a mental and spiritual paralysis I often despaired of surviving. In due course I survived it, barely, and went on to another life I will name "Safe Haven," my first marriage and my first sustained experience living safely outside the black box. "Motherhood" was another of my lives, in which I was taught often and radically by my mistakes and greatly inspired by my three children and dire necessity to grow up in leaps and bounds. "Working in the World" was the life that augmented my intellect and increased my worth outside of the home. Working in both worlds simultaneously tested the limits of my physical endurance; on the other hand, it brought me to a state of financial independence that allowed me to live independently, outside of the two marriages I chose to exchange for living free—and, finally, in solitude. "The End of Addiction" was a life with many happy endings; "Marriage Two" fared not nearly so well. I think it matters that, although I sometimes fell down and skinned my knees within a life, each life improved noticeably over the one that preceded it. What is curious, though, is that in all of my lives, save my present one, it never occurred to me to think I

Growing older: age giveth and taketh away

was growing older in addition to growing up. There were many things I did reflect on, including my own death, but never did I think about the process of aging—what it might do for me and against me on my way to the end that ends all.

⁂

Kunitz remarks of his many lives that only some of them were his own. Did he lament those he apparently considered not his own? Did he recklessly give some of them away—and was he mourning them still when he had reached his great age? I doubt it—or perhaps only as his life passed in review. He would be heart-struck again, perhaps, remembering the parts of his past that seemed bleak or inhospitable or lacking meaning in their time, so he honored them by writing them into his poem, but he would not linger there. "Some of them not my own," I understood to mean those times in a life when an aspect of the human condition gets lost from itself, wanders aimlessly away from its center for a time—weeks, months, or even years—until (though not always) it finds a road home, comes awake, and goes on with life. There is a part of us, it seems, that can drift again and again through miles of life and precious time without actually living as one's true self. Vulnerable and limited as we are in our human condition, can there be anyone who hasn't sometimes vanished from his own sight? Five small words: "some of them my own." I ached from the weight of meaning they brought back to me; my spirit lifted only as I remembered the times I finally caught up with myself—sometimes light-years down the road: fully found, wits recovered, ready to resume my life.

Some of my lives were not my own because I wasn't savvy enough to stake a claim on them and guard their perimeters, so I gave a couple of them away unconsciously, or out of brokenness or ignorance or naiveté. One life I gave away to the military because I needed a safer place to be than the big wide world I perceived was too feral to tame. Another life I gave away to my mother because I could find no practical or moral alternative that permitted me to do otherwise. I was still a patchwork of parts looking for the *real* me when I lived my "Motherhood" and "Marriage" lives; it was a time when making

Chapter nine

progress with my self took a backseat to treating the ten million things that daily skitter and skid all over the surface of a married-with-children life. They were important growing years, nonetheless, crammed full of love and pleasures and the pain of self-discovery. Mother and child, mother of two and then three, filled up a life all by itself. It was hectic, far too much so sometimes, but rich with surprise and diversity and individuation—theirs and mine.

"Marriage Two?" I won't say I gave it away—but I sure did make one highly irrational trade-off, perhaps the only one I've never been able to square with my reasoning mind. It was an emotionally expensive, paradoxically on-and-off-again handful of years, in which I was nonetheless able to matriculate a separate, parallel universe wholly new to me: a dimension of the relation-ship in which two bodies, deeply in love, reached for and found a level of physical intimacy and creative expression of rare and transporting pleasure. Yet, as I have written elsewhere in these pages, sex by itself does not a marriage make: eventually the magic show was over and the marriage crawled, ex-hausted from conflicted emotions, to an end. I would never deny and will never forget the "story" of that life; on the other hand, "Marriage Two" was also a serious off-road diversion for me—precious time away from my lifelong pursuit of whatever it was I felt so called to find.

So, if I gave a couple of lives away, the good news is I never gave away my soul. Start to finish, my soul was all I ever had that I truly revered, and I knew instinctively not to mess with it. I look at it this way: if I lost a life or two but kept my soul of a piece, those lives were not a total loss. It is years since I be-came enlightened enough to forgive and forget harm done me by others and claim full responsibility for my life. Now I feel moved to lavish my affection and forgiveness on the ignorant and awkward parts of myself in those years, to lament or deny nothing I might have done better, and to embrace every precious foolish move I ever made. I will fault them and myself no longer, because in truth there is not a time I can remember when my intentions were other than innocent, or urgent, or honorable. We are all the same: we process, pure and simple. Into and out of our many lives we process all the way to old, and then to quite old, and this much I know is true about me: the more I can profess awareness in the life I am living today, the more

I will come to "own" it—to live in and as the life I inhabit with confidence and competence and a willingness to trust. To trust is self-perfecting. When I learned to trust living in the now my mind grew peaceful. When I learned to take a long view on matters too many to count and then realized I was powerless to improve them, I came to trust our ancient, inspired universe. And now that I've grown used to surrendering to my willful, aging body to whatever "will be" and am habituated to the hard truth that "a time certain" is indeed on its way, I trust growing old, as well. When age gives and takes in a balance I find hard to justify, I try to remember how little in this life is subject to reason. Life *is*, however—the good, the bad, and all else—undeniably a *gift*. I didn't ask for the gift, but there has been no time—yet—when I would have willingly given it back. So far, the gift is still giving. So far, the give and take in my life proceeds in a ratio still in my favor.

*

"And I am not who I was," Kunitz says easily, almost casually—and I want to shout it from the rooftops, "Hallelujah! I am not who I was!" Could there be words of hope more validating for those of us who struggle to become more than we once perceived ourselves as being? I am not who I was, either, and though I am in one configuration merely a morphed collection of past lives and used-up identities, I am also much more than that: I am *essentially* different than I was. How so? My answer is intuitive and unscientific: A transformation occurs as the result of time passing and thousands of personal experiences, the only two yardsticks by which fundamental change is continuously measured in every human life. If we are open to change, our life experiences will seed a receptive mind with insights and wisdom sufficient to alter our perceptions in a process that transforms our consciousness, changes us literally from the inside out, a trace amount at a time.

I don't remember it as a consciously articulated decision, but it might have been. Arriving at some fateful crossroads in my childhood, the girl I was made a radical commitment to change her life altogether. I'll guess that—because she was an early reader and books meant everything to her—she was inspired to do so by some story that moved her deeply. It may have

Chapter nine

resembled her own story, perhaps, or served as a powerfully positive meta-phor. In any case, she was dramatically inspired to change everything about her life that worked against her naturally optimistic nature. Too young to think of failure, she committed to a harrowing task she could not have imagined, yet knowing—in the way a child believes its own truth absolutely—that she could and would one day pry open the cramped, airless quarters of her mind and walk away from the dark and discouraging family into which she was born. It made her happy just to think about it.

That's the best I can make of her in memory. The promise she made to herself—this child who felt chronically anxious in her circumstances—is the great reason why this story is happy to tell. My destiny was then in her keeping, and she could not have served us better, then to now. Looking back to that time, I surmise that in a single flash of imagination sparked by something I read in a book, I imprinted my mind with a purpose to achieve my life "without them." So began my life a second time, new at the root and strongly supported by the need to believe in myself—to "be there" for me. I was led all the time by an acute intuitive urge to pursue what was etched on my young psyche as my "true future," in which I would live free, whole, and happy. The urge, which never left me, is still the nearly perfect guide and the central player in my personal universe from which, or whom—like Kunitz's principle of being—I try never to stray. It is as close to God as I will ever get—it might even *be* God.

I was forty-something the first time I looked back on all there was to see so far—all of my lives with their troubles and treasures, all of the things and ideas I once defended and then gave away, and all of the people I had embraced or run away from, lost or let go of. All that time—so many heart-beats measuring time in millions of seconds—so many lives! I could see that I still had a long way to go, but I was not really discouraged by what I saw: "progress, not perfection," we say in the meeting rooms. It occurred to me, though, that the rest of my life was subject to a limited warranty and that I had never once considered all that was sure to come: physical limitations,

Growing older: age giveth and taketh away

fewer choices, declining energy, major shifts of perspective—all things not much fun to think about before (or after) they arrive. Oh, well—so what if I was surprised to find myself already at life's middle? If I had been consciously counting my years, I would not have been living in their present moments. Besides, I didn't *feel* old.

A few more turnings of the seasons, though, and I had come wide awake with body chatter—daily confrontations with the new reality that one has, in fact, "come of a certain age." There ensued many firsts—the first time I needed prescription drugs for this, that, and the other; the first time it registered that I was in bed with my book most nights by nine o'clock instead of ten; and the first time I looked closely and saw that my body had changed— not a little, but a lot. And for the first time *ever*, I peered into my future to see an "old crone" making her way up the road to me for tea and a little talk. I must remember to make her welcome, I noted—to be gracious and greet her warmly because it is she—principal actor in my last life to live—who will stand center stage at its curtain. Time to wake up and get smart about the last life of all: my self, my age, and my future were all on the same page at the same time and there was no looking back. Was it denial that even then I found it easier to think I would die tomorrow than in the old age my sensible mind was suggesting I think about? It was *not* denial, I protested to no one in particular—it is my body that grows old, not the rest of me. So persuaded, I made a respectful vow to study the old, do the research, and ready myself for a time I had just convinced myself was still well down the road. Soon, I was observing "the old" (those older than me) with great interest, learning unexpected things from them and finding some of them to be quite wise, indeed.

On the surface, life goes on pretty much as usual for the old who still live on their own; they have learned to tweak the days and their habits for survival to accommodate the special needs and minor challenges of their age group, extending their independence as far as it will go. They adapt, it seems. Yet under the radar of what seems to be, the aging live, in *fact*, in parallel

Chapter nine

universes. The old ones I know and observe wind down their time on the planet less committed to achieving worldly and material things. They are more pragmatic, more generally forgiving and—except for those who refuse to withdraw their allegiance to ego's vanities and ambitions—they are remarkably unassuming. Still, even as they linger lovingly on this planet they have forever called home, they are also "elsewhere," contemplating their end. Quietly, privately, often somewhat tentatively, they try to imagine what might come next—indeed, they wonder if there will *be* a next, as they check out all of their tender feelings about death and try not to fear. Every day, or as often as courage permits, they stick a toe or a nose onto "the other side" at the very same time they are feeling their special kind of gratitude just to be alive. Though bound fast to the earth which is sole support for the body they also call home, the spirit within, sensing freedom close at hand, agitates to detach and release into the spaciousness unimaginable to a body. Kunitz makes clear a view of the old as extraordinarily complex beings who daily live in the rich and extended layers of their long experience and whose focus of attention shifts between our small planet and infinity. I read one of Carl Jung's published letters, written when he was well past midlife, in which he said he felt he had one leg in each of two worlds and that his interest in the project of his life grew small while his curiosity about what came next grew great.

Certainly I do not find everything about the old to be excellent; they are the same imperfect human beings found everywhere. Yet, on average I find them to be at least as interesting as any other age group, and better than the rest of them at offering certain things only age can perfect—like kindliness, civility that is also graceful, interestedness, and respect for others—and wisdom, of course, greatly befitting the ancients they have come to be.

The aging body promises nothing. However well or long I have treated my body in the past, in the end "luck rules." Out of time and shorn of sentiment, it will give me little or no warning of its imminent demise and finally shuck the rest of me without so much as a by-your-leave. In truth, I hope not to resist it. When the time comes, I like to think I will give full cooperation to my body's inscrutable, irrational, and politically neutral timing. Why would I fight it? The Buddhists say about all things in the world, including old age and death: "It is what it is." I reacted badly to those words in the past because I hadn't yet plumbed the wisdom of their meaning; more than once I spit out in my ignorance—"Well, *damn* what it is!" But a fact is also a truth: the death of my body will come in *its* time, not mine; it will not care what I think or suffer what I feel, and will not in the end be tricked or tweaked or persuaded to stay. How, then, shall I philosophize my body's suffering, old age, and death? I shall refer myself to my own well-worn allegory: The fruit ripens as it grows, reaches for wholeness as it ages, and becomes full and rich before it drops from the tree. I will add that fruit can also wither on the vine when it holds overlong to the limb—or drop to the ground, rotten, in a refusal of its destiny. What else can I do but practice letting go of life's limb a little at a time and hope for perfect timing? If the god in charge of these things is listening: I would like to be picked from the tree just before the fall, please—full and rich and still looking good when the sun goes down.

❧

The poet Kunitz looked back on his life and saw his "milestones dwindling toward the horizon." He wondered how he might reconcile his "feast of losses" and grieved again the "dust of my friends, those who fell along the way." His heart was heavy with loss—and yet:

> Yet I turn, I turn,
> exulting somewhat,
> with my will intact to go
> wherever I need to go,
> and every stone on the road
> precious to me.[3]

And then he lived—his will intact—for another twenty-five years!

There is a stretch of miles along the road of growing older when the world, as you have always known it, undergoes a radical transformation. You might feel then as I did, that every single thing in your world is precious to you, every stone on the road, each separate cloud in the sky, and every tiny

Chapter nine

fleeting thought in your mind. If you are like me, you will comprehend in a blinding flash of appreciation that everything in your world has been a gift— on loan to you as part of the greatest gift of all, your conscious life. It was for me an achingly beautiful epiphany that said, with love: you are on your way home. I would not disown my past, especially the parts that hurt and taught me hard. Like the poet, though, I find no reasons to loiter there, to rehash the difficult times my mind has already scavenged for comprehension and closure. It is best to look straight ahead now, exulting somewhat that I still waken each morning fully resolved to participate in my life. There are always more lessons to learn, of course, though the big ones are likely done; more pleasure to be had, though of a quieter kind, and more anguish, too—though never again the searing pain and suffering I met with in life's earlier hells when I was innocent and ignorant. What's new that amazes me will always be precious to me, because while I practice living each day who I am for today only, I am also an offspring of the "big bang," so it is my metaphorical destiny to shoot for the moon—to move onward and outward at the speed of light into infinity, peeling away everything as I go except the totality of the present moment. From the beginning, my work was to jettison my junk—the clunky and depressing apparatus of my early conditioning—that I took from my well-meaning, wisdomless elders, who themselves had been taught nothing better. Jettisoning, peeling away, and traveling light: these are especially appropriate for the growing-older crowd: they are requirements, in fact, for a good and fitting end. So, the later it gets, the lighter I go, heeding a logic that perhaps speaks only to me: All I will ever need for the rest of my life is to be awake for it.

Should you think these words too simple or grim or off the mark to describe the unfathomable business of growing older, you could be right. I am well into the process of aging, and yet I walk new ground with it every day. Somewhere between *getting* old and *being* old, my thoughts are ten parts truth, five parts conjecture, and all parts intuitive, but I am far enough down life's road to feel the process deeply even if words are hard to find. It is not a "talky" subject to begin with—too deep—unless you are Stanley Kunitz, who seems to have lived through all of the layers of his lives without having once closed his eyes or refused his emotions—so gifted that when he

Growing older: age giveth and taketh away

had walked the walk he wished to write about, he sat down and wrote it to perfection.

Aging is a time when the heart is awash with poignancy, when the mind treads two worlds whose boundaries are fluid and unfamiliar, and when the spirit can flag and rebound a dozen times a day. Most of the time, it feels right to grow old—good to be doing the next indicated thing with a peaceful heart. When I am all lined up with my universe, I am struck dumb to think what gifts we get in exchange for our time certain—the love, and the loving, are different later in life; better for all the right reasons. I understand a bit of what Jung felt as he straddled his two worlds. I have felt it, too—though not often: a certain low-key excitement about the possibility of a "next" life, a tiny buzz of anticipation at the thought of meeting head-on whatever—if anything—is coming around the bend.

Chapter nine

Lose some and win some

The rain to the wind said,
'You push and I'll pelt.'
They so smote the garden bed
That the flowers actually knelt,
And lay lodged—though not dead.
I know how the flowers felt.

—Robert Frost

Was there ever a soul still lodged in its creature that was not at least once flattened—in spirit, at least—and left for dead? I too know how the flowers felt—I was one of them, pushed and pelted more than a few times, beginning right away in my life, losing this and that and the other thing. Looking back, I see that I have practiced the art and pain of loss throughout my life. By "art," I mean the ducking and dodging, the denial, compensating, self-medicating, and—with the face I turned to the world—conspiring to convince that I was really quite all right, thank you very much. Inside and in fact, I was navigating my world with blind instinct and a big stick, a quivering mass of uncertainty that belied my appearance. And by "pain," I mean a child's response to feeling alone, uninstructed,

and without the smarts to make her life work. Later, the child (incognito)—
still holding on to hurt like a teddy bear she couldn't put down—would badly
affect her adult self and add yet another layer of pain to a psyche splitting in
two. Nevertheless, pain can sometimes wring out of itself a new perspective:
an altered, objective truth that starts the healing to bring pain to an end. I
was lucky there, because the time soon came when, having used up the last
portions of my art and wit, I had faked my life all the way to the wall. Only
then did I think to ask for help, and not long after that I was sitting three
times a week face to face with the several causes and effects of my paralyzing
neuroses. Just in time, it seems to me now, because I had turned off the
voice that warns from within a long time ago. I was twenty years old with
one sibling—whose strange recurring behaviors would soon be diagnosed as
symptoms of paranoid schizophrenia.

✐

What was missing in me—and why? I was already looking for those answers,
kiddy-fashion, before I was in my teens; not consciously, but nevertheless
urgently, I went looking in books for anything leading to whatever it was
I had so unwittingly lost. At twenty, I was already combing the pages of literature, the world's religions, philosophy, and psychology, and shoveling my
thoughts and feelings into journals at night, hoping they would somehow
reveal the meaning of my suffering to me. In my early thirties, I embarked
on The Good Ship Psychoanalysis for a long, frustrating trip through cold,
choppy seas. Faced for the first time with my own contorted objective reality, I came to know the extent of my ignorance, anger, and humiliation. For
the longest time, it seemed to me I was merely trading one kind of pain
for another—and then came the day when I could noticeably feel myself
changing course in a slow turn out to warmer waters.

By the time I had completed my first, and longest, stint on the couch,
I understood that my old, untutored ways of gross self-survival had transmuted to a higher art: self-awareness, a longer view of things, and a clear
understanding that life worked in my favor when it was underpinned by
self-knowledge—the more the better. I learned about loss—all the big and

Chapter ten

little partings and deaths and diminishments we all face from birth—being one of life's few absolutes, insinuated into every existence as surely as the air we take in to stay alive—until, at some unspecific date, we suffer that loss as our last one.

One thing for sure about loss: it spares no one. Mine began where yours did, I suppose: in childhood. Some of my losses were routine, whereas others—like a drill bit pressing on a nerve—are seared into my memory. Yet, learning to mourn my early losses consciously and then release them to history could happen only after I had folded my forgotten child-turned-saboteur into my arms and healed her with the same love and understanding I was ready to feel for myself. Loving her first was the key to my understanding love at all; leading her out of the dark into my consciousness made possible the slow coming together of two split selves to make one whole person.

We all have known or will eventually know loss in many of its varieties, and we will suffer major loss as a life-changing experience at least once in our lives. My first loss was the absence of even one nurturing, mentoring caregiver, which set the scene for a whole gang of psychologically negative affects and secondary losses down the road. Then, probably common to most of us, was the loss of some childhood friends—when I, or they, moved away to a neighborhood with different schools, or when one of them betrayed my trust, or when our interests and our minds began to steal off in different directions, or when a sworn-in-blood, lifelong commitment to undying friendship began not to matter so much to either of us. A few friendships, significant in my early parenting years, were made and lost as I grew more discerning about friendship itself—about what I meant by that word, what I had in me to invest in it, and what I wished for and could reasonably expect to get from it. These are losses one recovers from, of course, but when I found myself commuting to a nine-to-five job instead of a college, I both grieved and resented losing something so huge as my further education—school being my best friend of all, the one *true* love of my life.

Lose some and win some

I lost boyfriends, too—one in particular, whose loss I needn't have endured had I been better "put together" at the time: not so shy and tongue-tied and scared to death. Sometime later, I lost a sister to schizophrenia in a slow, growing realization that her mind was drifting, cut loose, too far out to rescue. One doesn't shrug off a loss that big—not ever. I won, and then lost, two marriages. In the first one, I grew up quite a lot—and then away. In the second one—a bad judgment call based on a need to believe it would fix my life—I grew up even more, and away. I lost the two husbands, of course. Born and culturally conditioned in prefeminist modern America, both of them were good men and did their best to adapt to me, my enthusiasm for the women's movement, and our marriage. Yet those were the years when I was waking up to some of the more egregious gaps in power and equity and thinking between the sexes. At long last I was being mentored by the feminine principle—not by my one perennially "missing" mother, but by women in the dozens, including many who spoke and wrote from brilliant, unconventional minds. Without animus or conscious purpose, I discovered my own mind in the process, and subsequently dared to think there were certain things about the institution of marriage itself that might never be okay for me. Separate but concordant with that discovery was an emerging need in me to spend more time in solitude than is generally comfortable in a marriage. Perhaps a die is cast at one's birth for certain losses; do you think so? But that's another story . . .

I lost the total meaning of my life twice and found it again both times. The first time was when, in a singular act of grace and rescue, another Marine who bunked in the same wing of a military hospital in which I languished became concerned about my behavior. One day she hauled me out of the chair next to the bed where I had sat, depressed and catatonic, every day for weeks waiting to be discharged from my term of duty. Tall and imposing, with a beautiful smile and a convincing laugh, there was no resisting her. She threw an arm around me and marched us to the hospital coffee shop, where for several more weeks we, and whoever randomly joined our table that day, drank coffee, smoked cigarettes, and told our back-stories. Eye-rolling our black-humored, highly exaggerated individual tales of woe, we told "how I got here" for hours at a time and laughed until our sides split. In this way—her way—I inched myself back

Chapter ten

up the downward slope that had led to my psychic quagmire, and I gained a friendship that is still in full, brilliant flower. I reclaimed my life the second time—from alcohol—in the meeting rooms of Alcoholics Anonymous, where I was loved back to my better self by men and women who know exactly how to do that. There is no bond so strong, no healing so complete, as that which comes from the tolerant understanding common to people who have peered into the same abyss and lived to tell the tale.

A particularly serious and difficult loss—I have never suffered as much, before or since—occurred when one of my sons turned away from me in his teens and never came back. I see him rarely. He is always civil, if not conversational, but the chasm between us yawns wide and unremitting. Another significant loss—this one I am certain not to recover—is life without chronic physical pain. Vastly unappreciated were the years I enjoyed the unrestricted use of a supple, pain-free body having no reason to think twice about so great a miracle as that. Today I give it plenty of thought, plus hours of time and energy I would much rather spend on other causes. My body is my first nondebatable, rest-of-my-life test of courage and, while my condition is not life-threatening, parts of me are deteriorating ahead of schedule. So, I am left to make friends with my uninvited companion—"to follow my life force inward,"[1] as Stephen Levine suggests, and practice acceptance for the long term.

When I was finally able to look at my life from the top of a tall tree, I could understand that grappling with loss is something I share with every sentient being on the planet. It is a hard fact, no doubt about it, recurring all the way to the end for all of us, but the truth of it became easier for me to bear when I had grasped that loss was something essential to my personal growth, forever forging in its crucible its special gifts of detachment and acceptance. There was a time when I knew I had to depersonalize loss and expand my perception of it, to look outside of my life and my pain and understand that loss is an experience endured by every soul who lives. The more far-reaching my view of loss became, the less unique to me it felt: it simply is what it is for everyone. It hurts, the hurt diminishes; we survive.

Lose some and win some

Imagine with me that you are as yet unborn. What if God were to approach you holding in Her hands a big, beautiful box enticingly wrapped and beribboned, and atop the box was a gift card that read: "Your Life, Contents Unknown." Imagine further that, holding it out to you, making no promises and telling no lies, She said only this much: "If you accept this gift, you must agree to live every part of it." Would you refuse Her? Would you be so unwilling to discover all that you might find in the box that you would turn it down? At some felicitous time in my long history of healing, I came to think of life as a gift—not one *apart* from losses, for I found plenty of those in my box—but as a totality of everything I experience as I live my gift every day. I have come to think it is my painful experiences of loss that deepen my appreciation for all I have not lost—for all that *is*.

Were there no loss, I contend there could be no "found." The poet Robert Frost once said, "The best way out is always through." I have tested that bit of wisdom and learned that "through" is where one finds "found." Working through loss until I am safely on the other side of pain, which at the start might feel unbearable, is an extreme challenge but a sweet and singular achievement. It takes practice, yet there is no other way I know that will relieve the psyche of so much suffering. Consciously, in a quiet place, thinking, feeling, and writing my way to a new and more realistic perception of my loss, I can always find my way back to equanimity—though it might take years, as it did with my son. I learned from losing him that when I had done everything I could to repair our relationship, leaving no demands for self-scrutiny unmet as I measured my part in our estrangement—testing especially the quality and authenticity of my forgiveness of both of us—the rest was up to him. I learned, too, that it is in resisting the pain of loss, not loss itself, where suffering lives and thrives and can make me sick at heart. The truth is that loss will overcome itself every time if I will curse and cry and consult my loss until I'm done—then surrender as many times as it takes to the *fact* of that loss. Then I must set it aside, embrace life as never before, and honor both my life and my loss in acts of replenished compassion for others. Stephen Batchelor proposes, in *Verses from the Center*:

> Imagine a magician
> Who creates a creature

Chapter ten

Who creates other creatures.
Acts I perform are creatures
Who create others.[2]

One cannot "set it aside" until one is done with it, of course, which I found extremely difficult to do, especially in the beginning when my need was to justify my anger at my son, to believe that I had been unceremoniously deposed—to think myself a victim of circumstances beyond my control and deliberately thrown away. But my only way out was to keep pushing through the blinding intensity of my emotions, to suffer through, first my anger, and then the hurt—oh, the *power* of that hurt! On the other side of that long and difficult work, I found a better, more evenhanded truth and enough compassion to forgive us both and set myself free. Should the heartache of losing something so precious ever loom large in my life again, I might tremble and sway a while, anticipating more of that deep and memorable grief, but I would recover my psychic balance far sooner the second time. Having survived one "death-by-loss" has made me gritty and wise and has taught me that what I presumed to "lose" was never mine to keep, because every single one of us has an unchallengeable right to live life how and with whom we choose. There is nothing for it but to carry the weight of a lost love as gracefully as possible, until one is able to surrender it altogether. I once put to paper some words, burnished now from years of "climbing the mountain," to remind me how to begin again with loss each time I need to:

> Loss is a fact of life—for everyone. I will begin to detach from this
> loss by finding compassion for myself and for the other. I will
> surrender all desire to hold onto that which cannot be held—
> remembering that nothing in the world is mine for more than
> a moment. I will persevere until I can feel genuine gratitude that
> who or whatever I am "losing" was once in my life at all. I will
> reflect again on everything I have learned about loss—recalling
> how pain diminishes and finally dies and how my love for life
> fully returns and my equanimity is restored—every time. Right
> now, though, when the pain is fresh and its weight on my mind

Lose some and win some

and heart feels unbearable, I will keep this thought close by: The mountain of suffering I feel today is only my first perception of this loss, one I will reperceive a thousand times, if need be, until the mountain appears small and harmless in the distance, until my heart is light again and my mind is free again and what is left of my pain is easily borne.

Winning and losing are two sides of a single coin, flipped into perpetual motion at my birth in a continuous play of opposites: suffering and recovery, sadness and joy, frustration and contentment, anger and acceptance—all of them part of a process that is the whole time opening me, teaching me truth, and making me wiser. Of course, I wondered what had kept me playing the game in those early years. Why was I able to overcome my first great loss—surviving "abandonment" was no easy feat, after all—and go on to suffer so many more, without losing heart and folding my cards? Years later, when my psychic survival was secured and I was well into the habit of enjoying it, I took a long look back on my life and found two perfectly wonderful answers to my question.

The first one emerged quickly as a stunningly simple paradox: Every important loss I have ever suffered gave me something equally important in return—always a great surprise and a thing of beauty, always a gift dipped in considerable wisdom. For example, that first marriage I "lost" produced three children—beautiful, continuing presences in my heart—and how much joy it gives me even to think about who they grew up to be! And how could I have known that in "losing" their father I would gain, with the same man, a true friend in a lasting relationship? The second marriage served as the perfect context in which to rock and wobble my way through the last of my malingering neuroses and achieve a level of psychological stability finally worthy of note. Much later I came to think of this loss that once so bewildered me as the birth of my personal phoenix, truly the gift of a new beginning.

My friendships today, so different from the callow connections of my adolescence, are old and weathered, tried and true, comfortable and deeply comforting. They endure because I learned to select my friends thoughtfully, choosing them for like-mindedness, for characteristics I enjoy and respect, and for their energy and interest in the wider road we travel in tandem. These are friendships that grew deep and stayed, the friends whose loss I might someday feel big-time. What gift of equal value could ever replace the absence in my life of even one of them? I can't imagine it—unless I might feel their presence in spirit as I sifted through the many cherished memories of times we spent heart to heart and palpably in love with our friendship. We have earned our friendships so effortlessly, it seems to me, and I wonder why. Perhaps it is because we are free to be certain things in this world rightly accorded those who have finally let go of ego's need for appearances, whose needs are deep but few, and who have learned to accept "what is" with grit and a bit of grace.

It took years—decades, really—before I could drain the deep, recurring pools of suffering formed by my son's refusal of me. I did it by practicing surrender and by consciously giving him away to his wholly separate life away from me. I surrendered him to his own understanding of our relationship, knowing only that neither his understanding nor mine was right or wrong, only different—and so required each of us to truly forgive and truly accept the other. I yielded to the fact of that loss over and over again until I had finally surrendered every connection to him except my love. When I was finally freed of the long, searing experience of that loss, I found no need to "close the book" on him and our difficult past; rather, I felt a debt to both of us to remain open to every genuine possibility for reconciliation. My love for him grows deeper every day, as it does for his siblings, and I take great comfort in the unbreakable bond a mother forms with her child at birth: it is the one tangible connection to him that belongs entirely to me. Don't think I am not subject to flashes of the old hurt, but they are rare, easier, and quickly over. Mostly, though, I'm able to stand quiet in myself, infinitely patient at the distance he still seems to need, loving him in nonattachment and asking for nothing he is unwilling or unable to give. I have passed all my exams in forbearance, in loving from afar, and in the art of staying separate from the pain of "losing" someone so dear to me. I have gifts from this loss that will serve me, with others if not with him, for the rest of my life.

Much time has gone by since I "lost" my sister to her unthinkably radical destiny. It's not likely she will be redeemed to my world in our lifetime, but the passing years—and ultimately my success in relinquishing her to her world—have all but erased the cruelty of a loss I had so adamantly resisted. When it came to pass that I could no longer communicate with her mind, I learned to talk to her soul, reaching out to her in the caring, unspoken poetry of deep feelings and old memories. Though we live far apart from one another, I feel certain that distance is no barrier to my reaching her in spirit. So when she comes to mind, which is not so often anymore, I speak words of love to her, knowing that somewhere in her world she has heard me, is collating my words into her fractured memory and loving me back. I will never understand how I came to lose her, but I can easily grasp how so great a loss enlarged the landscape of my mind and caused my need to love her not only differently, but also better. She is lost to my loving eyes and tender touches, but she is not lost to my heart where we live—together still—in the brighter layers of our childhood.

So much treasure, sprouted and grown in the fertile soil of losses large and small, renews my conviction that there is a kind of divine, paradoxical parity that reigns in our universe: something lost, something found; sorrow, then joy; death, then renewal. The English philosopher and metaphysician Alan Watts said he believed the reason most people don't work very hard to get to heaven is because they can't imagine not being totally bored there. I suppose he was referring to living in perfect happiness. Life on our plane is not heaven—especially at this time; on the contrary, change and loss and suffering are strewn through our lives like the remnant matchsticks of civilization in the wake of a tornado. Random, unreasonable, disorderly: so much of life today gives us pause to reflect on its darker side, though our meditations yield few if any answers. Presented to us as metaphor and paradox, in symbols and always as mystery, the gift of life is complex. Even

Chapter ten

if we now and then glimpse a serene simplicity running through its deeper strata, life's dots on the surface are not easily connected—and certainly not the least bit boring.

⁂

A return to the question of what kept me playing the game of lose some and win some without folding my hand brings me to this second perfectly wonderful answer: I realized early in my healing process that my life was already radically changing for the better, which allowed me to think that, with patience, I might actually transform some of my loopy views of reality and find a happier life. That being my great hope, not to *finish* my work—to remain unconscious about all that I was dragging from my unhappy past into my present—seemed to be my worst possible option. Almost from the start, then, it was clear that my success would depend on my willingness to change, but I had to pray for it often and hard, because when willingness failed me, all forward psychic movement stopped. Worse than that, I discovered, is how the heart's inborn urge to flex, forgive, and stay soft seizes up with fear of change. Its crucial search to find the one nugget of beauty in every adversity—the insight that allows change to happen at all—stiffens and stops, dead in its tracks.

I'm not thinking of huge and monumental makeovers, but of changes that are small, numerous, and cumulative in their mission to keep me free-wheeling and adaptive. Going mostly unnoticed as I live the daily events of my life, I am at all times being modified by the people I meet and the words we exchange, by the media I watch and hear, and by the books I read and the music I enjoy. Consciously or not, I am altered every day by the increasing sum of my exterior observations and interior reflections—by everything that blinks a light in my brain or quickens my heart during the course of a day and the dreams of a night. It is the total of these ongoing, imperceptible changes that startles any of us each time we look back in review and see how different we are since the last time we looked and how all that while we had been morphing who we were into who we are now—except those of us who cannot or will not dare to change at all.

Lose some and win some

We all know them; there are at least one or two in every family, and we meet plenty more of them out in the world. They view our big, wide world through a small, tight aperture and their first response to anything that might change the status quo is a fearfully stubborn "No!" It is irrational behavior—trust that I know about that. There were years when I could do nothing better than to hang on to only what was familiar and under my control in fear that I would fall off the edge of my tiny world. The psychologist Carl Jung explains that recurring resistant reactions are warnings from the unconscious. They put us on notice that the psyche is off-kilter, headed for trouble, in need of help. Fear and discomfort function to save us, among other things, by urging us to dig deeply and locate the source of our discomfort—is it fear? Fear of what? We can then do the work to change the painful dynamic and find our "Yes!" to life. How long will the psyche beg for attention this way? How long do we have? How much pain will we put up with? When I jumped into the waters that would heal me a day at a time, I brought little more to the process than a broken psyche, some hope in my heart, and a prayer that I wouldn't drown. The work was slow, but success was sweet.

Sweetest of all was that time in my healing when I could think for myself where change was needed in me, and then make it happen. First, I had to say—and believe—that change was good for me, not something to fear and resist, but a means to personal growth and self-mastery. When I accepted that I needed change as a fundamental constant in my life and consciously embraced it, I began to improve the quality of my days. My growing willingness to change was the key that opened all the locked rooms in my mind, where, to my great surprise, treasure I hadn't known existed was stored. I remember well how tightly wrapped I was before I could make the changes that loosened me into my humanity—how I needed to plan and control and purposefully affect every hour of my day in order to feel I had earned my right to be alive. Behind an unconscious conviction that I was selflessly giving my life to my family's well-being every waking moment of my day, there lurked a deeper truth: I was in fact propping up my identity, proving my worth, and grasping for ways to make myself matter. I was exhausted by sundown every day from my own essentially more important survival drama.

Chapter ten

Attendant to this painfully distorted perception of my life were so many unhappy feelings of obligation to everyone except myself that I hadn't an inch of space to feel compassion for anyone who, like myself, needed it above all else. Forever stretched for time and trying to keep a lid on my resentments, my well-meant deeds often lacked enough warmth to define my act as a kindness. Yet, a simple change of perception, leading me to understand that I had the right to choose when, what, and to whom I wished to do good, lifted the weight of dreary obligation off my soul and changed my life. Taking care of myself first by acknowledging my limitations, then choosing where I wished to do good, unleashed a geyser of pure, guiltless consideration for others, which had lain buried all that time under my "should-do" thinking. Today, I have enough compassion for myself to see myself in everyone and to realize that we are all in this life together. We need support from one another, and to know that by changing enough, we become so much more than our terrified, grasping, self-judging egos.

There was a time when I had no worldview outside of my own personal survival. I have indeed changed. I say today that we are all peers in our humanity. We make our way through our days doing the best we can, and I love us all in our common cause to achieve whatever we believe will make us happy more than I have ever loved before.

I am also proven, unapologetic in my own eyes. As much as I can, I stay exquisitely focused on the present moment, engaged and fully attentive to whomever I'm sharing it with—and am no less attentive when the moment is truly dramatic: a great orange-red sun settling into the deep waters of evening, for example. I will never do it perfectly, but I practice the art of the present moment diligently, because I believe, mind and heart, that I am finally spending my precious time in exactly the right way. Now I practice a clear and simple philosophy; loosely constructed, it is this:

> I am alone in the universe in the sense that we are each separate,
> yet I can bear that because I know it is all of you who complete me;
> that we are alike—God-stuff at our core; and that we complete each
> other in every way. So I am not alone, after all. I am, as are we all,
> sentient energy on the move, responding to an intuition (God?)

Lose some and win some

that elicits my personal best because I believe that doing my best matters. Plainly, I am a woman housed in a body; exponentially, I am the whole, spiritually genderless body of humanity connected to every celestial body in the universe. If everything I once appeared to have lost I now perceive has come back to me tenfold in gifts of gain, and if I am open to changing as often and as much as will improve me even a little, then we can all be sure that my life has not been only about me, but just as much about what I am able to give back to you. To live my life this way is finally all I *have* to give.

There are a handful of words that have greatly influenced my life. First, Rainer Maria Rilke's:

> *Be ahead of all parting, as though it already were*
> *behind you, like the winter that has just gone by.*
> *For among these winters there is one so endlessly winter*
> *that only by wintering through it will your heart survive.*[3]

And this, paraphrased from one of Meister Eckhart's sermons: The ultimate letting go is the letting go of God.[4]

Subtle and powerful, those words informed me in no uncertain terms how my days were numbered. In the sixtieth year of my life, the idea of death pushed past fear to crack me open for some serious conversation. Our visits were infrequent and initially tenuous on my part, though eventually, as my courage and comfort with it grew, death was invited to come and go in my mind at will, and we became companions of a special stripe. And so it has been ever since, though I am apt to push too hard against the margins of reasonable discourse at times—such is my desire to know too much too soon in fits of the old fear. Then, my odd friend and I think it best we part company for a time, while I lean into the universe and breathe deeply until I can resume my ease in his company. I don't feel Rilke's endless wintryness yet—and perhaps I won't, having opened my mind to death early enough to be ahead of all parting, as he suggested. I have said before that I hope to let go of life with a peaceful mind, expecting not to know even then if there is more to come. And about Eckhart's subtle reminder—there is no having from God in this life even an *idea* of God because God is ineffable. Well, I have known that much instinctively since I was a child—that same child who could never seem to locate one of God's warm and reassuring hands to hold in times of trouble. Still, I have *experienced* the ineffable, so I think it's not possible that I will feel bereft when I hang up this worldly body of mine. No; I think not.

Accepting that I can know nothing with certainty, I am not much inclined to make predictions with so few facts. Even so, I will not be stopped from extrapolating from my own singular and treasured experiences of the mystery in order to pose this one fantastical question to the universe: Since every loss in my life has so far returned a gift to me in exchange for my suffering, is it possible to extend the possibility all the way; might there also be a gift waiting for me beyond my last loss of all, as death and I—odd couple to the end—exit to wherever-whatever-whenever?

We win some and we lose some as we go through life, and after a while we figure out that it is possible for the conscious mind distinctive to our species to—in the way alchemy sought to convert base metals into gold—alter our perception of loss, to extract the pure gold of its deeper lesson for us and call every loss a "win."

As the phoenix rises from its ashes, as the rain-pelted flower—"lodged—though not dead"—stands up in its roots again, we who have the imagination to transform our very selves can waken from the ashen landscape of personal loss to take pleasure in another day.

Lose some and win some

eleven

Control–ego's stage name

> Wholeness is a universal human urge or desire to fulfill
> all of oneself—all of one's potentials, all the aspects
> of ourselves as they have come into being or failed
> to come into being in our particular environmental
> circumstances—"the strongest, the most ineluctable
> urge in every being, namely the urge to realize itself."
>
> —Donald E. Kalsched

What hopeful, truly mysterious words these
are that can be said only about *us*—our species. That "ineluctable
urge" of which Jung speaks kept me afloat on the deep, murky
waters of my circumstances for years at a time. It was the urge to
open my eyes in order to see what was wrong with me. I knew by
the time I was seven years old that parts of me were inoperable,
frozen by unarticulated and inexplicable fears; I knew only by
instinct, intuition, and a God-given gift that kept me aware, on a
primal level, that I was in trouble until I had reached the age of
reason. The gift was that urge, the "force" that was with me.

This is another of Kalsched's "psyche sightings," one
which seems to be about only some of us, and its beauty is
strange, even a little menacing, until you dig into its meaning:

Less recognized is the idea that certain "anti-wholeness defenses"
may operate within certain individuals, conspiring to keep the
personality dis-integrated in the service of survival-in-pieces.[1]

Friend or foe, those defenses? They are both, I discovered. When a young
psyche is in trauma, feeling bereft of even minimal resources, these defenses
move in and become that psyche's "bodyguards"—always out in front, scanning the horizon, guns blazing at anything even resembling more hurt than
the child can handle in its already hurtful world. One is terrified to call them
off, these well meaning, heavy-handed, and extremely necessary defenders;
ultimately, though, one must go it alone. I know this in retrospect, of course,
having learned these things a long time ago, a little bit at a time. Knowing
too soon how much work lay ahead of me would have trampled my innocent eagerness to get started in therapy. Not only eager, but thinking myself
clever, I was sure I could wrap it up quickly: how long could it take? A year,
or maybe two at the most? Well, how about ten? I knew from the start that
I was one of those "certain individuals" Kalsched refers to, but retrofitting
the pieces of my "dis-integrated" psyche in fact took so much time that I
wonder even now how I stayed engaged with it. It is, in fact, work that is
never done. So I would need my rock-hard, reliable "bodyguards" for quite a
long time—to shore up my illusion that I was indeed in control of my world
and strong and bright enough to handle anything therapy threw at me. Oh,
what lies they told and I was so willing to believe, as we colluded to keep the
truth from me—all but those small bits at a time—until I could take the real
me in bigger bites.

Were you to ask me today how much control I think I have in my life, I
would say to you, "Not much—but enough." I would explain that my life is
less problematic when I simply go with the Tao, riding the river of my days
in an effort to keep them effortless, knowing from experience that when I
step out of the flow to "take control" of anything at all, I pay hell getting
back into the river. I would add that once I surrendered my ego's need to
be in charge—the same ego that once fought tooth and nail to control every
fragment of my waking existence—my life became a much smoother ride. A
controlling ego is a false prophet, I discovered; false, too, was all that power
I used to think was mine. So, "deep-six" control, I say, with two disclaimers:

Control—ego's stage name

"deep-sixing" is far easier said than done, and, in truth, we all need to have *some* control over our lives. And yet, because there is so little in my life over which I have consistent or unlimited power, I no longer bother to resist the way some things "just are." In theory, at least, I am liberated from the bondage of the illusion of control.

When I think about really important events and relationships in my life—marriage, children, friendships, careers, hard times—in the context of control, I vividly recall having acted on all fronts of my hectic, stressed-out life as though I were in charge of them all. Being "in control" was the bedrock characteristic of my daily existence. Long before I was ripe enough to know better, I assumed that my personal power was absolute for my lifetime. I never once questioned my right to think that way until I had to do so. The first time I ever felt outrage about a spanking I didn't deserve, it was immediately clear to me that I had no control whatsoever over anything at all. As a child, my life was monitored and micromanaged 24/7 by two overarching disciplinarians—my father and his live-in mother—and their ways were heavy-handed enough to incur huge, unhealthy amounts of both my fear and my wrath. Along about age fifteen, my silent, simmering fantasies about seizing control from them converted into actions. These acts were small and timid at first, to test the waters of parental backlash, then bolder and more frequent as I powered up a serious rebellion against restraints I felt were intolerable. But the time came (not soon enough by my lights) when I could leave my childhood and its cast of characters behind. Thrilling with plans for my shiny new freedom, my ready-to-go power and I swept each other into my future and never looked back. On that day, I believed from my head to my heels that I would have the reins of my life snugly in my hands and be fully in charge of every aspect of my unfolding destiny—yea unto the end of my days. In mainstream psychology, they call this "magical thinking."

Of course we all need to do that—separate, grow up, and get on with life so that the lessons of *real* life can finally begin. My lessons were all big because I had so much to learn, and I took some of them hard. One of the hardest, though not uncommon to anyone raising a teenager, was when my daughter added to my growing list of "teachers." Her lesson for me lasted long enough to finally break me down—and open me up. This lesson was all about "control," and it became a perfect model from which to learn about my every inadequacy, which in this case was an "unknowing" of such magnitude that it caused heartache, confusion, and hurt feelings all around for a long time to come.

My cautionary tale begins when my firstborn, fifteen years old at the time, was trying out her budding personal powers with small acts of defiance ("timid at first, to test the waters of parental resistance"), which grew in number as obvious tests of my authority. There were no shouting matches—we were both always "in control" of our decibels—yet in the end nothing I could say or do moved her even a little from her various positions. She dug her trenches quietly, but inexorably, I noted more than once. Did I connect her dots to my own history? It's hard to admit, but no, I did not. Rather, I took her assertive, burgeoning-selfhood behavior personally. I did not so much think about her defiance as *feel* it and then react disproportionately, certain she meant to frustrate my intent to protect her from making some of the same mistakes I had made at her age. It's an old story, isn't it? Lurking in the unconscious of every parent with a firstborn, there is an ancient, evergreen instinct instructing us to be and *know* and *do* and *give* more to the child than any-of-that was ever given to us. How often, I have wondered since, is that admirable "instinct" a cover for something else that is unconscious: a need to solidify parental control when there comes upon us a creeping suspicion that one is fundamentally powerless to control in the parent-child relationship? Rilke warns us to go carefully:

> Ultimately, and precisely in the deepest and most important matters, we are unspeakably alone; and many things must happen, many things must go right, a whole constellation of events must be fulfilled, for one human being to successfully advise or help another.[2]

These are words that make you think, make you cautious, make you wonder if you are grown-up enough to advise or help your own kids. Had I

Control—ego's stage name

come across his wisdom in time to adopt it as my own; had I known what his words meant in time to slip them into her mind, along with all the love and affection I felt for her, we might have healed from some of my unartful ways much sooner than we did. As it happened, her quite typical teenage need to challenge me at every turn caused me to feel threatened (read: not in control). I lacked the maturity—the grounded, intuitive authority—to parent her easily. The "power" she perceived I had over her was far less than wisdom rooted in experience—a truth that would occur to her eventually and bolster her advantage over me. This is what I know today: It is in the nature of puberty to reach beyond its dependence and make heroic efforts to close the power gap between the two generations—more simply said, to grow up. It is not enough for a parent to assume that he or she is "unquestionably" right, or that love is always enough; a parent needs insight—the kind of wisdom that is not only steeped in love, but whose ego stands separate, empathetic, and composed to receive a child's rebellion. If I am right about this, it is more than fair to say I was plenty short of requisites for my job. Having consigned to the dark hole of unconsciousness all the painful experiences of my own childhood in my race to get to better times, I was working with far less wit and wisdom than could qualify as the "artful" parenting I was eager to believe I was doing.

So there I was, stuck in my past, going "child to child" with my daughter in a power contest and completely unaware that her need to grow by testing me was far more important to our relationship than my need to hang on to control. Let me say now that, had I been totally "realized" and a saint, getting us through her teens unscathed would still have been difficult. She was ten years old in 1968, plenty smart and old enough to assimilate what most of the freewheeling, groundbreaking, drug-dealing sixties generation was up to—especially the drugs part, about which my generation knew *nada*. By the mid-seventies, there was already embedded in the teenage "counterculture" a whole new perception of its coming-of-age rights that left their elders drop-jawed and plenty worried about raising them. Many of us who were parenting our teenagers in those years automatically reined their kids in more than had been customary only a decade before—perhaps more than was necessary, but I can't blame us for that. Looking back, it appears even today that those times were far too complex for most of us to slide through unmarked by them. In any case, they certainly made clear how little I knew about navigating a sea of perils I couldn't have imagined when I was a teen.

Needless to say, it didn't matter to her that my reasoning was sound; that I knew what was best for her because I was older, seasoned by my struggles, mindful of the dangers that threaten youth's innocence, experienced enough to keep her from harm—and so on. (What a joke on me! I wouldn't have known a drug if I found one in my soup.) Every disagreement with her left me feeling bruised by her "stubbornness" and "lack of respect" for me. I couldn't tell her that, of course—I could only fall back and review my motives for the hundredth time: all of them good, all of them focused on her well-being—and how I justified my right to authority. Yet, I would learn that a thousand impeccable motives would do nothing to relieve our problem; in the end I felt let down, mystified, and a little cranky from it all.

When her time came to leave her family home with her shiny new freedom in tow, we loved one another in deed and in fact but spoke mostly "cordially," our unstated love filtered now through an uneasy truce. Though my heart longed to heal and return us to a "better, easier time," I still hadn't hit a wall, I was still trying to believe I was a good-enough mother, and I still hadn't a clue how I had "lost control" of our relationship. After that, I became afraid to say anything she might—and often did—take as criticism, which didn't help matters. It is accurate to say I felt estranged—lost from her and greatly perplexed. After a while, she moved to another town. We "kept in touch." I felt I needed forgiveness from both of us—and a good old-fashioned *satori* that would tell me why I felt that way.

Over time, I figured a few things out. So strong had been my need to protect her emerging destiny, and so sure had I been that I could lead her to it, that I hadn't given a thought to inviting her into "my" process. How had she perceived my role? It's not hard to guess this many years later, yet it's still a guess since we've never really talked about it. Did she perceive that keeping a tight rein on her meant that I didn't trust her? That might well have been the case. Had I hovered too close and too often, with too much advice not well proffered? Probably. Had I not heard her, this almost-woman whose most urgent need was to come of age and leave her home

Control—ego's stage name

clutching her freedom in her own hands? Not enough, probably. I will guess it was not really my "power" that she resented; in truth, she "won" more times than not when our wills clashed. More likely she perceived that I was insensitive to her needs, too ready to resist her, and not quick enough to make a bargain. I couldn't put a name to her frustrations nor help her navigate the peaks and chasms of puberty's hells and heavens. I could not, in other words, explain her to herself and I did absolutely fail her there. I stop to think how I once interpreted my father's intentions with me, and how I had once sassed him in my journal: "How mean and reckless you are with all your power!" I was sixteen years old, angry as hell, and already a piece of work. I couldn't say it out loud to him: I just wanted out. Much later, too late to tell him, I understood that that deeply troubled man was powerless to give me what I needed—a fact no doubt contributing to why I had been unable to successfully advise and help my daughter a generation later. That I was simultaneously struggling with a whole set of my own confusions—having nothing to do with her and everything to do with my ability to parent her—was only one of a dozen reasons why I couldn't meet a critical test of our relationship at a time when both of us could have used so much more than my meager stores of wisdom. None of this is "news," is it? We've all "been there" approximately, if not exactly. And while nothing about this is simple, I can describe it in a nutshell: I didn't know what I didn't know.

⚬

The eminent, now deceased, scholar, writer, and authority on Zen Buddhism, D. T. Suzuki, said about the individual quest for *satori*:

> Psychologically, this is accomplished when what is known as "abandonment," or "throwing oneself over the precipice," takes place. This "abandonment" means the moral courage of taking risks; it is a plunging into the unknown . . . and must be explored personally; and this is where logic turns into psychology, it is where [the intellect] has to give way to life-experience.[3]

Chapter eleven

Several years later and moving forward in my life, I am sitting in a fellowship meeting of Alcoholics Anonymous, marveling as I always do at all the ways the principles of our program work so well for us. We share our experiences to learn from one another how to pull apart, rethink, and work through the problems that finally caused us to "control" our psychic pain with alcohol: a "bodyguard" of a different stripe. We listen without comment or criticism to learn; we've all been in hell's reaches and are sober now to have a life, not to judge others. And while we would not presume to advise or instruct even the most recently arrived among us, we do give generously of our "experience, strength, and hope" by telling our stories— what it was like when we drank, what happened to turn us around and start us over, and what life is like for us now. Because our stories are all different, there is implied in our sharing an open invitation to "take freely what you can use, feel free to leave the rest." We avoid comparing because our differences are unimportant, but in fact we appreciate hearing anything that will lead us in the direction of humility: we know, or soon will, that there can be no surrender without humility. Control and surrender and humility are ubiquitous in our sharing because they are crucial to recovery. Suzuki says that surrender is also a prerequisite of enlightenment, "When all the traces of egotism are purged away . . . then all the contrivances cease, the purgation is achieved and the "abandonment" [surrender] is ready to take place."[4]

Nicely surrounded by the comity and purpose that mark these meetings, my mind is open, relaxed, and attentive. Suddenly—in the middle of someone else's sentence—I am experiencing my long-wished-for *satori*. It hangs gleaming in my awareness like a holographic jewel while time stands still. *I have only to apply these same principles in my relationship with my daughter and everything between us will come right.* Struck dumb by the suddenness and the ringing clarity of this epiphany, I understood at once that its wisdom was flawless. Like unraveling an impossibly knotted chain with the point of a slender needle, everything I needed to know was laid out, complete: no longer perplexed, no need for forgiveness, nothing to find and fix. My consciousness was changed in the moment and all was well. The experience was refulgent with symbolism. In the space between one moment and the next, I had released my daughter once and for all to her wholly separate life.

Control—ego's stage name

At the same time, I had also surrendered control of everything beyond the parameters of my separate self. So, this was made clear: if it was true that she and I stood separate in separate lives, and if it was true that each of our present moments had and will always belong only to our separate selves, then the same was true of every creature on the planet, giving me cause to respect each of them fundamentally equally. My liberation from the illusion that I had or could "control" any part of anyone else was now complete.

Suzuki relates how one old Zen master described enlightenment to his monks in the monastery:

> Think yourself to be down an old deep well; the only thought
> you will have will be to get out of it, and you will be desperately
> engaged in finding a way to escape; from morning to night this one
> thought will occupy the entire field of your consciousness . . .
> When one's mind is so fully occupied with one single thought,
> strangely or miraculously there takes place a sudden awakening
> within oneself. All the "searching" and "contriving" [to find the
> answer] ceases, and with it comes the feeling that what was
> wanted is here, that all is well with the world and with oneself,
> and that the problem is now for the first time successfully and
> satisfactorily solved.[5]

Yes. What was wanted—what I had waited for so long I had ceased thinking about it—had dropped into my consciousness as wordless, soundless, and weightless as a feather and gone to work in me. My thinking and behavior toward my daughter altered so organically, I felt I had always been who I had just become. Our relationship began to change—slowly, sometimes barely perceptibly; sometimes it went well and sometimes not. I had much to prove, it seemed. Yet, I sensed that she was beginning to trust that I had no other agenda for being in her life than to share it with her lovingly, with great respect for her separateness. Then and now, we have full lives to attend to, and we live some distance apart; but in every hour we have been together from that day to this, I have consciously practiced the "principles" that augured only good for our relationship. That our friendship and affection would grow over time is what I hoped would happen, and it has happened—happens a day at a time. "It's all good," to use a current turn of phrase.

Jung says in *Psychological Reflections:*

> The reason why consciousness exists, and why there is an urge to widen and deepen it, is very simple: without consciousness things go less well.[6]

You might ask why I had expected—no, needed—my daughter to go along with my thinking in the first place—to value my preferences over her own in the clothes she wore or the boys she dated or the schools she wished to attend—or for that matter, my insistence that she accept my word that black really was black and not white. What made me think I could save her from reinventing the wheel of life to suit her life, or from making mistakes to learn her life lessons her own way? Why would I not celebrate her desire to test and try my limits and wish her "good hunting" in her search for herself? I can only answer, "I didn't dare ask these questions." Having no other models for parenting save those I took from my childhood, I was afraid for both of us, nervous in a role I played mostly by instinct and with love—boundless love, yet not enough to do my job well. And why did it take so long to uncover the source of my incompetence? Well, that's a long, complex, very human story, but for now I will say that I was late plunging into the unknown—and when I did, it took a long, slow, breathtaking fall to get to the bottom of my unknowing and wake up.

Coming to consciousness is a process; it takes time and patience and courage—and at least one good, full-fledged epiphany. It is worth every effort I make. By the time I was safely certain I had no control over just about everything, I had also learned that I could *acquire* control over certain things about myself, especially my inner self, and the quality of my life. It is limited: I can't determine what might happen to my body or my brain or the planet, for example. Yet my earlier observation—"In truth we can and very

Control—ego's stage name

much need to have *some* control over our lives"—I can vouch for based on personal experience. To the extent that I have been willing to search for self-knowledge and self-awareness in my inner and outer worlds, mastery of myself has increased a thousandfold. Today I feel pretty comfortably in charge of my thinking, my behavior and emotions, and, on most days, my happiness. At some stage of my life, I chose to understand my limited power and control as having choices: the more I discover what is meaningful to me, the more choices and freedom of choice I can have to walk a meaningful path. Yet the work of "coming to know" is not done instinctively. Self-awareness is a gift of understanding I can give to myself, but I must choose to do the work of hunting it down. It is an option open only to our species, as Jung points out, "Man's capacity for consciousness alone makes him man."[7]

There are many ways to awaken, but the ones given most credit throughout history are ways that—pleasurably, or more often painfully—move us deeply, make us think and then go beyond thinking to reflect on the meaning of our lives. I think Jung says it better than anyone else:

> "Reflection" should be understood not simply as an act of thought,
> but rather as an attitude. It is a privilege born of human freedom
> in contradistinction to the compulsion of natural law. As the word
> itself testifies . . . reflection is a spiritual act that runs counter to
> the natural process; an act whereby we stop, call something to
> mind, form a picture, and take up a relation to and come to terms
> with what we have seen. It should, therefore, be understood as an
> act of becoming conscious.[8]

My son, the one who races cars professionally, came awake "all at once" a few years ago about two things that were crucial to his happiness. Still a young man, he came face to face with his mortality in a spectacular crash during one of his regular competitions. Another car clipped his from behind and he became airborne. His car took off at a right angle to the track and gained enough altitude to make three complete rollovers before landing hard. Somewhat stunned, but with his body and mind intact, he pushed himself out of the car's sorry remains and walked away. He told me that the experience so concentrated his mind on the two realities—life and the end of life—that both his choice to continue racing (were he to survive) and a clearer appreciation for the preciousness and fragility of his life burst full-blown into his hyperconscious mind as he was still looping to the ground. When "mother" renewed her concerns about his racing, he cautioned me this way, "Racing is my passion, and if I should one day die because of it, I want you, Mother, to tell everyone it was my choice to live my life doing what I love to do." I was awake before he finished his sentence. "It's my life to live," he was reminding me somewhat sternly—"my choice to make." I set him free of my concern for him immediately, and soon after that I could see the perfection in his logic. My fear for him finally seemed inappropriate to carry around, and I let it go—for the last time, I like to think. He was back in a car the very next weekend, fully conscious of his moment-to-moment mortality and full of joy doing what he most loves to do. Making his best choice to continue racing, he lives his life accordingly—following his passion, aware of the risks, true to his life.

Coming awake all at once is rare, even though Zen Buddhist literature is rife with examples of it; for people like me, who must first slash and burn their way through a critically compromised childhood, becoming conscious can be a long slog. Vaguely aware of how wobbly I was behind the screen of my persona, I gripped my illusion of control to convince myself that I was all right—safely centered in my world. That illusion doth make control freaks of us all, so I could really get into the "ego is might, right, and it rules!" mode whenever the truth about myself came too close for comfort. Today, when I see signs of that illusion everywhere, it is like looking into an old cracked mirror of myself. The wobbly-psyche population only increases in times like these, when nearly everyone in the world feels insecure. When an anxious planet suggests that none of us is in much control of anything, we react with justifiable fear. Yet, if I will summon my courage, let go of my mind's compulsion to run the whole scary show, and stay surrendered to losing control I've never had to begin with—my very perception of control will change and fear, and my illusion, will fade away. Coming awake *changes* me.

Control—ego's stage name

When I had accepted the concept that everything everywhere is changing uncontrollably all the time and that perpetual change is one of only two *fixed* facts of my existence, the jig was up with me; the illusion was over. The realization itself was a turning point in my life. I had awakened at a cross-roads in my life where "control" was a disputable concept, so which of the roads would I choose? Taking the one road committed me to keep moving into a level of reality where time and ego and all that we *do* drops away to allow an expanding experience of the mystery. The other road wandered off to nowhere in particular—places I'd already seen, things I'd already done, whole lives I'd already lived. This road, I guessed, was my one "opportunity" to quit the work: go for a walk, rock in a chair, have a beer, slip back into unconsciousness. My choice was so obvious that it hardly seemed like one. I have leapt off many a cliff since then, and I am still learning how vast is one's personal unknown, still surprised to find how much gold there is to troll in the undiscovered territory of self.

From my earliest stabs at awakening to the present day, I've sought to grasp—and finally did grasp with some precision—the tremendous meaning of Jung's words when he wrote:

> There is no other way open to us; we are forced to resort to conscious decisions and solutions where formerly we trusted ourselves to natural happenings. Every problem, therefore, brings the possibility of a widening consciousness, but also the necessity of saying goodbye to childlike unconsciousness and trust in nature.[9]

And as long as I have unfettered access and a desire to come awake to the wonders of my various worlds, I am happy enough to have a small degree of control over a limited number of things: certainly my attitude—toward people and things and life. I can choose to appreciate all of these things and feel gratitude for having them. I control my behavior, my mind, and my words pretty well, and I can make choices to have in my life people who will add love and friendship to it. Yet, whatever measure of control I appear to have, I say in all humility: It is small, it attaches to no one but me, and it works only in the present moment. My favorite Zen koan says it all:

If only death is certain
and the time of death uncertain—
what shall I do?

Am I right about control? Slippery as an eel, gone with the wind, wild as the weather, can't pin it down, and can't lock it up. We don't even have a say about the one thing we know is certain!

So . . . I spend a lot of time now looking into my "spiritual dimension," for lack of a better term. During quiet times of the day, I am again seeking gold in new territory and finding it, although only a little at a time. I am aware that the reason I do this derives from the same "ineluctable urge to realize *all* of myself" that spoke to me even when I was a child, and to which I feel deeply indebted and accountable. Moving into this level of awareness, I seem to occupy two separate planes at once: acknowledging in the more enlightened layers of myself that I have no control, nor any need of it—even as I live out my ordinary, extraordinary existence where having *some* control about only a few things is important and necessary. Rocking between the two worlds—consciously attentive to living and loving life's requirements in the one; surrendering everything I am and know to the mystery of the other—is the most interesting thing I have ever tried to do. And, wouldn't you know, the two worlds have a common denominator: practice, practice, practice.

Control—ego's stage name

twelve

Advice be damned!

> I am astonished, disappointed, pleased with myself. I am
> distressed, depressed, rapturous. I am all these things
> at once, and cannot add up the sum. I am incapable of
> determining ultimate worth or worthlessness; I have no
> judgment about myself and my life. There is nothing I
> am quite sure about. . . . and it seems to me I have been
> carried along. I exist on the foundation of something I
> do not know. In spite of all uncertainties, I feel a solidity
> underlying all existence and a continuity in my mode
> of being.
>
> —C. G. Jung

How Jung's words did surprise me, especially
since they were written at the end of a life extraordinary for the
size and brilliance of its contribution to the field of psychology!
Yet, he said on the same page and in the same breath, "The
more uncertain I have felt about myself the more there has
grown up in me a feeling of kinship with all things." This leads
me to think that his astonishment did not preclude his ability
to trust in "something I do not know" or his belief that his life
was deeply meaningful as he was carried along on a "solidity

underlying all existence." Wise beyond measure, he did not claim wisdom—only to have done the work that was laid out for him, which he must leave for others to judge because he could not. Given, so unexpectedly, the humility in which the aged genius so deeply dipped some of his last words, I would be reluctant to advise anyone other than myself—and even there I must be careful. I do think I know what Jung meant by being "carried along." Looking back at my life, I too will refute that I was in any real or authorial way in charge of my journey, feeling all along that my life has happened "to" me. My questions, choices, and decisions all seem to have been prompted by some source I often call "intuition," but, in truth, the source has always been a complete mystery to me. In review, my very self seems to have been magically constructed, deconstructed, and finally reconstructed as I twisted and wriggled my way through the years and torments of coming awake, until the day I simply found myself "at home." There was the process, of course, the work one does to become sane, but what was the engine that drove the process that I can only describe in metaphors?

What comes to mind as being symbolic of the first years of my life (I speak here of that accidental stranger we call our inner life) is a scene unrolling on videotape, let's say,—no sound—that, like a game of charades, represents my girlhood and perhaps says something about my character:

> She is a toddler, totally engaged in her effort to achieve satisfaction of some great need of the moment going unmet. She is thrashing her way through what the tall ones in the room might call a temper tantrum, expressing her need, with every ounce of her will and tiny stature and limited powers of reasoning, to have from the "powers that be" something she simply can't live without. Head to toe, her body is rigid, each hand a fist, both feet firmly spread and planted for battle. Her eyes are squeezed shut against a leaking waterfall of tears, the better to concentrate her purpose, which at the moment is to wail her misery all stops out and produce as many ear-piercing decibels as will make her case convincingly. She is warning her two persons of interest that she stands ready to punch them out should they refuse to accommodate what is surely the greatest desire she has experienced in her short,

Advice be damned!

wholehearted life. After awhile, fervor and decibels in decline and the sound of her breath-catching sobs barely discernible, she drops to her hands and knees—that classic toddler pose signaling the end of her causa sine qua non. Less than a full minute later, thoroughly exhausted from her epic struggle to overcome odds that were against her from the start, the sound of silence indicates she has fully accepted an unfavorable outcome. We see now all parts of her body loosely sprawled where she has eased them to the floor, and hear a long, final, shuddering sigh from her exhausted lungs. One of the tall ones covers her carefully where she lies surrendered to the deep and peaceful sleep that follows having given one's all, win or lose.

She fought the good fight, is how she would recall what happened; she hauled out every tool in her limited arsenal of years and experience and put them into service. Her victory, already forgotten yet embedded in her psyche for eternity, was not that she won the fight, because she didn't. It was the exquisite satisfaction she felt for having expressed her desire passionately—for having "gone for the gold" with her whole small self. Jung said, "The goal is important only as an idea; the essential thing is the opus which leads to the goal: that is the goal of a lifetime."[1] He was right, and although the work—her opus and mine—would indeed have its costs, none was ever too dear compared with the gains we made on our intention to live fully.

I am only one among many both cursed and blessed with a reflex to reenact this particular metaphor, which I have done one way or another from my childhood to the present day. In my youth it was an impulse to construct a more tolerable life, one with less pain and more substantive meaning. Later, the same passionate impulse, only more reasoned and self-assured, acted to preserve at any cost the reconstructing life of a psyche on the mend. My whole life calls for a much different metaphor—and this time sound tells all:

She is drifting and tossing the length of a river; shallow waters just down from its mouth froth up mud-brown and turbulent for miles and months and sometimes years at a time. In a deafening roar,

the river "takes her," and because the river is her life and there is
no going ashore, she rolls with it—soaked to the bone at times as
she struggles against drowning in the maelstrom of her fears and
resistance. Deep currents are moving the water beneath her at a
treacherous speed—plunging down waterfalls, into whirlpools,
and around immense rocky projectiles born in the river's bed,
immovable and eternal. Years later, half the length of her lifetime,
on a day rising clear, bright, and harmonious, the river relents, the
currents brake, the waters calm—undulating and buoyant still, but
no longer lunatic. Joy fills her: she and the river are one. Finally
afloat on her life, she seeks her center mid-width of the river and
rides effortlessly on its flow. Canyon walls of granite, once too
shocking and sheer to apprehend, give way to sunlight, sandy
banks, shade trees, and long stretches of horizon, emblazoned
with color. In pools coursing shallow enough to wade, time waits
while she stops to play and delight in them. She has found her
self—is now free and at home in her soul. Surviving the steep,
watery couloirs of her transformation, she is empowered, a self-
navigating life-stream focusing only on the now . . . and the now
. . . and the now . . . present moments coalescing, towing her in a
direction out to sea—those immense, borderless waters waiting to
transit her soul.

One does not survive one's watery unconscious underworld by following
the advice of even one hundred thousand wise ones. One rides one's river
alone and awakens, slowly, over time and confluent with the now . . . and
the now . . . and the now.

⁓

James Hollis:

Somewhere, in the collision between heart, which longs for
permanency and connection, and brain, which acknowledges

Advice be damned!

separation and loss, there is a place for us to find our personal psychology.[2]

I associate Hollis's "personal psychology" with one's "personal metaphor:" the ongoing many-layered story of a self we create in order to identify the meaning of our life and explain the mystery of our remarkable human consciousness. Our metaphors are unique; it might take a lifetime to unearth one, yet as it unfolds to *become* us, it is always only ours. If in some small way my metaphor shines a tiny light of influence your way, that's the most it will do. Though I can think of no one from whom I sought or took advice on how to make my metaphor, I can remember countless times when I vibrated head to soles to someone else's story, and in that way was graced to fill in some blanks in my own. And since I don't believe in tinkering with anyone else's metaphor, I'll say it right here: advice be damned! When is it ever appropriate, anyway, unless it is specifically sought—and paid for (think taxes, car repairs, and learning to speak Swahili)? When is it not just another word for "meddling"?

Shared thoughts and relevant observations, tales of personal experience, self-reflection, and conclusions drawn from the living and from literature old and new—the precious words that live and talk to me: these are the ways my personal psychology was reconstructed over time. I am thrilled to be "spoken to" in books written by so many minds that have never known me—yet know me through and through. From their truth I plucked the tiny glints of mica that I recognized as belonging to my own metaphor, as well, and I saluted them in thanks. I guess I could say that I am "advised" by self-reflection and by my intuitive responses to what others say—but there is that word again: intuitive. When intuition reveals something to me, I don't receive it as advice but as truth—fully formed and sacred: to intuit is to *know*, it has always seemed to me. All else aside, though, if I am not expanding my consciousness as a matter of habit, my "river" too could run wild and profligate out to sea, and I ponder how many of us are aware of the danger. If all the world's souls were given the opportunity, would they jump into the flow of their conscious energy—wet, messy, dynamic, and painful as it is—and construct a personal metaphor with which they could live happily?

Chapter twelve

This is a question each of us would have to ask ourselves—and answer only for ourselves.

Giving advice was always beyond my ken. Until my children were into their teens, I *instructed* them—about curfews and housekeeping chores and homework obligations, how to brush their teeth and towel between their toes: the basics. We "instruct" our bird chicks so they won't fall out of the tree before their wings can fly, am I right? Soon they were thinking for themselves and resisting all further instruction, and at that point, I tell you truly, they would not have dreamed of taking any advice from me that ran contrary to their already made-up minds. After they left home, I learned to stop tracking how well their wings were working and waited to hear from them—an enjoyable novelty I quickly became used to. I heard from them less frequently as time went on; when I did, it was mostly my ears they wanted as they searched for their own answers comfortably in the presence of someone who knew them well. The rare times they asked me for advice, I tried to relate similar situations or personal experiences, reconstructing what I'd had the luck to do right or the misfortune to do wrong, and in either case the lessons I had learned. Or, I would offer "best guess" scenarios for them to think about if I thought they might help. I think the most important thing I ever said to them was not offered as advice but as a statement of fact, "In the end, only you can decide what's best for your life." The older they became, the less I was called on to contribute to their lives philosophically, until finally we—some of us—began to "converse."

I for one appreciate the multitudes of talented professionals there are to choose from when I need advice, and they are usually paid handsomely for their specialized wisdom. So, even among my peers we might ask one another about this or that "What do you think?" But we never ask, "How would you advise me?" How presumptuous I would be to think I know even my best friends well enough to give them skilled, objective advice. And if they're like me, they wouldn't want the responsibility. Sharing similar *experience*, though—that's a different matter. Close, longtime friends and functional family members might seek advice from me or I from them, yet it is more often my undivided attention they are truly seeking—an honor I am pleased to earn. My experiences confirm that listening truly attentively to the other fills the underlying need to be comforted and often renders advice (from a nonprofessional) irrelevant.

◦◦◦

Least of all would I advise one of the opposite sex—now there is a slippery slope—though I might ask who of either sex knows enough about the opposite one to make so much as a dent of difference in their relations? There must be others in the world, but I have "met" only one author whose printed words taught me many important things about men. I came to James Hollis's *Under Saturn's Shadow* too late to benefit from his sometimes shocking knowledge about men while my two sons were growing up. I read it later, nevertheless, hoping to learn at least a little about what made them the men they are today.

Right from the start the boys walked and talked and behaved differently in every way from their sister, who (though no easier to bring up) at least offered me a familiar feminine sensibility to work with! Her brothers' responses to just about everything under the sun were so dissimilar to my own first impulses that I ultimately resigned myself to doing the best I could and hoping that luck and love would fill up the holes in my knowledge about what really went on inside of them. I played it safe by instructing them on the "big stuff"—tell the truth, play fair, don't bully, look both ways when you cross the street, the seven deadly sins—thinking that my "home-schooling," plus frequent visits with their father, would steer them to manhood in spite of their male gender "peculiarities." But I never once doubted I was flying blind with those boys. The only time I ever smacked my youngest one—he was maybe eight years old—he had just called his sister a bitch. How did he even know the word—much less at his age how to punish the opposite sex with it? In those days, I found males of every age truly stranger than fiction, too weird for words—indecipherable. So, it would take a man to break the masculine code and let me in on a few things.

My reward for reading Hollis's book was to understand for the first time how painfully ignorant I had been all of my life about the other half of my species and how sparsely defined in our culture is the male mystique below its surface. Hollis begins by revealing

Chapter twelve

that men, as well as women, labor always under the heavy shadow of ideologies, some conscious, some inherited from family and ethnic group, some part of the fabric of a nation's history and its mythic soil. This shadow is an oppressive weight on the soul. Men labor under it, oppressed and blighted in spirit. . . . The definitions of what it means to be a man—male roles and expectations, competition and animosity, the shaming and devaluing of many of men's better qualities and capacities—all lead to the crushing weight.[3]

He tells of the secrets men carry within, listing eight of them.[4] The first secret he lists is, "Men's lives are as much governed by restrictive role expectations as the lives of women." He elaborates on this with a depth of knowledge and compassion only a man who has done the long, hard work of moving toward the wholeness of his gender and humanity could possess. He describes a whole set of crippling psychic difficulties that differ only in detail from those women have suffered for millennia. I came away from his small, incisive treatise filled with compassion for the broken parts of both sexes and feeling the need to honor the immense truth that they suffer mutually—each at the other's unconscious hand and each at their own. How much work there is yet to do before men and women can meaningfully realize their potential for exquisite complementariness.

Another "secret within" is that men "collude in a conspiracy of silence whose aim is to suppress their emotional truth." Is there a woman reading this page who doesn't know at least that much about men—who didn't learn about it from a father or a brother, a lover or a husband, and who hasn't been frustrated by it at times to the point of rage? Yet, we have no advice to give to the "other" in these matters—no crash course to which we can drag each other and become enlightened. I realized early in the "relationship" parts of my therapy that the sexes will never fully respect and appreciate each other until individuals in ever-increasing numbers take up the task of understanding, first themselves, and next our intricate and elegant gender differences. We might then begin to instruct children down the generations—not teaching or advising them in classrooms, but by demonstrating genuine mutual

Advice be damned!

respect in our relations with one another. Is there any other way to discover the equal value and beauty of the sexes? I can't think of one.

Like other wise voices I have read, Hollis affirms what my psyche so often struggled to accept as I was trying to come awake: the wheel of life does in fact require each one of us to reinvent ourselves as we grow up and older—to step outside the habits of the collective and "go it alone" if need be until we find out who we are. Beginning in the late sixties and continuing full-throated through the seventies, many women tore themselves out of the "all-genders" mainstream and began—individually or with like-minded support—to assert ownership and liberation of their bodies and minds and souls. Hollis here encourages men to do the same:

> Men are now free to make their first secret known—that their lives are as restricted by role definitions as are women's—thanks to the courage of women who have protested at traditional roles and institutions that deny uniqueness and equality. Women have led the way. . . . That [men's] roles were oppressive and deforming did not occur to most men until women forced them to look more closely.[5]

Though many of the enlightened women of the those years are still actively working to preserve, protect, and improve on their hard-won gains, their work is no longer making headlines—perhaps because much of it has been integrated into our culture. Yet, there is more work to do, more headlines to be made—later perhaps, because certain "evolutions" are by their nature cyclical. Meanwhile, the much-needed men's movement sprang to life in the late seventies and grew a root system of support organizations, questing retreats, and a body of literature written by eminently qualified men. It is possible now for the sexes to study each other's literature and awaken to themselves for their own and their children's benefit.

The women of the sixties and seventies—the genies who refused to get back in their bottles—worked to free themselves for happier, self-fulfilling lives and caused a collective leap in consciousness that continues to serve all of us: men, women, and especially children. Now that both sexes are working hard—if not yet together or in great enough numbers—to better define and understand the importance of one to the other, there is reason to hope that both will come to value their differences as well as their similarities, their limitations as well as their strengths—ergo, their great need for each other. What is critical that we can all do is to change our thinking enough to find the deeper, gender-complementary meaning of our humanity, the inclusiveness that generates "bipartisan" gratitude that we are in each other's lives. Those of either sex who would in principle keep a separate power over the other hurt all of humanity by aiding and abetting our too-human tendency to resist change at any cost, to hide out in the status quo. Embracing change gives us access to the natural springs of human generosity that wait only on our enlightenment to serve us; without generosity we are individually and collectively stopped in our tracks from evolving. Jung said:

> I have frequently seen people become neurotic when they content themselves with inadequate or wrong answers to the questions of life. They seek position, marriage, reputation, outward success or money, and remain unhappy and neurotic even when they have attained what they were seeking. Such people are usually confined within too narrow a spiritual horizon. Their life has not sufficient content, sufficient meaning. If they are enabled to develop into more spacious personalities, the neurosis generally disappears.[6]

The die was cast by Jung in the last century for us in our century to look within ourselves for the answers we need to improve our species' survival. That we are never too old to "develop into more spacious personalities" and do right in our days and with each other is a happy fact only if we stay ahead of a collective inclination to ignore our history of self-canceling.

⟡

Speaking of gender, an interesting aspect of my growing older is finding out that in many respects I have become androgynous—not physically, of course, but psychologically, I would say in the way that infants, before their personalities differentiate into gender-specific attributes, receive their world "just as it is," though of course now I am able to articulate my world. I reason from this that most of the crammed-full, fast-moving, volatile years of an individual's development occur between infancy and late age. Following infancy, we accrete layers and layers of familial and cultural conditioning which go mostly unchallenged as we seek to adapt to society and get a grasp on our life. A few decades later, a time begins when it feels not only right but necessary to throw off all that conditioning, to withdraw from the collective mentality and define how we think and feel—which is to say, more deeply and authentically. Rilke speculates on this development:

> And perhaps the sexes are more related than we think, and the
> great renewal of the world will perhaps consist in this, that man
> and maid, freed from all false feeling and aversion, will seek each
> other not as opposites, but as brother and sister, as neighbors, and
> will come together as human beings.[7]

I wonder if Rilke's androgynous vision of world renewal is part of an individual's inclination to "renew" his or her perspective on life in general as the years pass. The process of authenticating myself is completing in me; I can feel it. I measure it by feeling less and less attached to my ego, more and more comfortable identifying as *everyone*—and in that way, androgynous: less narrowly woman, more broadly one-with-all in my relationship to the world. Or, as Carolyn Heilbrun describes it:

> [Androgyny] defines a condition under which the characteristics of
> the sexes, and the human impulses expressed by men and women,
> are not rigidly assigned. Androgyny seeks to liberate the individual
> from the confines of the appropriate.[8]

I experience my humanity as the one and only humanity—my consciousness spilling over, unconfined by self, spreading beyond my feminine boundary to become genderless. I am willing to posit that the consciousness we are today derives from the "androgynous" consciousness we manifested anciently, as

Chapter twelve

stars shooting through the heavens, clustering in hordes as galaxies, or as the sun rising and setting and the moon waxing and waning. I can easily imagine that long before our two-sexed, upright, *Homo sapiens* species evolved its capability for genius, it is possible that every last one of us was once singularly and ingeniously "awake" as a conscious constellation of stardust—outside of time's dimension and eternally part of the one consciousness. Today I imagine that while we continue to birth males and females who can't yet "get it together" on the surface of their lives, later in life we are acquiring a real knack for widespread "croning"—the ability to inhabit some deep or "other" dimension of the psyche with naturally occurring androgyny. What need for advice then—when we are no longer invested in power and all becomes—not "what should be" but the beginning of "what is"?

To read the Hollis book was to discover that, some details aside, no major distinction can be made between men and women at every age in their desire for happiness, freedom, and peace of mind. Transforming that desire into a quest—and then questing—and taking personal responsibility a day at a time for achieving what is meaningful to one's own life for the long haul: that is the nut of his message. It accomplishes nothing to advise another to quickly set sail and journey forth; that dialogue must happen with oneself. I can only contrast the before-and-after of my own journey and report back that my life was enlarged a millionfold by the efforts I made to achieve what I desired. I can barely remember today the tight little island of fear and fragility that was too long my home base—until my young and troubled psyche finally stepped off land to swim the deep waters of therapy. Even so, my present happy state is not guaranteed beyond the present hour; I am clear as can be that all things change all the time, that I must savor the moment or lose it altogether.

The very young and the very old "savor" their moments by living much closer to the ground of their being, I believe. Operating on fewer and simpler premises, and their egos now in retirement, the old love better and more carefully. They no longer sweat the small stuff, and are more willing by far to accept what they have no control over. Infants, because they are so close to their own beginnings, react to life organically. At some point, the aging tend to winnow everything they know—selecting, storing, and keeping close at hand only what truly matters to them now. In essence, they come (back) to their senses. It's a theory too simple by itself to answer life's bigger mysteries, but it nicely explains why I am so protective of what has once more become— this time consciously—my natural state: loved, loving, and lovable. It is in us to recapture our natural, lovable selves any time we are ready: I feel pretty sure of that. Now, when I am no longer naive in the innocence of infancy and when I have lived, learned, unlearned, and come back to my original self, what could I possibly be, other than loving of humanity? What more could I want than to be amazed—as I was at my beginning—at the risen sun and the thousand wonders of a day simply unfolding? And there is this, too: Not unusual in my late-age, androgynous, back-to-natural self is a feeling that I somehow know the truth—not as words of advice to dispense—far from that—but truth *as myself*, what I am made of, as having the same DNA—truth as perhaps what Jung meant by "the foundation of something I do not know."

There is no visible finish line in the long-distance run of a lifetime, of course—only the occasional rest stop and a glass of cool, pure water. Extending the adage "sunrise to sunset our work is never done," I would add to it "unto death's door" and say there remains the end game to address. The fear of death can loom large in old age. I have elsewhere quoted this advice I found embedded in one of Meister Eckhart's paradoxes: "The ultimate letting go is the letting go of God," by which I believe he meant to drive home that God is unknowable. To surrender the hand of a god that has so long symbolized the only end-of-life certainty we could conjure can be a scary proposition—though in truth it is faith whose hand we hold and we can be certain of nothing save an intuition of the soul's immortality. Each in our own way we seek comfort to alleviate fear of the death of the body; it is perhaps the last big opus of "overcoming" for the old. Yet, I have observed among friends my age—and it is my own experience, as well—that the intuition of "something more to come" seems to strengthen in one's sincerely humbled seeking of comfort, and that confronting death—if we will allow the confrontation—is the beginning of making friends with death.

So it seems to me that I am required to do at my life's penultimate juncture more of the same work I did when I decided to do my level best to begin to grow old gracefully. I am to wrestle my fears now just as I previously wrestled my anger and my pride and my ego—to fight them right down to the ground of my familiar, until I can find and feel gratitude for the gift of a miracle now coming to its end. Since I have not yet had the experience, I am the one who invented my fear of death, after all. Having thought all such prospects through, I can say that even death is beautiful when I find myself at times perceiving it that way; rightly understood, it seems to me death is worthy of celebration as the last act of my life as I know it. Can I do it well? Be graceful all the way to the end? Leave with a peaceful heart even if my body is more or less ravaged as death arrives? Who can advise me how to think and feel about death? No one. Here, too, I must do my work if I truly wish to live with peace in my old age—not resignation, a mind state not nearly profound enough for one's end—but the extraordinary peace of acceptance and an active readiness for whatever, if anything, comes next.

Beginning to end, there is no right, wrong, or one-way-only to live a life meaningfully and responsibly. I had to start somewhere and was fortunate that my early interest in psychology led me to a therapeutic process that literally saved my psychic life. I'm thinking, as I write, of how I had "his ears," yet I was never "advised" by a therapist. Hollis clarifies the process:

> The ultimate end of depth psychology is to stand respectfully
> before inner truth and dare to live it in the world. What blocks
> each of us is fear—fear of loneliness, fear of rejection, and most of
> all fear of largeness. We are all afraid to move from the confining
> powers of fate into the invitations of our destiny, afraid to step
> into the largeness of our calling to be who we were meant to be.[9]

Life is too individual, too singularly precious, and far too mysterious for me to think I might advise the aging of any age how to live through it. I

Advice be damned!

believe what matters the most in life is one's intention to live with purpose and passion and enough determination to quest out to its edges. Probably all that really matters is to "take it on" and shake out of it as much as we can. Yes, it's work—but it's interesting, fascinating work. I have known all the way to this day that every effort I made to shake out the treasure in my life was worth every candle I had to light when the dark parts fell out with it. Here's a metaphor that tells how little I know about life—and about how little that matters:

> Life is a kind of lavish gift box filled with every imaginable kind and color of things—scary, beautiful, wretched, and astonishing things; wonderful, terrible, sad, happy, boring, and exciting things—and at least two hundred simply amazing things you would never expect to find. So, tell me, if we would not shuffle through our life in a state of staring, wide-eyed sleep—well, what other choice do we have than to get in the box and play?

Chapter twelve

thirteen

Regrets? none but one . . .

> My body is a shell in which a chick lies closed about;
> Brooded by the spirit of eternity, it waits its hatching out.
>
> —Angelus Silesius

She was a beauty: at ten pounds, "half-grown and gorgeous right out of the chute," my mother used to say of her firstborn. The nurses held her by turn, showing her off because she was already smiling and because her beauty was so dazzling. Ten pounds going through the chute, she was also a mighty ordeal for my mother, causing her doctor and her husband to be greatly concerned when she told them six months later that she was pregnant again. She refused their strict advice to abort me. I wonder if you can imagine the immediate and enduring impact that fact has had on me and in how many ways—how it made all the difference in the way I was finally able to regard my mother, for example, and in how I came to terms with what happened to my only sibling.

My memories of my sister begin when I was four. She was five and already in kindergarten—the first of many "firsts" of which I would be jealous because being second garnered only lukewarm glory—and because she was so damned beautiful. When we were six and seven, I have a memory of my father admonishing her at the dinner table—not now and then, but every night—for eating too much, causing her to look sad and go silent and causing me to feel bad for her—and to not eat too much. Another vivid memory from that time is of my father scolding her for pulling out her hair a strand at a time from the top of her head. When she had finally pulled out enough hair to create a bald spot, my grand-mother knitted beanie caps for her to wear to school, but she figured out how to hook the strands through the cap and pull them out anyway. Later, when she was interested in boys, she stopped all of that, though try as she would she couldn't stop eating too much—nor could my father ever refrain from warning all of us at the table that she would soon be or (when it finally happened) was indeed—"fat."

We were perhaps seven and eight when my sister and I began to bond in a deep and particular way. Our parents frequently left us home alone in the evenings until well past midnight, so when the dark outside turned too black to see through we would stiffen our child-sized spines and pretend again that we weren't afraid of all those things going bump in the night that sounded like someone cutting open the screen to our bedroom window or for certain the footsteps of a burglar entering the kitchen through a rear porch door. Hardest of all to bear were the mute and shadowy figures—men wearing hats and waving their arms, we were sure of it—whom we watched even as they watched us through curtains not all that difficult to see through. We would turn up the sound on the radio, talk loud, and laugh a lot to scare them away while we huddled close to give and get from each other what little comfort we could fake. When the wind outside had finally died down—and the sounds and shapes that fed our fears had miraculously ceased—we would climb into a bed that filled up the one tiny bedroom in our very small house and pray for sleep to come. Out of such circumstances our sister-love grew deep and stayed for many more reasons yet to come.

As time went by our dissimilar personalities found different friends and separate things to do, though in that "particular" way our deeper connection remained. When we were fifteen and sixteen, the family moved across town to even smaller quarters and we transferred to a different high school. It was

Chapter thirteen

then that I began to notice some things about her I thought were kind of odd. As we talked, her eyes would sometimes cut away and peer into the distance, her full attention locked onto something she found "disturbing," I thought, because her face would tense and her mouth would move. Other times she would go to school unkempt and unprepared—hair not combed, shoes not shined, homework not finished—for several days in a row. When school let out for the summer, I would right away find some job or other that would take me outside the confines of our apartment to earn some spending money, yet my sister would beg to stay home and do chores for the pittance my father was able to pay her. I was baffled by these things, but said nothing about them because he was always on her case.

Sometime later I realized that she was afraid to go more than a few blocks from home by herself. Our parents thought her behavior was (although somewhat aberrant) indicative of a teenager in full puberty flower—but in her case, they were not even close. It never occurred to me or anyone else in her life that her occasionally eccentric behavior mattered much: "She'll grow out of it," they said. My father called her "lazy" and pretty much gave up on her. But in time it would matter, all right.

She lost some weight, was once again stunningly beautiful, and met and married a "career Marine" a month before she turned eighteen. They lived for a while on a military base with other career families, but she was unhappy with the lifestyle. Soon after that, her husband took her to a doctor because she was acting out in some negative ways. He resigned from the Marine Corps, earned an engineering degree, and built a tiny house for the two of them with his own hands. They settled into it and started a family: four boys, one right after the other. A dozen years later she was seriously unstable: undergoing electroshock therapy and receiving bleak assessments of her future. Soon thereafter she was institutionalized.

When I went to see her and "the keeper" unlocked the door between my sister and the reception area, she looked like a witch—crazy-eyed and talking to God and suspicious about who I was. Every time I left her behind in that place I cried all the way home, and after a while I stopped going because it hurt too much. I had children of my own by then and a full-time job and a marriage I wasn't sure was working. I was trying to find

Regrets? none but one

my center and couldn't take seeing her like that because she had no center at all: she was crazy and I was her blood sister and that scared me. More than anything else, though, the hurt was about losing her; after all we had been through together as kids, she would talk to God but she wouldn't talk to me.

I saw my sister one more time after that, when our aging mother wanted to see her beautiful firstborn before she died. My sister was taking her meds at the time (there were times when she refused to), so she knew who we were. We all went to lunch nearby and "chatted" for a while—artificially, bizarrely, desperately manufacturing simple little sentences that could pass as normal conversation—to fill the unnerving, disjointed, meaningless void that became our mother's last-chance meeting with her. In truth, I was probably the only one who felt crazy that day, but I could hardly wait to hug my sister long and hard—anticipating I suppose that I would not soon be seeing her again—and go home. That was at least fifteen years ago. Last year her oldest son sent me a recent photo of her. It took me several seconds to find my sister in the visage returning my gaze. She is no longer beautiful, not even recognizable. I quickly laid the picture facedown on my desk while something deep inside of me resumed its long, mournful cry of loss and regret.

I have heard from her husband that she's in a different halfway facility now—drugged, sleepy, wandering the halls, and still eating too much, I say lovingly. Of all the regrets I might have hung onto all this time and had sense enough not to, only one refuses to go. It sits on my soul, wide awake, is from time to time exceedingly heavy, and is not in the slightest bit diminished as the years go by. I regret that I lack the courage to go to her, wrap my arms around her, hold her hands, kiss her face, tell her how much I miss her, and say, "I love you." You would think I'd be strong enough by now to do that, but I'm not—and I may not be before it's too late, when, as unfinished business, I will regret all the more my resistance to her—to the memory of our entire miserable childhood for which she has become a symbol too powerful and too numinous to overcome.

Chapter thirteen

Except for her—not *her*, of course, but that one remaining regret—my past feels so *past* now! All of the super-sized emotions that once danced my feet or twisted my viscera have lightened up and evened out, mind and soul healed and whole and finished with their ancient interior psychodrama. I seldom if ever look back anymore, and when I do, the details of my life resist showing up for even one more minute of analysis. Yet, when it comes to regrets, there is much to say about how they can affect a life and how, when they are left "untreated," they can really bring you down. Sorrow and disappointment are synonyms for the word regret, and whom do you know who hasn't felt the meaning of all those words as they lived the circumstances of their life? I can think of situations in my childhood over which I had no control, yet I regretted my part in them, and later, there were times I regretted even more, because they were the direct result of actions I took knowing they would cause others to suffer. Recalling them even now tends to roll out their particulars. Regrets go deep and want to stay long.

We learn from others in the most casual conversations that regrets are universal barter exchanged between each of us and our particular reasons to suffer them—whether or not we are conscious of our reasons. To my way of thinking, regrets are usually self-inflicted—even if we meant no harm when we caused them to occur. They are also necessary instruments of enlightenment. The unawake will feel their regrets only after the dastardly deed is done and the chips have fallen willy-nilly. The young and the uninitiated are greatly inclined to pile up regrets because they take risks and bear consequences they aren't yet able to imagine. They make mistakes they come to regret by testing their own limits and pushing against the limits of whatever authority they perceive as too constricting—life's way of maturing them. I have known some extremely insensitive people who "apparently" feel no regrets for anything they do and so make no amends to whomever they hurt. The impression they give is "As long as I get mine, who cares what happens to you?" Yet, without knowing more of their story, who can say? Others seem born to risk and misstep and start over and over again—consciously, though, well-meaning and with a positive mindset. Should we suffer from their actions, they are quick to apologize—and just as quickly cease to regret. Young and old, male and female, they climb a tree every day expecting to fall out of it and to learn a thing or two in the process. Good for them, I say—we are all better off for their betting, gambling ways. Most of the rest of us, given the option, do our risking and misstepping in smaller and more measured ways. We are not so eager to gamble too big or too often, preferring to fall out of our trees as a matter of choice, not instinct. Each at our pace, we are mostly willing to make mistakes and suffer regrets when necessary—but even then sometimes not, I find, because some of what life expects of us is painfully hard to do.

When left to roost unattended in the hidden corners of the psyche, regrets will devolve into withering, contemptuous malcontents and wreck our chances for peace of mind. But there is also something profound about regretting if we use it consciously as a way to self-discover and forgive ourselves. Most of my big mistakes were made out of ignorance, innocence, inexperience, or immaturity—never malice; they were never purposely done to wound either myself or anyone else. Unintended as they were, I always deeply regretted them and wondered what purpose was served by my feeling miserable when I meant no harm. It seems the "purpose" is both profound and a paradox: it was precisely in the regretting of the negative consequences of my actions that I was relieved of my regrets.

Honesty was key. Not until I could confront my mistake truthfully would I begin to know why I had made it. Not until I could explore my misbegotten reasons for making it—with compassion for myself—would I experience the miracle of self-forgiveness that puts an end to regretting. Gathering the courage to accept responsibility and make amends, I learned the lesson that all mistakes will teach. It appears to me that sitting long enough with regret to understand why one feels it begins an elegant process of self-forgiving that removes regret. Coming to consciousness is a beautiful thing—the only way I know to shine a light on all that hides in psyche's dark and forgotten corners. And oh, the freedom! When all is transparent to mind-sight, life soars like a bird.

A person must sometimes break a commitment in order to grow. . . . Sometimes one must even become what in myth is called the Holy Criminal, one who violates the societal norm on behalf of

Chapter thirteen

a personal vision. Such a person is obliged to live out this calling even while bearing the burden of consequences as guilt.[1]

James Hollis says it straight in the language of his special expertise. My rough-and-ready translation of his wisdom is: Sometimes you gotta do what you gotta do to save your very self. I find it reassuring that he speaks to my own experiences of breaking commitments "in order to grow" and—like a dragon at truth's gate—of protecting my true self no matter the cost (guilt). He is no less resolute when he speaks to those who cherish a personal vision of themselves and their lives: "Such a person is *obliged* [my italics] to live out his calling."

The searing remorse I felt when I caused my children to suffer by divorcing their father—thereby radicalizing the established rhythms of their psychological underpinnings—is indescribable to anyone who hasn't had a similar experience. Their brave, unspoken, and thoroughly impotent sadness all by itself was so huge a burden to bear I can't think how I ever got through it—especially this divorce, when they were young enough to feel personally betrayed by my action and his consent to it. Yet, the decision had to be made, and once done, I never questioned it. Nor did I—for fear my knees would buckle—dwell on its consequences, because I knew—because it was my intention, and because I trusted myself and all the gods in their heavens—that we would all be all right eventually.

I had no illusions about the depth and breadth of my task; it was sweeping, it would test me in ways I couldn't foresee, it would change all of our lives forever. Yet I believed through and through that it was possible to mend our hearts and live happily. Paradoxically, given that my children would now need *more* of me, my first move was of necessity to reenter the workplace, and, like millions of other nine-to-five working mothers, I would have *less* time to be with them. Then it was a common nightmare for the nearly, or newly, female single parent who must agonize over the potential consequences of her actions. To stay in an unhappy marriage or leave it was the choice that haunted me—and in either case a painfully persistent conflict was already in place: if I stayed, the children would suffer the weight of my unhappiness; if we left, they would pay my price to regain authenticity. Hollis warns, though:

Regrets? none but one

As guilt binds us to the past, so it contaminates the present and the future, even unto destruction. For us to deal with guilt in a conscious way we must be able to differentiate the kind of guilt we are suffering. Real guilt is a mature way of taking responsibility.[2]

Guilt and remorse are close cousins of regret; entwined, they form a ball of separate hurts not easy to pull apart. Yet, when measured against the regret I would feel today if I had failed to acknowledge my intense desire to "right the wrong" in me—to fix that which I couldn't name but knew was so alien to my nature that my self was inconsolable—I did the right thing. My "radicalizing" actions were driven by a fear too powerful to ignore: my authenticity was in jeopardy and I was responsible for keeping it safe. Had there been a different choice to make either time, I would have made it gladly, but there was not—not for me.

Marriage and children, careers and personal values are extraordinarily important life choices. Ideally, they would come only after one has understood and identified one's most authentic beliefs, needs, and desires. Yet how many of us are mature enough to articulate what is essential to our happiness by the time we are expected to set our future lives in motion? My children were fully grown before I discovered that spending most of my time alone was my ideal state of happiness.

Hollis's "Holy Criminal, one who violates the societal norm on behalf of a personal vision," was hidden in me for a long time before I understood who she was, that we were one and the same and needed self-forgiving and "decriminalizing." Meanwhile, I carried the same burdens of remorse and regrets as do a great many others who get caught dismembering one solemn promise—to remain two until death—in order to rescue another vow they intuit is also sacred: to remain true to themselves. We dared to upset society's applecart at our peril in those days, "marked" for committing an act so unholy and roundly, if silently, rebuked by legions of our peers better equipped to keep their vows. We chided ourselves, as well, when children were involved. I can understand why conventional wisdom favors fighting for the status quo (fearing all of society will run amok) even if I couldn't then—and don't now—condone the harsh judgment of those who "fall from grace."

Chapter thirteen

Marriage vows are worth every effort to uphold, and the wedding ceremony is a lovely tradition; and yet the largely unreflected attitudes toward marriage and divorce even to this day don't come close to matching the reality of our human limitations. For most of us, it takes time, a measurable amount of self-knowledge, a variety of life experiences—and yes, some trials and errors in relationships—before we can expect to have a long and reasonably happy marriage. It is a published fact that today all but new late-life relationships are as much at risk of sustaining multiple fractures or complete break-ups as they ever were—so, isn't it time to think a little more deeply about some of our customs? One terribly scarring consequence of marriage-and-family traditions that are too idealistic for the innocents who commit to them is the number of divorced men and women who do and will—even if they remarry—carry guilt and regrets about their well-meant "mistakes" to their graves to "contaminate the present and the future, even unto destruction," unless they can find a way to carefully and consciously dispose of them.

For all that, we are a species remarkably adaptive to circumstances. When it became certifiably certain that my decisions and their aftermaths had apparently caused nothing even close to anyone's death or dismemberment, that the worst of our pain was a thing of the past and all of our clocks had reset to "life as usual," I was able to set my burden down. The question ever present in the mind of the divorcing parent—Am I sacrificing my children on the altar of my own selfish needs and risking outcomes that might gravely affect their lives?—finally withdrew from my troubled conscience, though it can never be fully answered, for how can I judge outcomes resulting from the course I didn't take? Although I continued to regret that my children were made to suffer at all at my expense, I felt not a single regret for having ended my marriages, because I had succeeded in righting my well-meant mistakes by reclaiming a self of far more importance than my errors in judgment. I suppose I could have gone on wishing forever that it had not taken a second marriage to complete the research on my need to live single; instead, I let it go, reminding myself that some mistakes simply have to be made twice and to regret that fact would have been sheer folly. Who can know what it takes—or how long it takes—to get where one needs to go?

Regrets? none but one

One of my great discoveries about our species, which endears it to me more than all the rest, is that we do not stop loving each other when we make mistakes, even big ones—at least not for long. During the years my children and I lived together, my parenting—the good and the not-good-enough—represented the best of what I believed was important. Those values that rolled on beneath the surface "messiness" of our daily lives were what I hoped would influence them to become uniquely themselves, to be someone in whom they deeply believed. Their exposure to the ups and downs of our circumstances and the complexity of our two-household relationships were so "up close and personal" that any serious mistakes I made I presumed would lead to serious consequences. Always the first to know when I hadn't done something well or right, there were times when I held my breath for all of us, yet as all children do so brilliantly, mine sensed that my motives were good, and so forgave me, as far as I know—or will eventually, I pray.

The fact that divorces today are as commonplace as marriages that "last" in no way diminishes the difficulties that proceed from a family's breakup. Nonetheless, my children grew up through all of the complexities occasioned by my decisions to live a life true to myself and became really beautiful people. Far more important than their "success," in the conventional sense of a word that is not always meaningful, is that they are good people, generous and fun-loving and doing well, perhaps as a result of overcoming challenges that tested their mettle early on. I didn't dare to imagine that all of our outcomes would be stellar, of course, but I hoped like any single or remarried parent does that my children would find their way to some good ones. Like all generations before them, they learned to process choices affecting them made by their parents over whom they had no control, so that—as they grew old enough to make and learn from their own mistakes and suffer their own regrets—they could choose and decide for themselves. When, one at a time, they had assembled a "starter set" of the data with which they were ready—or not—to go into the world, it was time for me to exhale and let them go, one after the other, along with any lingering worries about their need for more "adult supervision" and any lingering regrets about my shortcomings as a parent.

Chapter thirteen

A few of the lessons I had learned and could articulate to them more or less effectively were surely transferred to them in those years, if only subliminally. Chief among them was that making mistakes and wrestling with misgivings and regrets are inextricably threaded throughout the human condition and that one does well not to expect otherwise. Before we can know who we are, we must know what works for us and what doesn't, what is our truth and what is our lie. Then, if our intentions are right, we will learn from regretting our mistakes how to love and forgive ourselves, and others. I think we should treasure our mistakes—and treasure the resolution of them—the careful, exploratory wending our way through whatever ails us in search of the answer that transforms a negative into a positive. I have predicted that at the end of my life nothing will matter more than what my heart feels about how I lived my life. I will need to answer whether I was true to it: that my life was neither dictated to me, nor was its meaning diminished by my conscious actions, and that I harbor no regrets.

The same force that produced humans from amoebas produces adults from infants. That is, a person's growth, from infancy to adulthood, is simply a miniature version of cosmic evolution. . . . Now in psychological development, the whole of any level becomes merely a part of the whole of the next level, which in turn becomes a part of the next whole, and so on through the evolution of consciousness.[3]

I like Ken Wilber's view that human evolvement is "cosmic" in its reach for higher levels of consciousness; I have experienced my personal evolvement in the way he describes, and it is thrilling to think that one *becomes* with the cosmos. Wilber's quick-key phrase to describe a principal part of his widely respected theory about how consciousness evolves is "Include & Transcend," and it is perfect for describing how making mistakes and regretting them evolve each one of us as we "include and transcend" our experiences of them. Whatever stage of consciousness we currently inhabit, our first task with mistakes is to realize that we have made one and include it as a part of our known present reality. Next, we examine the mistake as a way to learn more about our actions and ourselves and to find self-forgiveness. We have now arrived at a new and positive perception of both the mistake (thinking of it now as a catalyst for growth) and ourselves (for having examined the reasons behind our mistake to expand our awareness). The stage is now set for us to end our regretting, integrate our new perception, and transcend our previous level of consciousness with our new, more enlightened perspective. All parts of this process seem exactly right to me, especially as the necessary prescription for making use of regretting in order to be rid of it. Once again, and heaven-sent, comes our "elegant paradox" to help us make sense of our species.

With the one exception you already know about, I feel caught up with my past: mistakes resolved, amends made, regrets no longer relevant, all important matters of the heart up to date. Today I could answer my heart and leave the planet by noon—but tomorrow? There is only the now. If I can stay awake and continue to include and transcend any mistakes, regrets, and sorrows sure to find their way into my remaining days, I believe I will have both found and given purpose to a life for which I must now finally thank my mother. She was so young and unschooled, helpless in so many ways throughout her long life, yet quite unafraid to defy more learned and urgent voices and give my life "permission to enter." She bestowed a gift she couldn't know she would be giving twice—to herself as well as to her only "surviving" caregiver.

◦◦◦

Turning again to the question that gave this chapter its subject, "How do you feel about your past . . . any regrets?" I could easily distill my response into a single word: No! In the beginning my life was difficult, but it was also extremely interesting and taught me many cogent lessons. I spent much of my past transforming its early effects on me; consequently, my past also evolved me to a peaceful place. I want for nothing more than I have and have no need to be more than I am. Reaping the benefits of my past in my present, I feel nothing but gratitude for where they came from. My joy is

Chapter thirteen

quiet and deep, and it comes as no surprise to me that, if I could wave a wand and change any of the circumstances of my past, I would not. Perhaps I lack imagination, but I would not rearrange one fact of my life, nor delete one mistake or sorrow or disappointment that brought me to this day—a day on which it is still my hope to remove from my conscience the one regret from my past still extant. How well I know that in the end, there is really only this to teach about regret: however often it visits a life, it is meant to be short-lived—to serve its purpose, exit quietly, and be gone for good.

Author's Note:

I'll go with you, *she said, when I picked up the phone (my best friend of all had just read this chapter).* We'll drive down together to see your sister—anytime you say. *[A long silence.]* Then, Yes, I said, let's go—if she'll see me. I'll need to find out. *[Silence again.]* Thank you, *I said, feeling both fear and redemption crowding into my heart and throat;* you are very generous. It's what we do, *she said, matter-of-factly:* we support each other. *Because of my friend, if there is still time, I will soon be a better person—if not in my sister's eyes, then in my own—and forever free of my only remaining regret.*

Regrets? none but one

fourteen

Turn, turn, turn

> Call the world if you Please 'The vale of Soul-making.'
> . . . Do you not see how necessary a World of Pains
> and troubles is to school an Intelligence and make it a
> soul? A place where the heart must feel and suffer in a
> thousand diverse ways . . .
>
> —John Keats

Ask any woman born in the last three-quarters of the twentieth century how much change women have undergone personally since that now-ancient time, and they wouldn't know where to begin. When I think about it, I can hardly believe it. First I want to cry, and then I have to laugh. Finally, I feel great and want to celebrate all over again!

How about this for a start? I received one of those "can you believe this?" e-mails making its rounds through the e-universe, and it speed-dialed me right back into the forties, when I was a kid, and the fifties, when I took up "wifehood" and motherhood. It was a 1955 magazine article titled "The Good Wife's Guide," which listed several of the ways a woman might ease the strain and stress of her husband's long day at the office ("greet him warmly," "quiet the kids," "make him a drink," etc.). Above the article was a drawing of an attractive, thirtyish, middle-class wife, with a couple of well-behaved youngsters playing together nearby. She is standing in front of a kitchen stove wearing a dress—calf-length, full-skirted, and starched; an apron, also starched, strings tied into a large bow at her back; and high-heeled shoes. My mind's eye instantly pictured what she wore under the dress: bra and panties, silk hose snapped to a garter belt (or a girdle—she's slim, though, so probably not a girdle), and one or two starched, white cotton petticoats, as was the style. She was making dinner wearing high heels?! I knew what was in her head, too—because she was who I was and who many other women of that time were whose highlight of the day was sitting down to dinner with her clean starched kids and husband—suit jacket off, briefcase aside—around a picture-perfect table. That's when I cried, I laughed, and I couldn't *believe* it.

Well, okay: So my father didn't work in an office and my mother saw no point whatsoever in starching her dresses. On the other hand, wishing a better future for her girls than the one she envisioned for herself, she did starch and iron *our* dresses. One way and another I zigzagged into the decade of the fifties and immediately bought into its zeitgeist, especially its two foremost and interchangeable conventions: "the perfect marriage" and "the perfect family." Failing at perfection, when the fifties became the sixties, I threw in my lot with the women who were kicking off their heels and wearing sneakers when they cooked—if they cooked. Sneakers were so much better for "coming a long way" over so much steep and contentious terrain. We made so many personal and collective changes during the next twenty years that it's hard to overstate how much influence women have had on our whole society—beginning with sex.

One of my just-married fifties friends, an outspoken, intellectual whiz-kid who never once pulled a punch as long as I knew her, called me right after her honeymoon and said, "If that's all there is to sex, what a bore." Other than her, none of the young married women I knew would have dreamed of trading girl-talk about their sex lives—good or bad—and without stories to compare, who could guess, on a scale of one-to-ten, how close she came to being perfect in bed? You probably noticed that even my one radical, truth-telling friend wasn't extreme enough to bring anything less than virginity to her wedding bed. That's because virtually every woman close to my age today was raised to believe that sex before marriage was absolutely out of the question—it was one of those really big sins that could ruin your "reputation" for life. Wait, they said; wait. The reward for waiting, as far as I could determine, was that the terrible taint on sex before marriage falls away, quite like magic, once the wedding ring is on the finger. Imagine that! Even as the bride and groom are pledging their troth, one of the seven deadliest sins of all will have become God-blessed (and guaranteed to bring connubial bliss) in time for tonight's bedding-down. Who knew the psyche could spin on a dime, when (I'm snapping my fingers now)—just like *that*—sex is no longer unspeakably wicked?

In the seventies, when women were talking to each other more than ever before, I was surprised to learn that a great many of us didn't rate the sex in our marriages "way up there." As one among the immaculate, uninstructed novices of a time when religious and social conventions required virginity from its women (though never its men) before her nuptials, I anticipated my "deflowering"—ummm, not so much. Conditioned since puberty to romanticize the wedding night all out of proportion, I recalled my "peak experience" the morning after the wedding feeling as though I had in some inexplicable way just gone down for the count—had sacrificed just-yesterday's venerated virginity for *his* pleasure, though not necessarily mine. "Yeah," I said to my friend after my honeymoon, "I'm disillusioned, too." And for the next fifteen years of our marriage, my husband and I never once talked about the first time or any other time we were "together" in bed; we never once asked each other, "How was it for you?" Our marriage ended before society had awakened to some of the flaws in its ideal matrimony mythology. When everything began to change a decade later, I learned to enjoy sex—though never as much or as often as our culture exploits it for gain. Yet, for a long, long time before then, I pretty much thought of the marriage bed as a responsibility—as a commitment implicit in my wedding vows as I perceived them—to satisfy his expectations for making love "on demand."

As if her super-idealized sexual "upbringing" wasn't enough dysfunction within a marriage, for any woman not trying to become pregnant there was the palpable fear that she might do exactly that—certainly the biggest

Chapter fourteen

deal-breaker of all for spontaneous and carefree lovemaking. "The pill" had not yet arrived, but when it did, in 1960, those marvelous little miracle tablets were instantly an integral and enduring part of a couple's intimacy, providing nearly total liberation from unplanned or unwanted childbirths. "The pill" opened up a world of possibilities to women, giving them much greater power over their own destiny almost overnight, and, while it was also the cause of cultural upheaval for a while, it lifted an anxious pall off the institution of marriage itself and changed all of our lives forever. Before the pill, it was easier to imagine that for some of us women already feeling not nearly enough in charge of our lives, much less our bodies, "making love" seemed more a euphemism for "rape." A harsh truth, that; it took me years to allow it into my consciousness, to say the word aloud and reflect on its implications. I think it explains almost everything about sex for many married women in those years: so deeply connected to her body are a woman's emotions, so personally does she feel her body is hers to give or withhold, that there is nothing quite so conflicting or enraging for her than perceiving she doesn't have the first and last say about it.

Needless to say, these had all been my perceptions, not those of the man I married. Nor had my perceptions ever been his intentions. He, too, was a product of the time in which we married, one among droves of middle-class, upwardly mobile, ambitious, and career-competitive men who went no deeper into the female psyche than men have ever thought was important—which is to say, minimally. Unschooled in love, not yet in therapy, I was hopelessly unconscious in the marriage bed—and I would never know what he thought about us in that setting. I often overreacted to (as I perceived them) his long-held masculine-gender assumptions about his rights to my body, and our lovemaking produced little joy in my experience of it. He was caring and thoughtful in many ways, yet I couldn't say he ever looked at "us" through my eyes to find a perspective different from his own. This is not a judgment of him: men of that time didn't need to, so why would he? If only we had known how to talk—but we didn't. It would take years—more years than we were married—before I could articulate myself to *myself*, much less to anyone else. Though we both finally went into therapy, we never discussed our sex life straight out, never got beyond our equally inchoate discontents—all of

Turn, turn, turn

which went so much deeper than our sex life. So we blamed one another—
civilly, of course, always peripherally, or implicitly, or silently. Eventually, for
all the reasons born of the impossibly unenlightened customs of our day—
and for the usual "insurmountable differences and mutually unmet needs"
that came to light in our separate therapies—the marriage ended. It was one
of thousands and thousands of fifties marriages that had their demise in the
sixties; we were the generation of couples who started a trend in divorce that
eventually ran away with itself.

So it was with great care that I extracted my particular points of view from
the maelstrom of partisan opinion swirling around the Women's Movement
at its peak in the seventies. I worked my mind steadily in those days, trying
to clarify my feelings about the girl-woman I had been and the maturing,
"coming awake" woman I was becoming. The public "battle of the sexes"
was daily polarizing the gender issues I thought were probably best discrimi-
nated by me—personally and privately and for my life only—because whatever conclusions I drew I knew were going to influence the rest of my life
and all of my relationships. Women were rewriting conditions for their sex
famously and fast, and, while their cause and much of the reaction against it
were both emotionally charged, progress was also apace. Women of my age
were already feeling better about sex when I married again in 1974. Feeling
free, even teachable, after all that therapy, I was eager to participate and
experiment as a full sexual partner in my second marriage, celebrating the
sexual encounter, discovering the joy of surrendering my body to love and
finding the rapture in love returned. Yet, a passion pitched so high could not
be sustained forever—only for as long as I was in love and in lust and blithely
believing that all the lessons I had learned in my first marriage would guarantee success in the second one. When my ardor had cooled and taken its
rightful place among my other passions, our differences took their places
front and center.

It soon became clear how important it was to him for our physical relationship to continue with the ardor and frequency he desired. Just as important

to me was that we discover other ways of loving, as well: less hot-body passion, more affectionate companionship; less physical prowess, more intellectual exploration; and far less time out in the world of people, more time in the quiet pursuit of our separate interests. Too simply put, he complained, I balked, and the marriage unraveled. Was his version of "love" generic to his maleness, so primary in his gender that he could not accommodate our differences? Or was it more his preference for a sexual lifestyle he was determined to keep? And if I asked those same two questions about myself, would I find the lifestyle I favored equally important to me? I believe today that he was, consciously or not, serving not a preference but a psychological need to have me in bed at his pleasure. Certainly I was serving, consciously or not, a need with a different objective: to cool down my life, to breathe and to *be*—separately. When the surface of our relationship finally cracked open to expose our different fundamental life requirements—more important to both of us than the marriage—his was to have the sexual life of his imagining, mine was to live alone.

Both of my marriages ended not just because of my differences with the men, both of whom I had loved dearly before we parted. They ended because marriage is a complex emotional arrangement; it has parameters and mutual responsibilities—and it is conditional, requiring two separate souls to give and receive from one another in a delicate balance of mutual desire, communicating with an intent to learn, and a willingness to accommodate one another. I once believed that I had needed from marriage—and was willing to give back in return—only what was "fair" to us both: acknowledgment of my value in the relationship and respect for my needs as a separate person. Had I expected too much?

But wait: there is more to this story. Even as I struggled to make marriage work, I was itching to live by my own lights—to break free, grow up, get sane, and quest for the "more" of my destiny I felt certain was waiting to be discovered. In my heart, but still "unknown" to me, I was chafing at partnership. Like staying too long in the heat of the sun, I was burning out from the extraverted "togetherness" of marriage; it pulled me out of my *self*, where I had unfinished business I was longing to complete. I was not a brat with an attitude about marriage; I was not threatening "my way or the highway" for eighteen years the first time and eleven the next. I had twice hoped—assumed—that marriage was what I wanted—so why had both of mine been such a struggle? Or was I struggling against myself? Down the road, far too late to save either marriage, I finally had an answer to my question. As far back as memory will take me, I've been a little "dorky," ever the serious-minded introvert: a reader, a writer, a thinker, a walk-on-the-beach-and-never-cook-another-meal "loner," who does great with one or two good friends at a time, yet is lost in a room full of people at a party. So, *yes*, I had expected too much of marriage—and both husbands—and myself.

More change was in the offing, and to my way of thinking what happened next to my "woman" was so radical there can be no way—nor enough time left—to top it. The background: It is nearly twenty years after my second and last marriage ended. I have been living alone and loving my life ever since and am now working part-time in brand new surroundings. I have just made a move that would make almost any heart sing—four hours away from the hot, sprawling, overpopulated city down south to a charming, unpretentious coastal community halfway up the state. More a village than a proper town—one post office, one stoplight—it is friendly, cooler by far than where I came from, and walkable from end to end. My modest, smallish, three-level dwelling is a cedar house planted in a small forest of tall trees, themselves "home" to sundry four-legged critters. When a family of deer passes under my kitchen window on most mornings, I am never not astonished; I hold my breath when all at once they stop to watch me observing them, and I wave good-bye when, again all at once, they step out on their artfully chiseled leg bones and disappear into the trees. The considerable charm of my little sanctuary springs from the simplicity of its architecture and two west-facing windows, one upstairs, the other down, through which I might, if I so choose, observe a gigantic ball of fire-red sun: slipping . . . slipping . . . now slipped altogether into a darkening sea to trade the day for yet *another* star-filled night. Life is very, very good in paradise. I am each day amazed to be one of its occupants, grateful beyond words, and as certain as one can be that I will be watching

Chapter fourteen

the deer right here in the trees all the way to check-out time. You can see how it is that *I want for nothing* (remember those words).

Before long, and against all odds in a town of its size, I meet an interesting man and we are immediately mutually attracted. We are close in age, he is nicely conversational, and I am soon persuaded that he is more than smart, maybe even "enlightened"—could this be? Old, familiar feelings haul themselves out of a deep, lengthy slumber and wander back into my second chakra. A year later we become intimate, and the first thing I notice about our special times together is how out of the ordinary they are. Everything about them, especially my feelings, is new, for there is a certain rarified quality to them I can't seem to describe. But, never mind—because after a half-dozen of these now-and-then times, there comes the first "uh-oh" in our relationship, followed by a series of accelerating "uh-ohs" that finally bring an end to our intimacy. What can I say? You know how it goes: things about us are not as we had once imagined them to be. Nonetheless, the rest of our relationship survives and we become friends—which I am pleased to think confers a certain cachet of maturity on both of us.

Off and on for a year and a half following our last time of intimate togetherness, I wondered what it was about those close encounters that had seemed so special. In a way I could not explain, they symbolized something of great importance to me, the meaning of which I seriously needed to explore. So I began to write about them. I wrote and rewrote and wrote again about those curious times, until I had come as close as I could to the truth and to uncovering the meaning of my part of our story. Our stories were different, you see: I once asked him if he experienced our times together the same way I did and he said, "No, that's not how they are for me."

It was the *love* that was different—the kind and quality and inexplicable totality; I had not known this love before. It was not love as in the way we "made" love," which was always tender, respectful, and (for me, anyway) never about sex *per se*. It was not about being "in love," which we knew from the start didn't describe our feelings; we were quite content to think our

Turn, turn, turn

attraction was more about lust, at least for the time being. Finally, it was not ego's tendency to dramatize our sexuality—we had no larky need to prove that we could still "get it on" even-at-our-age. So now I will try to capture in words this "love of another kind" that happened only to one of us, though it is indescribable and I have no hope of doing it justice:

> My observing "I" is barely present, recording only liminally for memory these feelings that slowly overtake me—sexual and at the same time not; remotely familiar, yet in some way too rarefied to recognize. My body, wrapped around and joined everywhere with his, becomes one body—and merely a body: a "vehicle" for an experience unconscious of itself in a long "forever" moment outside of time. Is it our one body who is so deeply silent, resting, feeling intensely gentled by the long chords of a particular energy pulsing through it—or is it me who rides the current of this tremendous beauty through a space so silent and so beautiful I dare not speak? The pulsing, barely there—unheard yet unmistakable—emanates from and is integral with the same starry black and plangent silence that floats the universe. The one body comes awake to an energy pulsing love into the vastness of eternity. I am deeply moved by the stillness of this love that stills even my breath, as though to breathe now is optional or irrelevant. I am fully present and involved in the experience of love where time is not and I have always longed to be—yet, soon something in me yearns to leave, to be free of this love because it is more than I can carry: too tremendous, too beautiful to bear. Though my eyes were never closed, they open now; in the distance, I hear a door close, softly, and am returned to time.

I have said this "love" seemed to be the energy of existence itself: impersonal, all-inclusive, pulsing and streaming through the one body, and naming *my self* the same love as *its self*. Yet, in each of these encounters there came a time when I felt my heart breaking apart from the weight of so much "transcendent beauty." That a love such as this love was the sum and

Chapter fourteen

substance of every atom in the universe was unfathomable; that it was everywhere at once—or, if not everywhere, then issuing from a stratum of depth beyond the known universe; and, if not that, it was love as the ground of all that moves up and out of our apparently inexhaustible unconscious: who can *think* like that? Was this love I felt using the one body to demonstrate the fact of itself—or was it *me* in those moments who was that very love as a fact? Sexuality had in some sleight-of-hand "vanishing act" transcended the dimension of my physical self to expose the universal love I was truly made of—where I had come from and where I am to return. I was the literal anatomy of a love so huge I could grasp its import only for minutes at a time. It's not likely I will experience more of those minutes, and I am pleased to think so: if a heart can break from feelings of love too powerful to prolong, and if memory can conjure the beauty of that love only from a tolerable distance, one is not apt to beg for more. James Hollis says:

> Wheresoever we intimate the presence of depth, in cosmos, in
> nature, in others or in self, we are in the precincts of the soul.[1]

Why were my experiences mine alone and not, in some degree, approximated by my friend? Apparently we were not in the same "psychospiritual" neighborhood, not nearly as alike even then "as we had once imagined." In time, it occurred to me that two bodies—one male and one female—were required to create "the whole body" necessary for those experiences, which made it easier to sort out the meaning of our encounters. Each of them began with an expectation of sexual union, which in itself can be a spiritual experience: "Sexuality by its very nature is transpersonal libido [energy]," according to Edward Edinger, and when sexuality engages the whole person, it plumbs profound depths of the psyche."[2] Yet the original expectation was each time quickly displaced and subsumed by a "larger" experience unbounded by sexual intent, therefore limitless and ultimately much more profound. It was as if the whole of my psyche had been penetrated by a love that was also whole—that is to say, by a love that was total and complete, all other forms of love being a part of its wholeness. I was able to confirm then what it was "of great importance" that those times had symbolized for my life and to rest my case: during those times when I felt myself and the love I described to be one and the same thing, I was experiencing the "wholeness" of my self. For no more than minutes during each of those extraordinary half-dozen encounters, I was able to feel the unbearable beauty of being completely aligned with the unfathomable love that is also my very being. One does not will, or choose, or even hope to have such minutes, but a single glimpse into the mystery that is me—of all of us and every thing—is worth the work of yet a dozen more difficult lifetimes.

⚬

One of my favorite friends, who is both a clinical psychologist and a spiritual retreat master, puts this question to his congregants: "If you had planned your own life, could you have imagined it any better than the way it is today?" To answer his question, I ask myself one of my own: "Would I change anything about my life today?" My life, especially my interior life, has not been easy, yet, over and over again, I have answered both of our questions with a resounding, "No," because the truth is, my life is perfect today. I haven't always thought it perfect, of course, yet there was never a day when I would have exchanged my life for another's. When I look back to see how many ways I have changed over time—the hundreds and hundreds of tiny ways and a few crucial ways—I am dazzled by the artistry, imagination, and skill that go into the creation of an always changing life. Believe me, I claim none of those attributes in amounts that could have imagined my life so skillfully—or so much to my liking as it has become. So, as ever it was, the mystery of the miracle of me—and us—remains unsolved.

Turn, turn, turn. The three watershed changes in my sexual life occurred over a span of decades. During that time, they were fusing with other changes that were occurring simultaneously on different levels of my psyche, to create a transformation impossible to describe all at once. My conscious desire to become a whole person persisted when many women like myself were seriously discontented with the roles society had assigned to them, perhaps especially with their role as sex objects, centuries ago. Later, midlife in my case, when women set out to change the accepted view of women's sexuality for one with considerably more autonomy, conditions changed for the better. I, too, changed, and eventually became that fully sexual woman I had wanted, and needed, to be. Then, as I grew older and sex took a lesser place among my needs, I changed again, this time moving beyond gender boundaries and more fully into my personhood. The merger of my inner male and female characteristics now offers me a less bounded, more androgynous perspective on life and—in those few reassuring glimpses of my own personal wholeness—a somewhat "proven" link to the spiritual "ineffable." Change is Psyche's motor, surreptitiously effecting, with our permission, the slow, quiet transformation of our lives, minute by minute. The pages of this book have pulled on many separate threads to unwind the never-ending, shifting story of change that begins on the day we are born. I have followed its trail, done its bidding. That's *all* I have done.

Admitting to no certainties, I continue to believe that the love channeling through me in my encounters with my friend was sacred love, and that my extraordinary experiences were not only spiritual in nature, but also perfectly timed for the next watershed change in my life. When I moved out of the big, hot city down south and into my "paradise by the sea," *I wanted for nothing*—do you remember? Ending the intimacy in a relationship that I was not "wanting for" to begin with made room for our friendship, which I think today was always the more appropriate gift we had to give each other. Yet, if his was the gift that allowed me to experience that "different kind of love" I will cherish as long as I live, it will have been greater by far than any others we exchanged.

Turn, turn, turn

fifteen

The not immortal coil

> When I was young, immeasurably and unimaginably
> far ahead was a landscape of aged people with white
> heads and blotchy hands tottering on walking sticks. . . .
> How I did fear this place, old age, and particularly the
> old women, each one of whom I knew (theoretically)
> to have been once like me, young and pretty. . . . I was
> determined never to be like that. "I will not, I simply
> will not," I muttered to myself.
>
> —Doris Lessing

As Shakespeare, quill in hand, sat writing
of Hamlet's agony of indecision about whether or not "to be,"
whether or not to end "the thousand natural shocks that
flesh is heir to" and "shuffle off this mortal coil,"[1] there's not
a doubt in my mind that the good bard's body was in a world
of hurt. If you're like me, you have to think his arthritis was
flaring or his GERD or his gout or his sciatic nerve was in full
frontal attack, nailing him to a state of morbid depression. If he
was somewhere past fifty when he put those inspired words into
Hamlet's mouth—giving everyone thereafter a landmark funk
with which to identify—he would have been acutely aware of

how different his mortal body felt at fifty-plus than it had when he was a carefree youth.

Had I been close in age to Will and serving him tea as usual on the day he was writing Hamlet's angst, I would have suggested I pour us some of his hard stuff instead. "Set your manuscript aside, Will—let us kick back and commiserate on our aging bodies and allow your excellent brandy to work on our pain," I would have said. Needless to say, it is the world's good fortune that I was not there to divert him from his legacy, and my own good fortune that chemistry—too late for Will, poor Will—has since given the world its recipe for five-hundred-milligram tablets of acetaminophen.

Some of you living in a body past its prime know the story all too well. Even so, let us set aside for the moment fearing this place, old age, and bemoan the inevitabilities of the body in good humor—and because the details of our stories are probably alike enough to be too tiresome for words, let's leave them out. For now, remember with me as I tell you how, in the old days, my head rode high and mighty atop a body it held in servitude and misused in the extreme, slaving its parts night and day and year after year without mercy. Sound familiar? Today, the aging framework from which hangs my battered collection of bits and bones pays me back for my foolishness with a vengeance. That same blithe body of yesteryear now yanks me back from truly more worthy diversions a dozen times a day, shouting out to me in full-throated pain just whose fault it is that my life expectancy is recalibrating yet *again* to shorten the span of my days.

Nevertheless, I have endured the prickly thrusts and stabs of this body's pique so often and so long that I have actually become accustomed to them. I have to credit whichever god in his pantheon gave our species physical pain with which to contend, because he was not "out to lunch" when he also threw us a bone for adapting to it. I am, in fact, so used to hurting more or less that my psyche is lined wall-to-wall with enough antibodies—and medication—to keep pain down to a low, throaty croak. More unacceptable to me than living with chronic physical pain is the time spent with all the medical specialists who seem determined to treat its usually "unspecific" causes. Do they who plant their flags all over my body ever consult my intimate knowledge about it? Not on your life! Perhaps their professional

The not immortal coil

expertise so far exceeds my paltry symptoms they have no need for my humble input. Well, whatever. In fact they expect little of me beyond bringing my body to them: I run errands—filling prescriptions, going for blood tests, having MRIs, and the like—while they at their leisure ponder the origins of my problem. I'm asked to stay on the alert for further symptoms, of course, and to calendar return appointments for quite a long time, really—until they say, "There's nothing more we can do." How boring is that? I say it's much more interesting when one is a subject instead of an object. No wonder old people "forget" their appointments and self-medicate—or refuse to medicate! It is time that has all the power now, not my still perfectly adequate reasoning mind. Time and an aging, errant body take their turns at the wheel of my life, while ego adjusts to riding passenger. I counsel myself: "Get a grip, my friend, learn to live with it," or, as some new part of me adds its problem to my lengthening repertoire, "This, too, my dear; this one, too (sigh)."

Those among us who remember to be kind say things like, "Some days are better than others," when asked how we feel. Why is that? Because the reply is short and true and obstructs all further conversation on the subject. In truth, it is a rare day when there is not some degree of body ache getting my attention, even when it is blessedly minimal on the "better" days. Only in memory now are the years—seemingly endless as I lived them—when I toddled, kicked the can, hid-and-sought, skated, biked, danced until dawn, worked out, child-bore, child-reared, and drove L.A.'s freeways *every day*, for God's sake! All of my body parts, separately or together, moved in synchrony like a well-oiled machine to get everything done by dinnertime, and my body never once crossed my mind. Now, when every four hours on cue, pain scatters through my consciousness like a horde of needy addicts looking for their fix, I pop my pills and feel bad about Will (poor Will), though I confess I am bored stiff by the routine. How profligate it seems, spending so much treasured time on all the fixing, fine-tuning, and maintenance necessary to preserve the human body. Like an older model car for which new parts are no longer available, so my own original parts no longer reconstitute, and there is nothing for it but to carefully coddle them along. It is a hateful comparison, but a perfect metaphor.

Chapter fifteen

In "Being 80: Old Age Is Not for Sissies," Doris Lessing says:

> If I am not dwelling on the innumerable ignominies that go with
> being really old, like me, which creep up on you, then that is be-
> cause I feel we dwell on them too much already.[2]

Between ages fifty and sixty, I both noticed and resisted the changes in my
body. No matter how many times I looked in the mirror, hoping this time
not to see them, they were there: few in number and barely noticeable to
begin with, more of each as the decade wore on. Well, they would be my
dirty little secrets. Between sixty and seventy, I scanned the landscape of my
peers and found them as shocked as I was—but they were airing their grief
in public! Hearing a breathless recitation of some new failing body part one
too many times brought an absolute end to my patience. I didn't need everyone else to tell me what I already knew! So prevalent was the tiresome topic
of their health among my cohorts that in my sixty-fifth year, I gave birth
to The Mother of All New Year's Resolutions: I alone of all aging bodies
everywhere would find a better way to think and feel and act my age besides
talking about it. How might that be? Mother of All New Year's Resolutions,
Sub-section (a): I vowed to get right down on the ground with aging—the fact
of it; to deliberate what it means to grow old, how aging changes a life—and
to accept the naturally occurring limitations of my body with compassion.
I quickly understood that how I tackled adjusting to growing older was going to describe the psychological and spiritual quality of the rest of my life.
Although I had no control over the catastrophic events that can happen to a
body at any age, I thought it possible that with practice and determination,
I could grow old gracefully—noticeably more gracefully, I hoped, than some
among my peers who seemed to be in perpetual shock and awe about the
insolent—nay, outrageous—march of time that was leaving its footprints all
over them. I knew how they felt—and I needed a plan!

Admirable intentions frequently end up as roadkill for a good reason:
they are more easily "intended" than carried out. With practice, I did manage
to acquire a certain knack for aging—though it begs for improvement even
now. To stay awake to my primary objective to age gracefully was the first
step I took toward accepting the process of aging. When fully parsed, there

The not immortal coil

is much more to the word "graceful" than first appears. For me its meaning began with discipline and it proceeds even today as art. The discipline was to respect aging: to avoid fearing it, ignoring it, resisting it, or denying it. It takes time and practice to believe that every part of one's life is—or can be—beautiful when it is rightly perceived. Once there, the art of gracefulness quickly began for me: acceptance on a spiritual level of not only aging, but of death itself.

Facing facts—getting down and dirty with the many kinds and levels of surrender I was required to make as I grew up and older—was the hardest part of the process. There was so much more in my world than aging over which I had not one bit of control; talk about shock and awe! It is revelation of biblical proportions to discover how many of one's assumptions about control are at best, childlike illusions, and at worst, arrogant pretensions. In the end, one is relieved to let go of them all and accept the truth of one's life appropriately. "Appropriate" is to life what "centrist" is to politics: "The Middle Way"—some of the Buddha's best advice. The way I comment on the beauty of the day when I am asked about my health, is, I believe, appropriate. I've had little use for this clever response, however; it seems that most folks already know, when it comes to people my age, not to ask about their health!

One tries—indeed needs—to be lighthearted about bodies wearing down and out, yet the subject merits a serious response, too. How does one deal with a body that grows older faster than the mind? Greatly ignored by society at large and the medical profession in particular, which tends to treat the aging body and mind as a single set of collective symptoms, in that our elders are purged of their individuality—reducing the worth of the whole life to little more than that of a body nearing its end. Treated this way, how can the aging regard their bodies with respect and care for them affectionately as they undergo quite natural changes? I'm grateful that my health issues are merely various attrited bones and stiffened limbs—still pretty much the usual, inevitable concerns—and not life-threatening diseases. Chronic pain is real enough, though, and takes up serious space in my head every now and then; those are the times I stay home, read *Doonesbury*, and keep my reputation for graceful aging intact.

Chapter fifteen

From childhood until I was about fifty, my body was wiry, well proportioned, and—the ultimate "slim test" in those days—skinny enough to display its hip bones. That was a blessing in our America, of course, where the cultural standard of ideal bodies for both sexes, the female in particular, was virtually impossible to meet. Women of every age did their damnedest to meet the standard in spite of the odds—and all these years later it is still the same. Ours is a commercial culture that sells youth to every age, and in which being "imperfectly perfect just as I am" is still not taught even in the home.

Another of my blessings congruent with society's ideals was to have a face, post-acne teens almost all the way to fifty, that met its criteria for beauty—a bit of luck I might have taken lightly and did not because I relied heavily on my looks. For the generous span of years I was granted them, how I was seen on the outside camouflaged a rudimentary inner self that was frightened to death. I understood perfectly that, while luck might be shoring me up in the short term, it would desert me eventually, and that it was how I felt on the inside that would—or would not—ultimately render my life viable. I learned early that everything "out there" was not only transitory, but also illusory, and that—just like Cinderella—one fine day at midnight I would be returned, in much plainer clothes, to an exceedingly unpretentious pumpkin.

So, if I appeared to the world to be sitting pretty on a couple of prime assets, it was the world's illusion, not mine. To survive the fleeting appearances of today's body for the longer haul, I would need less a good-looking body and a pretty face than a heart and mind intact and fully operational. The work ahead was to toughen up at the cellular level and to cook up the superglue that bonds a psyche to its soul. Making my way to and through midlife, I acquired much of what I lacked, enough that when time's pumpkin arrived to collect Cinderella—whose lucky good looks were fading right on cue—my soul life was largely of a piece and reflecting the inner advantages so necessary at my age. The timing was perfect and the trade-off was exquisite. I would not today exchange my humble Honda Fit pumpkin or my livery of blue jeans and sweatshirts for all of the glass slippers and horse-drawn carriages that once filled the dreams of a hopeful and determined young girl of meager psychological means. Now, repeat after me: Inner life rules!

Today I compare nothing in my present life with earlier times. It is enough to have had them, good and bad, and to have learned all the lessons they

The not immortal coil

held. I harbor no anger or disappointment about any part of my past or its players, nor do I feel bereft of the strong, healthy body that once was, because what could I possibly change or gain by mourning it? Memories of "the way we were" or "the life we lived" are not worth keeping for many reasons, but mostly because I can remember no time in my life when I felt as pleased and grateful to be alive as I do this very day—aches, pains, and all. While time was quietly making changes to my body, I was growing myself up—clearing out the underbrush of suffering, altering my perceptions, and searching deep and wide for a generous and forgiving view of my past and present worlds; in other words, uncovering the unutterably beautiful gift that my life was becoming. It seems to me that if one lives each day fully awake to whatever it brings, one will reap a thousand-thousandfold in profit over what happens to the body in the natural course of things.

When I hurt enough that I am compelled to reflect on this physical form, now so clearly in its decline, I do so with compassion and in gratitude for its yeomanly past performance. Though it frequently chatters its pain to me, how can I not marvel at the miracle of the body? It is a brilliant work of art, a complex respiration tool inside an "envelope" that travels the circumference of the planet and as far into the universe as our probing brains will take us. Who will deny that the body conferred on our species is the most incredibly imaginative composite of interactive parts in the world? And who will not lament that its magical properties—like all else made of matter—will eventually break down? It is already inconceivable to me that every face on the planet differs significantly from every other, but a single illustration detailing the body's clockworks interior leaves me speechless. We earthlings, and our "housing," are designed with *such* elaborate and versatile panache!

Who or what is this lucky "me," who lives beneath her no longer snug-fitting body wrap, peering out to see everything that falls within her sight line? At my merest whim, an incomparable wizardry puts into motion the countless precision tools stored in my "house"—for tasting, smelling, and hearing; for crying and laughing; for thinking and walking and talking and loving and yearning and too many others to name. Because I inhabit my body in space and time, I can only speculate about the limited lifespan of our species. It seems as if the body starts us out, serves us beautifully for a while, can and

Chapter fifteen

often does become problematic, then eventually and without exception lays itself down. Some contemplate what happens when the body dies, but everyone knows it's a miracle while it lives and breathes and serves our purposes. I'd say that's about all we know. As for me, though I might, with the poets and the mystics, glimpse intimations of my spiritual immortality, I seem to walk daily on the edge of a great big mystery about the body's "inferior" status in the overall scheme of things. Since it is not for me to know, I carry on with coddling my body's parts, knowing even as I do that, however carefully I attend to them, they will not make good on my hopes for their longevity.

When I moved into my seventies, where I am now, my body changed quickly and noticeably. The lines in my face are deeper today; my hair—no longer blonde and "having more fun"—is gray-turning-white. My spine has collapsed by three discs and two inches—so that my top and bottom halves no longer face the world proportionately. The bones in my fingers—and countless other places I can damn well feel if not see—are "arthritically inspired" to change their structure. My energy is less and demands a shorter day, and my gait sometimes models the tension of chronic pain; add a dozen less notable "etceteras," and you have the picture. I can still feel my hip bones, and I do still walk two miles a day con brio—even if the brio flatlines right after dinner. So I keep dancing, if a bit more slowly, though I expect I'll be subject to more of poor old Will's "natural shocks that flesh is heir to" before I shuffle off the stage and into the wings.

When and where and *how* my body will shuffle off, I have no way of knowing. I take my instruction from that deeply meaningful fact and live—body and mind fully attentive—inside every last present moment. Even Shakespeare, perhaps soothed by a roaring fire and two extra-strength brandies, had the prescience to give Hamlet some words of pause in his suicidal maunder, a moment to get a grip and for God's sake leave death alone until it arrives:

> But that the dread of something after death,
> The undiscovered country, from whose bourn
> No traveller returns, puzzles the will,
> And makes us rather bear those ills we have
> Than fly to others that we know not of.[3]

The not immortal coil

I probably react in the same way most others do whose mortal bodies are aging much faster than their immortal spirits: I push my "envelope" as far as it will go, pay due diligence to all of its parts to keep them moving, and send my mind to the ends of the universe whenever I please. How perfect for us is this age of electronic virtuosity! My age group is computer-enhanced—we carouse around "in the now" more than any generation before ours. Use a walker? Never mind: you can shop 'til you drop on broadband. We can go to London's BBC for the news, attend five concerts a day courtesy of iTunes, travel to every country we've never been free of charge. We can Google the entire world, earn a dozen degrees, read every book ever printed, and have cartoons for dessert. I could easily "check out" still in my chair at the computer were it not for thunderstorms and power outages in my neck of the country. Those are times I move out of my chair and onto my bench and meditate in all that rain-whipped thunder on the power of the Mystery and the continuing gifts of my days. Or, quill in hand, I might write a book!

A little, telling tale: My friend and I, both in our early thirties, would go out now and then to wine and dine and catch up with each other. As the evening wore down and she was climbing into her cups, like clockwork her mood would turn quiet and serious and intense—this to signal the importance of what was coming: "Life is ver-r-r-r-y daily," she would say, though never more than twice. That was it. Matching her mood, I would nod slightly—as if to say, "So true, my friend, that is sooooo true." Soon after this little ritual moment had passed, we would gather our things and take our leave.

Whenever I think of my friend today—those few carefully articulated words, the way she looked into my face to see if I had grasped the depth of their meaning—I feel the wonder: How did she know so much when still so young, and then fit it all—a book's worth of wisdom—into six little syllables? And why did it take me so much longer to reach that same "altered" state of mind that sees life's treasure in every hour of every day? But never mind: I finally got here—along with my aging body, with whom I remain friends though she be far, far older than my mind.

Chapter fifteen

sixteen

Death

More a Perception Than an Experience

> Faith is not equivalent to mere belief. Faith is the
> condition of ultimate confidence that we have the
> capacity to follow the path of doubt to its end.
>
> —Stephen Batchelor

Climbing up the trail through a cloud
of distant memory, I come upon her: She is no more than six,
walking hand in hand with a counselor at the rear of a long file
of campers. She is younger than the others by a year or two—is
that why she seems not a part of them? A trail guide leads them
up a long mountain slope, suitably benign for their ages. The
group, all girls, is thrilling to a moonlight hike, the featured
event of their stay, which will end tomorrow when they all board
a bus for home. This is the first time her parents have had
enough money for so grand a treat as summer camp, yet I see no
signs in her of the lively pleasure so apparent in the others
about going home. Following closely, I try to recall what is behind the sweet-faced silence she keeps. I sense that she is not
so much unhappy as unusually reticent—and then, suddenly,

I remember it all: she is feeling a universe apart from the others, in some unexplainable way "different" and alone in a world of strangers. This feeling is nothing new to her. Moving quickly to avert the panic that used to overwhelm her, she straightens her spine, takes a deep breath, and dives deep into the center of her silent, private being. Once inside, she feels "at home" and comfortable with the only person she trusts. Head back, she looks into the mute, black, star-laden immensity overhead, shivers, wraps her hands into the pockets of her sweater and tries to imagine how this time she might stay "inside" for as long as she lives—because "in here" she is safe from whatever it is "out there" that troubles her so. "I know—I won't talk anymore! I'll write everything down, but I won't say a word." She means never again to utter a sound, never to talk until she dies! She has reasoned that the breath she will "save" by keeping silent will add years and years to her life—and by that time everything will be fine. She is well pleased with her plan—feeling better already about living "in here" for as long as she likes—and commits to it immediately. Later, when her parents threaten to punish her for such "stubborn and ridiculous behavior," she makes only one small concession: "If I must speak, I will use the least amount of words possible"—and again she is pleased. I can hardly believe what I'm going to say next: In unwavering obedience to her own rigorous self-discipline, and by not telling her secret to even her closest friend, she continued her near-perfect silent retreat for more than six weeks. Only when summer was over and the new school year had begun (she *loved* to be in school) did she allow her spoken words—which were never many in any case—to represent her again "out there" in the world.

The experience remains vivid in memory. In telling of it here, my feelings from that time are reproduced in me precisely, surprising me—telling me that the psyche is an ever-completing collection of life's most symbolic moments, always "on call" for us to pull up and make sense of. My memories of summer camp dropped into my unconscious the minute school began and two decades later my analyst explained the child's curious, though some-what classic, behavior to me this way: A frequently abandoned child feels the fear of her aloneness as though she is receding from the world helplessly "untethered" from terra firma. Her experience is one of floating away, or falling into an abyss from which there is no return; ingeniously, she will find a way to rescue herself. My seven-year-old mind had made a plan that was complete and logical for its age to prevent a "death" the child unconsciously felt was imminent. There is a downside to so much self-protecting when so young, he added: Every time she "invented" her survival, she added one more brick to a fortress of defenses that, while protecting her in the moment, was also toughening her resistance to healing influences later on. I recounted to him then how she was happiest at that age sitting by herself on the porch of her tiny family home, head tilted toward the sun for its warmth, eyes closed against every kind of intrusion, as waves of nearly unbearable pleasure surged through her body. Today, many years and several psychic "homes" later, I sit on a bench by the sea and enjoy the sun on my face, just as I did as a child. Today, though, my eyes are open wide on a view the child could not have imagined: the brilliant light of a white-gold sun dancing on waves of deep green sea in a world that no longer intrudes and a "death" I no longer fear.

The first death to register in my psyche was President Franklin Delano Roosevelt's. I was thirteen, old enough to be deeply moved by the quality and quantity of human sorrow that poured in rivers from everyone I knew and millions of others worldwide I didn't know. They keened their grief straight into my young, confused, and reluctant heart with a collective sadness that overlaid the whole land for weeks and months and—for some—years. Later, when I was an adult and able to keen with my mind as well as my heart, shockwaves from the death by assassination of President John F. Kennedy careened around a world immediately transfixed by television coverage that went on seemingly forever until it finally numbed the collective grief of the nation.

Three days after Kennedy's death, my father died. My unseemly lack of response to it one way or the other was notable even to me. I was thirty-two and still too hurt and angry about most of our history together to feel sad that he was gone. The stubborn, steely truth is that my father's death was

Death: more a perception than an experience

not nearly as painful to me as my memories of the early and frequent "near-death" experiences I had suffered from his clumsy, insensitive parenting. My heart was hard when he died. In truth, I felt that justice had been perfectly served when I could spend all of my sorrow on that most beautiful family from Camelot rather than my own.

My feelings about my father at that time were, of course, self-referential. Not yet having come to terms with him, my thoughts were conflicted, narrowly subjective, and graceless in the extreme; anger was my backbone in those days. After a while, when time had softened my anger and I could think about some of the early times, when our love had been mutual and sweet, my memories of him recalibrated to ameliorate and expand my view of our relationship. The day came when I could describe my father with compassion, give him his due, and grieve his death appropriately. To forgive him and forget the past in a long moment of silent surrender was the way I finally reconciled our differences—a homecoming of the heart that tragically did not include his presence. The other tragedy about us, which I suppose I will always mourn at least a little, was how blind he was to the clear and present danger of a chronically dying psyche in the growing mind of an innocent child.

⁜

Once my father was gone, it seems to me I thought of my physical death seldom and never for long, so absorbed was I in the business of keeping my uncertain spirit alive. Then, full-blown and unannounced on a day in my forty-first year, my mortality fell on my mind like a meteor onto earth. Never before had I acknowledged a reference point for my death; I simply moved along through the years assuming I had "the rest of my life"—a length of years vaguely approximating forever—in which to do everything in its time to the end of time. Since then, I have not celebrated a single birthday without calculating the statistical average number of years I have left to live. The truth is, I experienced mortality's dawning as a profound loss of innocence, quickly realizing that if my life were bounded by a limited number of years, every thought in my head would have to accommodate my brand new accep-

Chapter sixteen

tance of that reality. And since I had long ago put away my childish fantasy that hoarding one's speech adds length to one's life (even if it is still an oddly beautiful idea), I was made uneasy by mortality and took it as an imperative to Study This! If death were as close to me as an uninvited thought, I had better make friends with it or be uneasy for the rest of my life.

Krishnamurti taught me best how to think about death:

> Death must be something extraordinary, as life is. Life is a total thing. Sorrow, pain, anguish, joy, absurd ideas, possession, envy, love, the aching misery of loneliness—all that is life. And to understand death, we must understand the whole of life, not take just one fragment of it and live with that fragment, as most of us do. In the very understanding of life there is the understanding of death, because the two are not separate.[1]

That "the two are not separate" is a concept I took on in earnest; like a dog with a new bone, I chewed on it for years trying to understand exactly how they are not separate. In all that he says about death, Krishnamurti hammers home his primary point: we fear death only because we wish ourselves to "continue." "So what we are concerned with is continuity, not death,"[2] he says. Fearing that my "I" will not survive my death, I insist that it will and must do so; when my body dies I will reappear on the other side of life much the same as I am on this side: body, mind, spirit, and soul all in some way reassembled and ready to finally roll out the good times. If we could fully believe our case, there would be no reason to fear death, no waking in the middle of the night sweating our existential angst. We could all bump along doing our best for now, shift gears when the body dies, then carry on—only this time joyfully, or peacefully, or perfectly—in any case happily ever after.

If we even have a version of the hereafter, it's an easy guess that most of us don't fully believe it no matter how hard we try. So we set aside the subject of our death, thinking we will come to terms with it—and our fear of it—later, deciding to drag it along with us "out of sight" of consciousness until, terrified, we are looking death straight in the eye. After awhile I took

Death: more a perception than an experience

Krishnamurti's point that fear, indeed, is what breeds our need to believe—not in the mystery that we cannot fathom, but that we will somehow prevail beyond our bodies, even if we can't quite imagine how. "So we have beliefs, dogmas, resurrection, reincarnation—a thousand ways of escaping from the reality of death."[3] And yet, he says:

> You do not actually know what it is to die, and until you do, death has no meaning whatsoever. What you are afraid of is an abstraction. . . . Not knowing the fullness of death, or what the implications are, the mind is frightened of it—frightened of the thought, not of the fact, which it does not know.[4]

Krishnamurti takes no prisoners and suffers no fools. Learn to live in the present, he says—as have all the wisdom teachers I have read. The past is dead, it comes "alive" only in present memory; the future that never arrives is anticipated only in the present; so in fact there is only the now. At some point it became natural for me to wake each morning being immediately aware that another day had arrived to deserve my appreciation, and to die to my life each night trusting the universe to return it to me in the morning. In that way, death is both "real" when I close my eyes, and eventual when I open them—a psychology that allows me to live in the present, without fear of a death whose arrival time is still uncertain. Similarly, to live and die to each present moment—to see things that way—finally made clear to me how life and death are not separate: it is because they are never apart—each present living moment is simultaneously dying to the next one. When I consider how willing I am to renew my body and mind with blessed sleep at the end of the day, can death—at least in principle—be much different? There is another huge incentive for living and dying *right here and now*: If I am not in the present moment—that is, not consciously experiencing it—it is lost to me: I have wantonly rejected a precious fraction of my priceless life.

Krishnamurti was a disciplined man with a brilliant mind, one of a small group of sages to have lived habitually in their spiritual depths. He is a difficult teacher, often cranky and impatient, but always extraordinary and worth every effort I've made to comprehend his wisdom as I sought

Chapter sixteen

to calm my existential flutters. Yet, despite his counsel to all within his reach to reflect on death, doing so is not our natural inclination. Our minds are easily diverted and notoriously undisciplined, and since to die is more or less imminent—and thoughts of death more or less frightening—we need great amounts of patience and persistence to keep death in our minds long enough to tame our fear of it.

⁂

A few years ago, hoping to improve my progress in neutralizing death, I enrolled in a hospice training program, the better to study death in proximity. My hope was to learn from those who could teach me the most about what dying is like in the "home stretch," in return for giving them the best and most I could in their circumstances. I had in mind how the venerable teachers of certain Eastern spiritual traditions instruct their monks about death, which is to have them consciously contemplate all aspects of their own death until "to die" is neither more nor less important than being alive. The monks sit squarely before the public pyres where the corpses are set ablaze while attendants stoke the fires. They are told to pay particular attention to the smell of burning flesh and the sight of charring bodies as the dead are slowly returned to emptiness, leaving behind only their ashes to float on the fire's wind. Contemplate death with all of your senses, they are taught—think it is you who burns in the flames, your bones that mingle there in the ash that was once the body with which you now observe your death. To meditate like this, they are told, is to free yourself from death's repugnance and make you at peace with "all that is, just as it is."

Rites and rituals that signify the end of life and "passing over" differ widely among the world's cultures, yet it seems to me that the underlying intention in all of them is similar: to honor the individual who has died and to honor the mystery of death itself. Of course, I did not choose to systematically study death without hoping to benefit. I took it on because I could imagine nothing worse than to arrive at my death terrified of its prospect, and I had learned from "doing time" in psychotherapy just how steep the price—and how hard the work—can be when one ignores that which needs

Death: more a perception than an experience

to be dealt with consciously. My greatest wish—then and now—is to arrive at my death fully awake—to be present for my death in the same way that, in living "awake," I am present for my life. I think forty-one was not at all too soon to be shaken awake to my mortality. It seems I have needed all the time I've been given to bring death out of the dark, to probe and delimit my fear of it, to study and refine my perceptions, and to practice my acceptance of it—perhaps even to *befriend* death and discover that, as with life, death is, after all, something extraordinary.

Words fail to convey my deep spiritual comfort when I am able to say, at the end of a long, thoughtful surrender to my powerlessness over so much in my life, but especially my death, "It is what it is." These five words are among the smallest in the dictionary, yet they comprise the answer to everything we spend our entire lives questioning. There is no right or wrong way to face the fact and fear of one's death; even so, when I can meditate on the truth of things—surrendering my whole self to the reality that I will one day die and not feel fearful—I know that I am in my soul because there I am authentic, resilient for what remains of my journey, living and dying well. Fully accepting death, the bliss of being alive rushes through my psyche and fills its every crevice. It is the ultimate paradox to feel nearly ecstatic just to be alive at the same time I am feeling at one with my own death. "Practicing" death these many years so transformed my fear of its once-notorious power that today I dare to imagine a time when, in radical need of it, I might welcome death as my last, best, paradoxically perfect friend. This more enlightened perspective would soon lend itself to a circumstance that might otherwise have been far more difficult to endure . . .

Melissa was new in town—living with a sister who would be her caretaker until she died from the cancer metastasizing in her body. I met her in one of our local A.A. meetings on the same day she received her prognosis from the oncologist: three to six months to live. She introduced herself to the meeting group, explained her condition, and smiled when she said she hoped her doctor was wrong about the time, because there was a lot to do and she needed more. She told us plain and straight—just the facts, no theater, no self-pity—and asked for our support "because I want to die well, with courage, and I need all of you to help me do it." After the meeting I introduced myself, told her I was in hospice training, and offered her my time and transportation if she should need them. Soon I was driving her to and from doctor appointments, and it was during those hour-long rides that we told each other our stories and came to know one another. Melissa was an intuitive; she was also completely awake to her life, so it was not long before we were aligned on the deeper levels of a close and caring friendship. Always conscious of the specter of her limited time, we talked freely, holding nothing in reserve for the "later on" that was never to be. How she did impress us all, shimmering vibrancy like a human tuning fork almost all the way to the end. We laughed a great deal—she was tiny and spirited and loved to laugh so that even as we talked about her death, she was serious, yet never somber. I took her lead in all things, especially when she fell silent, slipping into herself to wrestle alone with the hard, uncompromising fact of her imminent death. I waited, comfortable in her quiet. She grieved not for herself as much as for her sons, nineteen and twenty-one: they would suffer when she was gone and it was breaking her heart. At the end, when neither her words nor mine could overcome the enormity of her psychic pain, I "spoke" to her with my hands: touching and holding, hugging, pressing, and stroking human warmth onto her body, affirming that I understood and cared, that she was not alone and was dearly loved by many.

Melissa stayed alive for fourteen weeks and was viable for all but the last three; by then she was in pain most of the time, being attended to with opiates, communicating little of anything except her pain. A few times, when she was conscious enough to perceive the love I could send only through my eyes, she managed to return a few emotionally powerful "last words" of her own—a look of recognition, a touch of her hand on mine, a sound I knew to be my name. They are gifts I treasure still, passed heart to heart in those last days, while I sat before her "pyre" waiting to catch whatever keepsakes would now and again ride on the wind of her "burning" body. The time I spent with Melissa confirmed to me that birth and death are not two separate events but a single destiny in continuum. Fear tends to follow us where we go, to confront

Death: more a perception than an experience

us when we most need to be reminded that there is no way to know before we die whether our destiny exceeds the life-death experience. I witnessed Melissa "taking it on," witnessed her courage to accept that all knowledge stops this side of the body's death. Her "intimations of immortality" were enough to keep fear at bay. She thought to tame her fears by moving in on death—consciously and courageously getting close enough to her preconceived idea of death to "reperceive" it, yank its fangs, and die in peace.

Stephen and Ondrea Levine:

> When you start using death as a means of focusing on life, then everything becomes just as it is, just this moment, an extraordinary opportunity to be really alive.[5]

I was lucky to have had Melissa as my teacher; the dying are not always able to be so brave or as spiritually "together" at life's end, nor as determined to model dying well—not just for her sons, family, and friends, but for herself. Her work to achieve acceptance and equanimity on the way to death was an act of conscious participation in her own demise, and her last meaningful gift to her sons: an image of her soul they could love and honor for the rest of their lives. I have always thought that living one's personal best streams a message into the universe and adds something of value to the ages; I'm certain that Melissa's intentions are even now reverberating up and down the generations. She came to us in the meeting rooms plainspoken, without guile, and spiritually brilliant, and stayed long enough to inspire every one of us who shared in her rite of final passage—which surely must have been the most poignant and deeply significant event in her too-short life.

There was a time when I assumed that death was "the enemy." Watching Melissa die confirmed to me that it is not. Death lifted Melissa out of her cancer-ridden body and brought her peace: cancer was her enemy, but death was not. Were I to be the victim of a senseless death, my death would be tragic, yet death itself would not have been my enemy. Disease, brutality in all of its forms, the madness of war, ignorance and unconsciousness—all of these tell me that we must look closer to home for the enemy, because it is not death. While it is no less a mystery than it has ever been, death seems to me now—though I look "through a glass darkly"—to promise things I sense are profound and intimately related to the life from which it will one day separate me. Were I to stand on the lip of a massive black hole in space and peer into its long, seductive craw, I would be less amazed than I am by death's enigmatic relationship to the meaning of consciousness in our species.

⚬⚬⚬

Are there any harder or more momentous questions than these asked by Ken Wilber?

> Once you have developed an accurate and healthy ego, what then?
> Once you have met your egoic goals, once you have the car and the
> house and some self-esteem, once you have accumulated material
> goods and professional recognition—once all that, what then?
> When history runs out of meaning for the soul, when material
> pursuits in the outer world go flat in their appeal, when it dawns
> on you for certain that death alone awaits you, what then? [6]

For anyone who has yet to examine death as a given, Wilber's questions pack enough voltage to start them off on a task that is both urgent and unique to our species. It is said that the deeper we go into ourselves, the more we discover we are the same, that at the very bottom we are one. I think the same can be said of the wisdom traditions, all of which seem to me to rest at their depths on some simple and sensible premises. By the time I came to Wilber's questions, I had already decided that my own "free-floating midlife anxiety" was, deep down, the fear of my mortality. In the search for a remedy for my fear, I was led to Buddhism, and there I found two-centuries-old teachings about suffering in general—impermanence and nonattachment—to which I immediately responded.

Everything in life is impermanent, goes the teaching. All that we experience with our senses and our intellect rises and falls, forms, and dissolves. Nothing is "fixed" in time or space, because all things, even those that appear to be permanent and enduring, are always dying to change; either obviously

Death: more a perception than an experience

or imperceptibly they are recycling birth, death, and regeneration. I like this teaching because it is clear, simple, and logically obvious. We fear impermanence because it is a harbinger of our death, for example. We counteract that fear—in the face of all we know to the contrary—with a deep desire for permanence. By denying or repressing what is perfectly clear, we create a psychological contradiction—desiring the impossible—that becomes the cause of our suffering. So especially strong is our fear of losing our life, for example, that we attach to anything we can hold onto and claim as our own—God, relationships, our youth, power, money, prestige, material goods, ideas—only to discover that all of these are also impermanent. Over and over we are returned to our suffering—running from our angst by chasing anything that will fix us "out there" without considering that whatever we attach to will sooner or later disappoint our intention to permanently endure.

I don't doubt for a minute that I was enlightened by these teachings; they felt "right" at the time and continue to be a compelling influence on both my worldview and my personal psychology. Along with Krishnamurti, they answered my questions about why we are terrified when death finally gets our attention. I learned from them how to think anew about attachment, how to practice nonattachment, how to think in depth about the negative power attachment generates in relationships. Overcoming an unconscious tic to attach to *anything* for fear of losing that thing is ongoing work to which I am devoted—having once too often felt the misery that "clutching" has left on my heart.

Stephen Levine wrote that "detachment" means letting go of a thing, and "nonattachment" means simply "letting a thing be"—not attaching in the first place. I might resist "detaching" with all my might; I might prefer believing I can "have and keep" all that I love. But I would be wrong. How can I refute impermanence? Our bodies grow old and weak, the world rumbles and quakes, loved ones die, life circumstances implode or explode, and I am guaranteed nothing—not even my life—for more than a millisecond. So far, this is the truthiest truth I know. Getting used to this truth is the practice—remembering to accept it as my reality and to stay in the now—where fear is *not* and joy is plentiful. I have learned not to fear suffering, but to suffer appropriately (not exceedingly) when it arrives,

Chapter sixteen

because suffering is merely a part of life, not all of it. Life and death, including my own, is the way things go in this world—where I am ever so briefly a guest. No matter which way life cuts, I tell myself to rejoice! It's a gift—say "thank you."

It is empowering to know that as an individual I have it in me to conquer my fears. At the same time, I have far less power to control *collective* fear. Remembering the war in Vietnam, I recall being so afraid my boys might be drafted into the military that I vowed we would all hit the road for Canada should "serving their country" in that war become even remotely possible; it did not. That war ended, as have some other "skirmishes." Now we are in the midst of at least two other wars, and I discover again how attached I can be, not just to my own flesh and blood, but also to everyone on the planet. Yet, my attachment is nothing to fear—nothing when compared to a collective fear that becomes so big it has the power to run away with a country's morality. I don't pretend to have easy answers to complex problems, but I can tell right from wrong and feel pretty certain that our species does not solve problems by warring against itself. If I can, we all can imagine the terror we would feel anticipating our death for reasons that—on all levels of our being—are incomprehensible. Given that each of us shivers at the thought of his or her own death, I can only wonder at the irony in our history that proves we have so little trouble—collectively, impersonally, and willfully—killing our own kind. We can all agree that the death of the body is inevitable in its time, but unnecessary death is tragic—a blunt, insensitive assault on every god in his heaven, a crime we commit against ourselves. It is not so easy to practice detachment from so much suffering—which one must do or become deeply dejected—unless I stay conscious about the dark side and darker deeds of our humanity and find compassion for us in our unenlightened brokenness. It helps me to remember that the present time is no more than a comma in history's timeline and to continue hoping that we, and our gods, will, one by one, continue to evolve beyond our propensity to self-destruct. This, from Stephen Batchelor:

Death: more a perception than an experience

Fixed ideas of permanence
And transience,
Finitude and infinity,
Have no place when all is well.[7]

Why have the sages of contemplative spiritual traditions throughout the centuries testified to the usefulness of spending some part of every day in quiet self-reflection? It's a great question deserving everyone's consideration. To reflect on all manner of things evolves our consciousness, for one thing, helping us to choose life over the deathly perils created by an unconscious mind. Sitting before the private "pyre" of my mind to watch my own bones burning inspires me to love every minute of my life. Intertwined and symbiotic, there is less than the breadth of a single hair between one's life and death at any given moment. Contemplating that fact is how I memorized death's contours until she was familiar and harmless, until my dread was benign and I could say without fear: "When you come for me, I will be pleased to have you teach me." When all of its drama is unwound, death is entirely without malice; she merely waits for a signal to quietly claim my body. By practicing death, I see her for who she is—a moving, permeable "cloud of unknowing" that floats in and out of my mind as a thought, as death imagined—and am moved to celebrate my life. It was I who arranged for my body to be burned and its ashes cast out to sea—just enough rite and ritual to suit me. Meanwhile, when I am quietly moving around in my depths, tentatively and intuitively feeling my way into my most interior truth, I am sometimes drawn into a delicately beautiful feeling experience: a multidimensional inscape of extraordinary humility—all essence, poetry without words. At those times, I find it easy and natural to think that death is hollow, a concoction of residual fears and my fecklessness—more a perception than a reality.

I hear you asking, "Do you really believe that?" It is different than "believing." It is a *knowing*—a distillation of all the words I have ever read and heard and feared about death and an instinct to conclude that death is not a negative. Not always do I know—only at those times I can genuinely let death go. Rilke says what I mean more eloquently:

Chapter sixteen

I love the dark hours of my being.
My mind deepens into them.
There I can find, as in old letters,
the days of my life, already lived,
and held like a legend, and understood.
Then the knowing comes: I can open
to another life that's wide and timeless.[8]

Death: more a perception than an experience

seventeen

Searching for soul in the cul-de-sacs

> The boon of increased self-awareness is the sufficient
> answer even to life's suffering, otherwise [life] would be
> meaningless and unendurable.
>
> —C. G. Jung

When I was six and my sister was seven,
we were sent walking each week to a nearby Pentecostal Church,
wearing clean starched frocks and black patent Mary Janes. Two
dimes apiece were tied up in white linen handkerchiefs and
tucked into our Bibles: one dime for the collection basket, the
other to buy a double-dipped ice cream cone on our way home.
This weekly ritual effectively killed three birds with one stone
for my parents, who gambled at poker palaces hours into the
morning several times a week: forty cents on Sundays bought
them two hours of priceless undisturbed sleep, the gratitude of
my grandmother who was alone in caring that her son's children
grew up with God in their lives, and a guarantee that my sister
and I would receive a "proper Christian upbringing." The day
came when we were old enough to attend the church service for
grown-ups, though I say in hindsight not old enough to hear the
good preacher's sermon on hell and damnation for the devil and
the fallen. Some in the congregation who heard a thing or two

about themselves in his rant sprang to their feet from the pews to repent their sins right then and there. Arms and eyes reaching to heaven, these clamoring waywards begged for God's grace to change their too-human, unholy ways: "O Lord Almighty," they would cry, decibels ascending apace with their fervor, "won't you please, *please*, Lord, save this sinner and keep the devil away from my door!" The sight and sounds of so many God-offenders all dressed up and pleading for their souls in such a ruckus of fear so terrified me that I took leave of the church through a side door and ran away from their god forever. As fast as feet can go at that age, I fled to an earthling's paradise: ice cream, double-dipped and stacked on a sugar cone in exchange for one dime and all further thoughts about God or religion for many years to come.

My sister did nothing of the kind, perhaps sensing early that only God could save her from herself. She, in fact, attended those Holy Roller services every week without fail, and pretty soon the whole congregation witnessed her baptism by total immersion—not once, but twice. The second dip was arranged at my sister's request soon after she surrendered her virginity in an ecstasy of submission to her lover's beseeching, to his promise of undying love, and the very real possibility that her parents would be home from their card games "any minute now." Soon tormented by her shameful betrayal of the Lord's offer to love her eternally, she confessed her terrible secret only to me. Of course, God knew, and when she rose up from her baptismal waters the second time, she swooned in a fit of gratitude for another chance to make good in spite of her wicked ways. Looking back on it later, I thought she probably could not have waited for a kinder god or a later time to have her spiritual needs met, because—though no one we knew could read the signs—she was already on a long, rocky road of incurable troubles.

In her late twenties she was diagnosed with paranoid schizophrenia and eventually institutionalized. Your heart would break to see her in that setting—talking to angels and scorning the heathen. Once more she confided in me—showing no remorse this time, instead proud and defiant—that at least twice by her recollection she had been made pregnant by the son of her god. After awhile, I "ran away" from her, too: the specter of their insanity—God's and hers—was moving into my space, crowding my exits, swarming my need

Searching for soul in the cul-de-sacs

to be separate. I didn't know then that later I would have to sort out every-thing I ran from in my fear. Nor did I know when I exited the door of that Pentecostal church in my childhood that I had made my first about-face from one of our culture's most hallowed conventions in a search for my self and my soul.

❦

> Even in the most privileged of childhoods, life is experienced as traumatic. Connected as we were to the heartbeat of the cosmos, we are cast into the world as exiles who wander in search of that lost connectedness, suffer estrangement from self and others, and absorb "the thousand natural shocks which flesh is heir to." Most survive as neurotic, merely, carrying with us the shock of child-hood as a memory, a psychic reflex, and as a perception of self and world.[1]

No author I've read better describes the setting in which I struggled to overcome my acutely unhappy experience of childhood than James Hollis, the Jungian psychologist whose brilliant explications of the psyche have been pulling me out of rabbit holes since the first time I opened one of his books. His words elaborate both the form and substance of my psychological "liv-ing quarters" for the first twenty years of my life. My life, which began three years after the 1929 stock market crash that by 1932 had been renamed the Great Depression, had not been prudently or otherwise planned, needless to say. Late in the year of my birth, more than twelve million of the country's workers (that's one in four) were unemployed and by the next year, Califor-nia, the state my family called home, counted one-fifth of its population on public relief. Among lower-middle-class, blue-collar families like mine, fear and failure were commonplace and persisted throughout an era of world-wide misery that first flooded and then drowned many of its victims.

They were too young: sixteen and twenty-two. Inexperienced, still newly wed, and ignorant in their innocence, my parents produced two babies within fifteen months. Those ineluctable facts, dropped into the crucible of an era that was taking no prisoners, eventually robbed my parents of their youthful optimism—turned their mouths down, scrubbed the light from their eyes, and ground them into clinical depressives. I don't recall ever going without dinner, but I remember well that there was never enough money. Inspired to survive by any means possible, my father took to gambling in poker houses after work and was soon addicted to an illusion that, over time, he would turn a profit from his folly. Adrenaline rushes fueled his compulsion and made his dreary life seem worth living. Soon they became his best, and then his only, reason to get up in the mornings. By day, my mother fantasized better times between the covers of thinly plotted novels, generously populated with money, glamour, and bright, worldly people who toasted their lives in happy endings with flutes of expensive champagne. In the evenings, though we were still too young to be left alone, she went with him to his card games—"desperate for a little fun," she would say, as she kissed us good-bye, insisting there was nothing to be afraid of. Everything finally fell apart, of course, into bankruptcy, divorce, and sadness too deep to describe. They could have made it through those terrible times, I often thought—and yet, how? They practiced no religion, studied no philosophy, and pretended to no god. Laconically treadmilling time on the flat, hard surface of mere existence, the meaning of their lives ran out of reasons to stay. When the nation got a boost over the top with the outbreak of World War II and its killing-machine economy, I was ten years old and plotting my escape from the whole family into a world of my own making, because whatever awaited me in the future had to be better than my life so far.

James Hollis observes:

> One may even say that the unexamined adult personality is an
> assemblage of attitudes, behaviors, and psychic reflexes, developed
> before consciousness, to manage the anxiety that threatened the
> fragile existence of the child. Those behaviors and attitudes evolve

Searching for soul in the cul-de-sacs

before the age of five and are elaborated in an astonishing range of strategic variations, which are properly called neuroses.[2]

Indeed, yes! But do you think I would ever again grace God with my trust, complicit as he surely was in the unspeakable disease that was twisting my sister's brain? I had better things to do, and only myself to trust, as I set out to find some skillful way to manage the anxiety that by now was threatening my own psychological existence. I was in my late teens, and, though I was clever enough to appear otherwise, I was painfully introverted and disconnected from almost everyone in my world. One day, among all the closed doors of my debilitating stuckness, the right one opened and I tumbled through it and into a new beginning. Browsing the stacks in a bookstore— searching, as ever, for some author who could fix everything about me that felt so broken—I chanced upon a title that caught my imagination: *The Three Faces of Eve.* Jung would have called it synchronicity: when an interior intention or need meets an outer reciprocation. I read, in one sitting, the story of a woman with multiple personalities that was based on a case history documented by two psychiatrists. Vibrating in every corner of my psyche and loosely identifying with Eve's inner chaos if not her specific pathology, I was so enthralled by the complexities of a mind so much in trouble with itself that I plunged immediately into a "home school" study of all things psychological, reading wherever I could find "me" and wherever that led next— because all of it was manna. Somehow I had made a connection between Eve's story and the unconscious subtext of my hunger to understand the workings of my own fraught mind and—just like that—I had kicked off a search for my sanity.

⚬⊷⊷⚬

If in the beginning I was led by my reading, I soon learned that books would not be enough. It takes more than a good neurotic mind to prognosticate the findings of its own autopsy. To overcome the child's breathtakingly skillful defenses against a childhood that had been too hot to handle would require a baptism of my own—a diving deep into the waters of my uncon-

Chapter seventeen

scious to retrieve my psychological salvation: piece by piece. I would have to learn just how close to the edge of familial madness I had drifted and how—in halting, baby steps—to back away from its precipice. Dipping deeply into the wretched pool of my early memories, I would have to chip away at feelings that had long ago turned to stone, to flay open the wounded heart of a child and stitch it back up with love and compassion until she could walk and talk and breathe on her own again. Well, I was more than ready to take the plunge, more eager than I can say to become something more than "neurotic, merely."

Thirty-something and mother of three, I embarked on a long and stormy psychoanalysis with a black-belt by-the-book Freudian. Freud was The Man in those days—my generation's trendy new savior. In the sixties, nearly everyone I knew in my upscale neighborhood was simultaneously getting a divorce and undergoing Freudian analysis. I stayed the course longer than most of them—ten years, one way and another; my divorce came somewhere in the middle of that decade to extend my couch time by many months, needless to say. I've no doubt the analysis saved my sanity, but *only* that. It had been a complex and grueling undertaking, and since my efforts had been unstinting it was hard to believe I was not thrilled to death with the results. I knew, without knowing why, that a part of me, still unexamined, was floating around in my psyche like an orphan waiting for me to claim it. Was I hopeless? Mad as hell, I hurled my questions into the black hole of Universe: What is wrong with me? And what now, dammit? It was a long time before I heard back. According to Ken Wilber:

> Freud ended up confining his remarkable and courageous investigations to the ego, persona, and shadow. But Jung, while fully acknowledging these upper levels [of consciousness] managed to push his explorations all the way down to the transpersonal [levels]. Jung was the first major European psychologist to discover and explore significant aspects of the transpersonal realm of human awareness. Freud could not comprehend this, confined as he was to the upper levels, and thus the two men traveled their separate paths.[3]

Searching for soul in the cul-de-sacs

Wilber is referring to a major "doctrinal disagreement" between psycho-analyst Sigmund Freud and depth psychologist C. G. Jung, who had worked together closely for a half-dozen years before parting company over their differences. Freud, an avowed atheist, once famously said that religion was "the universal obsessional neurosis of humanity,"[4] whereas Jung proclaimed that God's "existence does not depend on our proofs"—that God was in fact "one of the most certain and immediate of experiences."[5] This was how I learned that, after ten long years and a black-belt diploma, I had been a disciple of the wrong master—that Freud's psychology had failed me both purposely and significantly. I was complicit in the crime, of course; at no time during my therapy had I been interested in the only God I had ever met and dismissed at the door of his church; hence, the subject had never come up. Later, I thought it had all been for the best; if, in Freud's psychology, a yearning for "God" figures only as a symptom of the analysand's neuroses, think how I might have been led away from the discovery of my still hidden, free-floating soul. But oh, the irony! I would have to turn again to this matter of God, walk myself back to the church I had sworn off "forever," crawl back into my mute and fearful child, and painstakingly put words to her story. Casting a wary eye on the past, I reluctantly reentered the cul-de-sacs Freud and I had passed by too quickly so many years ago—there to knock again on the doors of my yearning and beg to know: Is this where soul resides?

⌘

Jesus said unto him, If thou canst believe, all things are possible to him who believeth. And straightway the father of the child cried out, and said with tears, Lord, I believe; help thou mine unbelief.

(Mark 9:23–24, King James Version)

Catholicism had been my first conscious turn toward spirituality. Soon after I married, I began a study of that venerable institution because (went my logic) it was oldest and closest to Christianity's beginnings and surely the most reliable crucible in which to sink my heart and mind to assuage them. I read thirteen volumes of its history and studied the ecclesial dogma with a local Paulist priest, a giant man with a giant heart and intellect who believed in his god with an awesome certainty. I came home from a meeting with him one day in a fit of amazement and said to my fallen-away Catholic husband: "I can be baptized in the Church and take Holy Communion if we agree to live celibate in our marriage." He looked at me for a long moment and then turned away without comment. We never broached the subject again. Forfeiting my goal to join the Church formally, I decided instead to have my three children baptized all at one time when the youngest was an infant: I would raise them as Catholics—and feed off of their faith vicariously, I must have reasoned. Then, as my children grew into the rituals and the doctrine, I waited for my own hunger to be fed, some meager faith of my own to materialize and speak to my expectant soul. Three years later, having "heard" nothing from God in the interim, I thanked the Paulist priest for his prayers on my behalf and walked away—a silent, seething, full-blown insurrectionist. What I had once wanted so much, I would not have given a nickel for then. The children would find their way—and God in his sanctimonious church would once again become my adversary.

⁕

I said to my friend: *What is the inner impulse that pushes us to know more, to go always deeper to find what we can't even come close to naming? Why do we keep looking for an answer to this yearning of such unbearable beauty that it is wrapped all around with pain?* I don't know, he said.

⁕

My career was going well, which is to say I was remarkably focused and functional in the workplace, if also acutely aware of the existential loneliness parked more or less permanently and easily within reach of my awareness. I was not lonely for people—my days were filled with people—and it certainly wasn't God I missed anymore, yet my unidentified longing hovered, always nearby, like a ghost of myself. The single glass of chilled white wine—a singular comfort at the end of my day, its effect being both pleasing and harmless—increased to two, then two plus exactly half a glass more, then three, as I played the classic fractions game of denial. Yearning for surcease from the nameless yearning I could not objectify, I was relying on flutes of magic as false and dark as my father's addiction to gambling. Years later, I read in one of Jung's published letters his description of an alcoholic who sought Jung's counsel about his drinking problem: "His craving for alcohol was the equivalent on a low level of the spiritual thirst of our being for wholeness, expressed in medieval language [as] the union with God. . . . You see, alcohol in Latin is 'spiritus' and you use the same word for the highest religious experience as well as the most depraving poison."[6] By the time I read these words, I had already discovered their implications: to find one's spiritual home in a world with so few pointers and no quick fixes that are not also personally destructive is an imperative both daunting and essential to life. Another marriage. Another divorce. No longer searching for God, I was beginning to question the value of my struggle—why is it I'm getting up today? Working to pay the bills began to seem a meager incentive for so much effort. Sliding down a slope, chronically aware of how much trouble I was in and having not the glimmer of an answer to my predicament, I set aside my Bloody Mary one Fourth of July weekend and made a telephone call. Four days later I was interviewed, professionally assessed to be a "problem drinker," and enrolled in a hospital outpatient program. Eight weeks after that I was regularly attending meetings as one among a large fellowship of Alcoholics Anonymous. I sat myself down in their chairs and listened hard to these people in whom I was investing the dwindling stores of my energy and optimism. After awhile I began to hear the miracles in their stories, and, when two years had passed, my joy and gratitude for being alive had rekindled. I learned to value the present moment as the only one that mattered—each one a new beginning—all of them in some way "spiritual," as I was beginning to understand the layers of meaning in that

Chapter seventeen

word. A day at a time my life came back—but better and deeper and richer than ever before.

The second great gift of the program was my introduction to the works of C. G. Jung. Ultimately, I understood perfectly why so many of these brilliant, funny, grateful, serious, sober, and life-loving people were familiar with the psychologist who, had I met him earlier, would not have steered me wrong, as happened when Freud and I crossed stars those many years ago. Jung is familiar to Alcoholics Anonymous, because his psychology is based on a fundamentally spiritual premise that locates a God-image archetype, to which we all refer whether or not we are consciously connected to it, in every human psyche. Referred to in the meetings as "the God of my understanding," it is a bedrock principle of the Fellowship's twelve-step program and it was the start of my long and happy apprenticeship to the mind of a man who was able to finally help make me whole.

> The manifestations of the spirit are truly wondrous, and as varied
> as Creation itself. The living spirit grows and even outgrows its
> earlier forms of expression; it freely chooses [any] who proclaim
> it and in whom it lives. The living spirit is eternally renewed. . . .
> Measured against it, the names and forms which men have given it
> mean very little; they are only the changing leaves and blossoms on
> the stem of the eternal tree.[7]

So it was that I picked up Jung's books and learned my way through more of them than I can count. Studying his psychology every spare moment I could steal from my workday, I felt the same thrill of discovery as I had when, as a teenager, I'd read *The Three Faces of Eve*. The depth of Jung's intellect, shot through with the rich spiritual metaphors that are hallmarks of his psychology, fed my thirst to know more. His theories are complex and his books are not easy reading, but my brain was on fire. I was responding to his ideas with every part of my psyche, absorbing them readily because they met my needs exactly, and pleased to be searching out every aspect of my long-suffering soul in order to finally do right by us both. Reading Jung expanded my curiosity, leading me ever outward for new ways to think—yet all of them taking me inward, and, inevitably, deep into the numinous ground of the mystery. Shifting between psychology and the transpersonal, I discovered deep new pools of intellectual content in a veritable ocean of new (to me) and traditional spiritual literature—mythology; the Christian mystics, especially Eckhart, John of the Cross, and the Gnostic gospels; Buddhism East and West; Hinduism; Sufism; Krishnamurti; Ramana Maharshi; Alan Watts; Lex Hixon—the list is long. Never have I been happier than at that time when, for months on end, I was rolling around in a virtual heaven of inexhaustible riches at fever pitch.

Finding my spiritual roots by way of psychology—Jungian psychology, specifically—and the psychoanalytical process was an admittedly arduous, at times overwhelming, task. It is not the only way to seek one's soul, and it's not for everyone. Yet, the language of the psyche was the only medium in which my greatest need—to make plain the meaning of my life—could be met; any less arduous way would not have brought me whole, because my defenses were nearly shatterproof. I always felt there was a catalyzing influence working with me during those years—over and over again picking me up, starting me over, sending me forth. Perhaps it was the elemental psychic suffering—the need to find my *meaning*—I was never able to suppress. John of the Cross would say "Oh, happy fault" that I could feel it deeply, because suffering was the agent that kept my struggle alive, the grain of sand that ultimately produced the "pearl of great price." Attention to my inner needs was sometimes diverted when my outer-world priorities took precedence, yet I never deserted pain until I was conscious of its cause and could heal it: to heal was always my overarching objective. Embedded somewhere in the psychic wounds of every human being, there is a counteracting psychic need to access the healing spiritual perceptions that make pain bearable.

Somewhere in the heap of our unconscious, unattended ashes, our personal phoenix waits to be acknowledged and made whole—to launch its flight to freedom from the worst of our suffering. This is a truth we can count on, one more of those breathtaking paradoxes in which are hidden the poetic constructions of the wisdom of the ages. "Only paradox can express the transcendental," Jung said. "Only the paradox comes anywhere near to comprehending the fullness of life."

Chapter seventeen

If I accept the fact that a god is absolute and beyond all human experiences, he leaves me cold. I do not affect him, nor does he affect me. But if I know that a god is a powerful impulse in my soul, at once I must concern myself with him, for then he can become important.[8]

Jung's words alluded to my most important question concerning the nature of spirituality, and suggested that I go to the sacred space within and study its signs. I knew the territory: the private place behind closed eyes where one finds respite from the unfathomable daily wounding in our world. But did Jung mean I would find God there? Who has not felt the powerful impulse of which Jung speaks yet failed to recognize its source? By following Jung's clues, I was coming closer to "home." Others were leading me along, as well. Fewer than a dozen words, written by the early Christian mystic Meister Eckhart, traveled up through time to a meditation retreat I attended to have an immensely compelling effect on me, "The ultimate letting go is the letting go of God."[9] From them I understood—and have never questioned—that God is ineffable; what we *name* God is *not* God but a metaphor for something we can only intuit or—again in Jung's words—feel as "a powerful impulse." Impressed by his concept and sensing its value, I scooped up the word "metaphor" as I would a priceless jewel. Sure enough, there came a day when it dropped into place with something I was reading and rocketed me to a new dimension.

I have never enjoyed the comfort of a handholding "I-Thou" relationship with God, yet I have experienced some indescribably moving moments from time to time. Although their effect on me was powerful, I had never thought to call them "spiritual." I was always alone at these times—my mind at peace, my brain at rest, my "I" surrendered to its fundamental powerlessness. Looking up now and then to watch the restless, sun-flecked sea and be moved by the teeming fullness of my inner life, I was reading Jung when I lifted off:

Searching for soul in the cul-de-sacs

The question of religion is not so simple as you see it: it is not at all a matter of intellectual conviction or philosophy or even belief, but rather a matter of inner experience. . . . The inner experience . . . shows the existence of personal forces with which an intimate contact of a very personal nature is thoroughly possible. Nobody who is not really aware of an inner experience is able to transmit such a conviction to somebody else; mere talk—no matter how good its intention is—will never convey conviction.[10]

And there it was! God as *metaphor!* My "indescribably moving moments" were in fact Jung's "contacts of a very personal nature" with the "ineffable" God of my understanding. Do not hesitate to characterize these events as religious in nature, he went on to say: when genuinely felt as numinous, the presence of the divine at these times is assured—and we are the sole arbiters of our truth in these matters. Again, Jung:

Religious experience is absolute; it cannot be disputed. You can only say that you have never had such an experience, whereupon your opponent will reply: "Sorry, I have." And there your discussion will come to an end.[11]

So, metaphors, metaphors, let me count your ways: any or all of the religious and spiritual traditions, love, art, music, and nature in all of its resplendent renditions. If I experience any of these at any time as an experience spiritual in nature, I may say that I have met the Divine in a metaphor of itself in one of those timeless present moments eternally revealing themselves as I write (and you read) this. Metaphor has served me ever since as a freedom from the need to know if God exists; God is the face of all that is "just as it is." That's how I see things today. I've had a few more encounters with God-metaphors since then, and they all pretty much knocked my socks off. One of them left me literally moaning on the floor when it revealed this bit of truth to my ecstatic heart: I *am*—and you *are*—the overarching love we feel when we are in our souls: *we are made of it.* Rare and fleeting are these times in a life, yet how well and eloquently they argue on behalf of the eternal mystery.

Chapter seventeen

Jung and his colleagues have not, in any of my readings, explicated my child-hood god the way institutionalized religions have taught him to their Sunday congregants: reifying, personifying, and literalizing the Christian mythology and its literature until, for people like myself, it is wrung dry of the spiritual-ity it once held for major populations, East and West. Every one of my au-thor mentors—and some well educated, deep-thinking, straight-talking other folks, as well—have led me in my spiritual needs to a concept that acknowl-edges a direct and personal relationship with the ultimate. This perception of the mystery adds to life the inner strength, spiritual beauty, and inimi-table meaning for which I believe we are all born yearning. I speak of a psy-chopoetic "I-Thou experience," which defies translation to anyone outside of it. Eastern traditions call this experience "satori" or "enlightenment"—an intimate flash of insight that takes place between one's self and the unseen "other." My own few utterly mysterious moments of this kind are seared on my brain, totally recalled, and infinitely more moving and meaningful than the Sunday morning church services I sat through with my children, seeking some sign that surely here God was present in our lives.

The God-image in each of us is constellated—meaningful still for many of us—in religious traditions celebrated all over the world, permitting us to love, pay our respects to the god of our preference, and worship as we choose. Yet, as all else changes and evolves, so must we allow for the natural evolution of our traditions and a reworking of our sacred symbols in order to keep them qualitatively inspirational. If it has been crucial to my own spiritual survival to keep the mystery alive, would it not be true for all? When we allow our conscious yearning for the ineffable to become the Sunday morning rote of unconscious habit, our souls are stripped of the "feeling experiences" we call "God." A mythology that no longer works for the many will pull down with it the uplifting principles and guiding sym-bols that once attached to it. History records such events and—according to a concerned Jung in the year of his death—it could happen again in our own time if too many individuals fail to pursue a conscious life and nurture its spiritual component. Left with nothing larger than ourselves, nothing but ourselves, we lose the game. Better by far to find our metaphors for God, it seems to me—to live not squandering our genius, but richly and full of amazement.

⌘

Remember the alcoholic who was seeking a remedy for his oncoming personal disaster? Here's what Jung said about him:

> I am strongly convinced that the evil principle prevailing in this world leads the unrecognized spiritual need into perdition if it is not counteracted either by a real religious insight or by the protective wall of human community."[12]

Of the two, "the protective wall of human community" served me first, keeping hope alive as a countervailing influence against the possibility that my self and soul would break away from my center and float forever lost in the ether. When I entered into the caring kinship of Alcoholics Anonymous, my nearly inanimate psyche began to recover immediately. These were in no way "ordinary" people who shared their stories in the meeting rooms with such remarkable honesty. I listened and related, understood them perfectly, and was myself perfectly understood, until a whole new perception of my own history was revealed to me. Their accounts of what their lives used to be like were blunt, searing revelations of the deep, personal pain they had suffered as a loss of meaning in their lives. Some more quickly than others, all in different stages of recovery, each looking for a god of their understanding, these amazing and courageous people were climbing back a day at a time from the physical and spiritual defeat that had once brought them down. Surrounded by people who truly cared whether I outlived my addiction and who knew all about the spiritual and psychic suffering that finally brings one to these rooms of last resort, I began to heal. In each survivor's tale, I traced the single thread we all had in common: the pain we had self-treated with the devil's own anesthetic—because it worked every time, until it stopped working

Chapter seventeen

altogether. I remembered anew my father's addiction and denial, how he would "swear off" the gaming tables in the morning and return to them in the evening—to bet against his pain one more time, until he had lost everything *except* his pain. It was in the meeting rooms that I learned to forgive my father for just about everything.

Healing in the refuge of this compassionate community, I emerged from the kind of quiet, subtle despair one can only point to and describe when it's over. Today I can spot that kind of trouble in the flicker of an eyelash on a face that would have once mirrored my own. Returning to myself— breathing easily, light of spirit, humor restored—I walked back into life embracing the entire universe. Though I continue to see and feel and hear God in their stories, it is not God that evokes my whole heart's response; it is the men and women who dare to share their rock-bottom truth with me. Through them, I experience the ever-perfecting infinite that has no name; they shimmer with authenticity and image God for me in metaphors so sweet and powerful I need little else to make my day.

I have no more questions for or about God. Liberated from the hand-me-down hell and damnation of my beginnings, I frolic and rollick to my own much prettier tune—not "out there" and obvious to the eye, but "in here," where it sustains me. At long last I am not only "ept," I am seriously okay. That is not to say I have shucked off every last husk of my existential angst. I have plenty in reserve for those times of loss and doubt that so famously mark our species all the way to our end. I have to remind myself often that my soul is not a philosophy or a belief, but rather a matter of inner experience. Who or what am I *really?* In a perfect and palpable silence, to which I am more and more drawn, I am dipped in a presence I can finally call "God." Sometimes I am spilled—like water rushing from the mouth of a river in which flows all that I have been and continue to become. I am nothing I make happen: "It is not I who create myself, rather I happen to myself," Jung said. So I merely follow on—*from* myself in one moment *to* myself in the next—as I ride the river of my life down and out to sea, where I will join up with . . . who can say? Will my spirit float free of the sea? If so, what then? Will it find another river mouth? Or will "I" locate in a different dimension of the many-planed mystery? Why speculate, Jung would ask:

No one can know what the ultimate things are. We must therefore
take them as we experience them. And if such experience helps
to make life healthier, more beautiful, more complete, and more
satisfactory to yourself and to those you love, you may safely say:
"This was the grace of God.[13]

There are no guarantees, he reminds me, no promises to be made; there
is only the proof of my own God-given, soft-spoken inner voice to tell me when
I am spiritually connected. I am content with that, comfortable trusting
my own intuition—which I might easily call God. Have you ever seriously
reflected on the mystery and miracle of intuition? What is not mysterious
in the least is that we are cast to remain in our present form only briefly—
blink an eye and we're gone. I have known for a long time that nothing
material or corporeal has ever belonged to me personally, and that "what is"
will become "what was" in a heartbeat (the last one) and return me to the
emptiness from which all forms endlessly recreate—or *something* like that. I
say Jung was right about this:

I would only remark that our proper life-task must necessarily
appear impossible to us, for only then can we be certain that all
our latent powers will be brought into play."[14]

Like, just play this game for all it's worth. And wait—without waiting, of
course—for whatever comes next. How would *you* say it?

Chapter seventeen

Appendix

The Harvesting Wisdom Interview

(Courtesy of Roberta Forem)

1. What gives meaning to your life?

2. What does success mean to you? What is your definition of a successful life?

3. How important has your work been to you? What aspects of work are your favorites? What aspects most difficult?

4. How have your relationships changed over the years?

5. How important are friendships to you? What do you look for in friendship? What do you try to offer as a friend?

6. How do you see your responsibility toward others, the world, and the universe?

7. Who are the happiest people you've known? In your observations of people, have you noticed any common qualities among happy people?

8. Wisdom.

   Whom do you know that you consider to be wise? What is it that makes you think they are wise?

   How would you describe wisdom?

   Where do you think wisdom comes from? How do you think people become wise?

Can wisdom be taught? What methods could be taught that would help people develop wisdom?

What do you think wise people offer to society?

Do you think wisdom and happiness go together? Why? How?

Do you think wisdom and peace of mind are related? How? Why? How do you describe peace of mind?

9.   How do you feel about getting older?

10. Do you see the later years of life as mostly loss? What losses have you experienced and how do you feel about/understand them? What gains have you experienced in the process of growing older?

11. What do you believe you have control over in life?

12. What advice would you give to aging people to help them age peacefully, happily? Do you have any specific advice you would direct toward women? Toward men?

13. How do you feel about your past? Do you have any regrets? Do you think you can resolve them? How?

14. Have you observed any changes in the way you experience and identify yourself as a female? As a male?

15. How do you feel about your body? How have your feelings about your body changed over the years?

16. Death & Dying:

Did you think much about death as a child? What experiences of death have you encountered and how did they affect you?

Are you afraid of dying? How afraid? Do you have thoughts about what happens at death?

How do you think your understanding of death translates into the way you live your life?

How big a part has the contemplation of death played in your life?

Do you think the wise fear death? Why, or why not?

17. Spirituality:

What, if anything, catalyzed your interest in spirituality?

How do you consciously put attention on your psychic and spiritual development? How do you nourish your soul/spirit?

How important is God to you? What is your current understanding, concept, or experience of God? How has this changed over the years?

How has your spirituality changed over the years?

What do you see/feel/understand to be your essence, the core of yourself, your own depths?

Notes

Chapter one: What do you mean?

Epigraph: Paul Elie, *The Life You Save May Be Your Own: An American Pilgrimage* (New York: Farrar, Straus and Giroux, 2003), 29.

1. James Hollis, *Swamplands of the Soul: New Life in Dismal Places* (Toronto: Inner City Books, 1996), 71.

2. Hollis, *Swamplands*, 7.

3. James Hollis, *Creating Your Life: Finding Your Individual Path* (Toronto: Inner City Books, 2001), 102.

4. T. S. Eliot, *Four Quartets* (Florida: Harcourt Brace Jovanovich, 1988), 28.

5. Hollis, *Swamplands*, 145.

6. C. G. Jung, *Memories, Dreams, Reflections*, rev. ed., recorded and ed. Aniela Jaffé, trans. Richard and Clara Williams (New York: Vintage Books, 1989), 340.

7. Hollis, *Swamplands*, 71.

8. Hollis, *Swamplands*, 141–42.

9. Peter Kingsley, "Common Sense: An Interview with Peter Kingsley," *Parabola* 31, no. 3 (2006): 24–30.

Chapter two: Success as different from dollars

Epigraph: Shunryu Suzuki, *To Shine One Corner of the World: Moments with Shunryu Suzuki*, ed. David Chadwick (New York: Broadway Books, 2001), 9.

1. *Merriam-Webster's Collegiate Dictionary*, 11th ed. (Springfield, MA: Merriam-Webster, 2003).

2. C. G. Jung, *C.G. Jung: Psychological Reflections: A New Anthology of His Writings, 1905 — 1961*, sel. and ed. Jolande Jacobi in collaboration with R. F. C. Hull (Princeton, NJ: Princeton University Press, 1978), 131–32.

3. J. Krishnamurti, *Total Freedom: The Essential Krishnamurti*, ed. Mary Cadogan, Alan Kishbaugh, Mark Lee, and Ray McCoy (New York: HarperCollins, 1996), 295.

4. J. Krishnamurti, *Krishnamurti: Commentaries on Living: Third Series*, ed. D. Rajagopal (Wheaton, IL: Quest Books, 1967), 110.

5. Rainer Maria Rilke, *Letters to a Young Poet*, trans. Stephen Mitchell (New York: Vintage Books, 1984), 34.

6. William James, *The Letters of William James*, ed. Henry James (Boston: Little, Brown, 1926; repr., Whitefish, MT: Kessinger, 2003), 2:90.

Chapter three: Life's labor, mindfully

Epigraph: Helen M. Luke, *Such Stuff as Dreams Are Made On: The Autobiography and Journals of Helen M. Luke*, ed. Barbara Mowat (New York: Parabola Books, 2000), 140, 158.

1. James Hollis, *Swamplands of the Soul: New Life in Dismal Places* (Toronto: Inner CityBooks, 1996), 24, 26.

2. James Hollis, *Creating a Life: Finding Your Individual Path* (Toronto: Inner City Books, 2001), 92.

3. Hollis, *Creating a Life*, 92.

4. Hollis, *Creating a Life*, 92, 93.

5. Hollis, *Creating a Life*, 94.

6. Luke, *Such Stuff*, 158.

Chapter four: Relationships

Epigraph: J. Krishnamurti, *On Relationship* (New York: HarperSanFrancisco, 1992), 123.

1. Aniela Jaffé, *The Myth of Meaning in the Work of C. G. Jung*, 2nd ed., ed. and trans. R. F. C. Hull (Zurich: Daimon, 1986), 56.

2. Helen Luke, *The Way of Woman: Awakening the Perennial Feminine* (New York: Doubleday, 1995), 196.

3. Marie-Louise von Franz, *Projection and Re-Collection in Jungian Psychology: Reflections of the Soul*, trans. William H. Kennedy (La Salle, IL: Open Court, 1988), 6.

4. Helen Luke, *Way of Woman*, 196.

5. C. G. Jung, *Psychological Reflections: A New Anthology of His Writings, 1905–1961*, ed. Jolande Jacobi and R. F. C. Hull (Princeton, NJ: Princeton University Press, 1978), 225.

6. J. Krishnamurti, *On Relationship*, 7.

7. J. Krishnamurti, *On Relationship*, 23.

8. Jaffé, *Myth of Meaning*, 138.

Chapter five: Friendship–the best of all the 'ships

Epigraph: Helen M. Luke, *The Way of Woman: Awakening the Perennial Feminine* (New York: Doubleday, 1995), 37.

1. Sidney Creaghan, "Letter Written by the Sea," *Psychological Perspectives/A Journal of Global Consciousness Integrating Psyche, Soul and Nature* 39 (Summer 1999): 60-61.

2. Marie-Louise von Franz, *Projection and Re-Collection in Jungian Psychology: Reflections of the Soul*, trans. William H. Kennedy (La Salle, IL: Open Court, 1988), 177.

3. J. Krishnamurti, *On Relationship* (New York: HarperSanFrancisco, 1992), 2.

4. Creaghan, "Letter Written by the Sea," 60-61.

Chapter six: How much do I owe?

Epigraph: Aniela Jaffé, *The Myth of Meaning in the Work of C. G. Jung*, 2nd ed., ed. and trans. R. F. C. Hull (Zurich: Daimon, 1986), 150.

1. Annie Dillard, *Holy the Firm* (New York: Harper and Row Perennial Library, 1988), 11-12.

2. Dillard, *Holy the Firm*, 12-13.

3. Stephen E. Whicher, ed., *Selections from Ralph Waldo Emerson: An Organic Anthology* (Boston: Houghton Mifflin, Riverside Editions, 1960), 148.

4. J. Krishnamuri, *Total Freedom* (New York: HarperSanFrancisco, 1996), 129-30.

Chapter seven: The happiest people I know raise a glass half full

Epigraph: C. G. Jung, *Memories, Dreams, Reflections*, rev. ed., recorded and ed. Aniela Jaffé, trans. Richard and Clara Winston (New York: Vintage Books, 1989), 269.

1. Stephen Levine, *A Year to Live* (New York: Bell Tower, 1997), 18.

2. T. S. Eliot, *Four Quartets* (New York: Harcourt Brace Jovanovich, 1971), 29.

3. Anthony Storr, *Solitude: A Return to the Self* (New York: Free Press, 1988), xiii.

4. Storr, *Solitude*, 21.

5. Storr, *Solitude*, xiv.

6. Rainer Maria Rilke, *Rilke's Book of Hours: Love Poems to God*, trans. Anita Barrows and Joanna Macy (New York: Riverhead Books, 2005), 67.

Chapter eight: Wisdom

Epigraph: C. G. Jung, *Memories, Dreams, Reflections*, rev. ed., recorded and ed. Aniela Jaffé, trans. Richard and Clara Winston (New York: Vintage Books, 1989), 355.

1. T. S. Eliot, *Four Quartets* (New York: Harcourt Brace Jovanovich, 1971), 59.

2. Stephen Levine, *A Gradual Awakening* (New York: Doubleday, 1989), 80.

3. Levine, *A Gradual Awakening*, 7.

4. Aeschylus, quoted by Edith Hamilton, *The Greek Way* (New York: W. W. Norton, 1943), 257.

5. J. Krishnamurti, *Total Freedom* (New York: HarperSanFrancisco, 1996), 346.

6. Krishnamurti, *Total Freedom*, 347.

7. C. G. Jung and C. Kerenyi, *Essays on a Science of Mythology: The Myth of the Divine Child and the Mysteries of Eleusis*, trans. R. F. C. Hull (Princeton, NJ: Princeton University Press, 1969), 97–98.

Chapter nine: Growing older

Epigraph: Florida Scott-Maxwell, *The Measure of My Days* (New York: Penguin Books, 1979), 42.

1. Stanley Kunitz (http://www.poets.org/poet.php/prmPID/2).

2. Stanley Kunitz, *Passing Through: The Later Poems, New and Selected* (New York: W. W. Norton, 1995), 107.

3. Kunitz, *Passing Through*, 107–8.

Chapter ten: Lose some and win some

Epigraph: "Lodged" from *The Poetry of Robert Frost*, ed. Edward Connery Latham. Copyright 1928, 1969 by Henry Holt and Company. Copyright 1956 by Robert Frost. Reprinted by permission of Henry Holt and Company, LLC.

1. Stephen Levine, *A Year to Live* (New York: Bell Tower, 1997), 159.

2. Stephen Batchelor, *Verses from the Center: A Buddhist Vision of the Sublime* (New York: Riverhead Books, 2000), 113.

3. Rainer Maria Rilke, *The Selected Poetry of Rainer Maria Rilke*, ed. and trans. Stephen Mitchell (New York: Vintage Books, 1989), 245.

4. Meister Eckhart, *Meister Eckhart: A Modern Translation*, trans. Raymond B. Blakney (New York: Harper Torchbooks, 1941), 204.

Chapter eleven: Control—ego's stage name

Epigraph: Donald E. Kalsched, "Wholeness as Image and Clinical Reality in the Practice of Analytical Psychology," *Quadrant, The Journal of the C. G. Jung Foundation* 37, no. 1 (2007): 29–48.

1. Kalsched, "Wholeness as Image."

2. Rainer Maria Rilke, *Letters to a Young Poet*, trans. Stephen Mitchell (New York: Vintage Books, 1986), 14.

3. Daisetz Teitaro Suzuki, *Essays in Zen Buddhism: Second Series*, ed. Christmas Humphreys (New Delhi: Munshiram Manoharlal, 2000), 70.

4. Suzuki, *Essays*, 71.

5. Suzuki, *Essays*, 71-72.

6. C. G. Jung, *Psychological Reflections: A New Anthology of His Writings, 1905–1961*, ed. Jolande Jacobi and R. F. C. Hull (Princeton, NJ: Princeton University Press, 1978), 29.

7. Jung, *Psychological Reflections*, 29.

8. Jung, *Psychological Reflections*, 32.

9. Jung, *Psychological Reflections*, 33.

Chapter twelve: Advice be damned!

Epigraph: C. G. Jung, *Memories, Dreams, Reflections*, rev. ed., recorded and ed. Aniela Jaffé, trans. Richard and Clara Winston (New York: Vintage Books, 1989), 358-59.

1. C. G. Jung, *Psychological Reflections. A New Anthology of His Writings, 1905–1961*, ed. Jolande Jacobi and R. F. C. Hull (Princeton, NJ: Princeton University Press, 1978), 225.

2. James Hollis, *Swamplands of the Soul: New Life in Dismal Places* (Toronto: Inner City Books, 1996), 43.

3. James Hollis, *Under Saturn's Shadow: The Wounding and Healing of Men* (Toronto: Inner City Books, 1994), 9-10.

4. Hollis, *Under Saturn's Shadow*, 11.

5. Hollis, *Under Saturn's Shadow*, 130.

6. C. G. Jung, *Memories, Dreams, Reflections*, rev. ed., recorded and ed. Aniela Jaffé, trans. Richard and Clara Winston (New York: Vintage Books, 1989), 140.

7. Rainer Maria Rilke, *Letters to a Young Poet*, trans. Stephen Mitchell (New York: Vintage Books, 1986), 41.

8. Carolyn G. Heilbrun, *Towards Androgyny: Aspects of Male and Female in Literature* (London: Victor Gollancz, 1973), x.

9. James Hollis, *The Archetypal Imagination* (College Station: Texas A&M University Press, 2000), 103-4.

Chapter thirteen: Regrets? none but one

Epigraph: Daniel J. Meckel and Robert L. Moore, eds., *Self and Liberation: The Jung-Buddhism Dialogue* (New York: Paulist Press, 1992), 19.

1. James Hollis, *Swamplands of the Soul: New Life in Dismal Places* (Toronto: Inner City Books, 1996), 34.

2. Hollis, *Swamplands*, 34.

3. Ken Wilber, *The Atman Project: A Transpersonal View of Human Development* (Wheaton, IL: Quest Books, 1996), 2.

Chapter fourteen: Turn, turn, turn

Epigraph: John Keats, *Selected Letters*, rev. ed., ed. Robert Gittings (with a new introduction and notes by Jon Mee (New York: Oxford University Press, 2002), 232–33.

1. James Hollis, *Swamplands of the Soul: New Life in Dismal Places* (Toronto: Inner City Books, 1996), 13.

2. Edward F. Edinger, *Transformation of Libido: A Seminar on C. G. Jung's Symbols of Transformation*, ed. Dianne D. Cordic (Los Angeles: C. G. Jung Bookstore, 1994), 10.

Chapter fifteen: The not immortal coil

Epigraph: Doris Lessing, "Being 80: Old Age Is Not for Sissies," *AARP: The Magazine*, May/June 2006, 55.

1. Hardin Craig, ed., *The Complete Works of William Shakespeare* (Chicago: Scott Foresman, 1961), 920.

2. Lessing, "Being 80," 55.

3. Craig, *Shakespeare*, 920.

Chapter sixteen: Death

Epigraph: Stephen Batchelor, *The Faith to Doubt: Glimpses of Buddhist Uncertainty* (Berkeley, CA: Parallax, 1990), 17.

1. J. Krishnamurti, *On Living and Dying*, 1st ed. (New York: HarperCollins, 1992), epigraph.

2. Krishnamurti, *On Living and Dying*, 50.

3. Krishnamurti, *On Living and Dying*, 50.

4. Krishnamurti, *On Living and Dying*, 6.

5. Stephen and Ondrea Levine, *Who Dies?* (New York: Anchor Books, 1989), 30.

6. Ken Wilber, *No Boundary* (Boston: Shambhala, 1985), 119.

7. Stephen Batchelor, *Verses from the Center: A Buddhist Vision of the Sublime* (New York: Riverhead Books, 2000), 122.

8. Rainer Maria Rilke, *Rilke's Book of Hours: Love Poems to God*, trans. Anita Barrows and Joanna Macy (New York: Riverhead Books, 2005), 51.

Chapter seventeen: Searching for soul in the cul-de-sacs

Epigraph: Aniela Jaffé, *The Myth of Meaning in the Work of C. G. Jung*, 2nd ed., ed. and trans. R. F. C. Hull (Zurich: Daimon, 1986), 140.

1. James Hollis, (1989), "The Myth of the Tragic Flaw," *Quadrant: The Journal of the C. G. Jung Foundation for Analytical Psychology* 22, no. 2 (1989): 25–35.

2. Hollis, "Tragic Flaw," 25-35.

3. Ken Wilber, *No Boundary* (Boston: Shambhala, 1985), 124-25.

4. Sigmund Freud, *The Future of Illusion*, trans. and ed. J. Strachey (New York: W. W. Norton, 1961), 43.

5. C. G. Jung, *Memories, Dreams, Reflections*, rev. ed., recorded and ed. Aniela Jaffé, trans. Richard and Clara Winston (New York: Vintage Books, 1989), 62.

6. C. G. Jung, *Selected Letters of C. G. Jung, 1909–1961*, sel. and ed. Gerhard Adler (Princeton, NJ: Princeton University Press, 1984), 198.

7. C. G. Jung, *Psychological Reflections: A New Anthology of His Writings, 1905–1961*, ed. Jolande Jacobi and R. F. C. Hull (Princeton, NJ: Princeton University Press, 1978), 271.

8. C. G. Jung, *Psyche and Symbol: A Selection from the Writings of C. G. Jung*, ed. Violet S. de Laszlo, trans. Cary Baynes, R. F. C. Hull (New York: Anchor Books, 1958), 344.

9. Meister Eckhart, *Meister Eckhart: A Modern Translation*, trans. Raymond Bernard Blakney (New York: Harper Torchbooks, 1941), 204.

10. Jung, *Letters*, 128-29.

11. Jung, *Psychological Reflections*, 350.

12. Jung, *Letters*, 198.

13. Jung, *Psychological Reflections*, 346.

14. Jung, *Letters*, 16.